D0945253

MY LIVES

MY LIVES

FRANCIS MEYNELL

THE BODLEY HEAD
LONDON   SYDNEY
TORONTO

BY THE SAME AUTHOR

The Week-End Book
The Typography of Newspaper Advertisements
The Nonesuch Century
Fifteen Poems
English Printed Books
The New Week-End Book
Poems and Pieces
By Heart: An Anthology

© Sir Francis Meynell 1971
ISBN 0 370 01303 4
Printed and bound in Great Britain for
The Bodley Head Ltd
9 Bow Street, London WC2
by William Clowes & Sons Ltd, Beccles
Set in 'Nonesuch Plantin'
First published 1971

CONTENTS

ILLUSTRATIONS

/continued

[9]

I

Heredity

My father kept a box file for each of his children. On the cover of mine he wrote:

Francis Meredith Wilfrid Meynell

Born noon 12 May 1891

Baptised 16 May 1891

Called Francis after his godfather, Francis Thompson

„ Meredith after his Parents' favourite novelist

„ Wilfrid after his father.

So there I am. With all my life—my lives—before me: typographer, politician, journalist, Nonesuch Press-man, film publicist, advertising agent, civil servant, man of business, broadcaster, gamesman, poet. And my more private lives . . .

'Our father works in us' is a line from one of my mother's poems. Certainly my forefathers and my parents have worked in me. Even now a visit to the National Gallery is a visit chiefly to the pictures my mother showed me there. In my book-designing and publishing I followed my father's principal interest. All my life I have, like my parents, been a lover and writer of poetry.

My parents established a literary, journalistic, mostly Catholic circle in the midst of which their children grew up. Their lives and work were the major formative influence on me.

My mother's father, T. J. Thompson, was a close friend of Charles Dickens and in 1844 they went together to the Mechanics Institute in Liverpool, where Dickens was to give one of his readings. Also on the programme was a young girl, Christiana Weller, who played the piano. Afterwards Dickens wrote to T. J. Thompson: 'Good God, what a madman I should seem if the incredible feeling I have conceived for that girl should be made plain to anyone'. But in the event it was Thompson and Miss Weller who fell in love and Dickens who dealt with Thompson's doubts—was he, a widower and fifteen years older than Christiana, a worthy suitor? The following year Dickens was a guest at their wedding, wearing a striking waistcoat copied from one owned by his friend Macready, the actor, so that (he wrote) he might 'eclipse the bridegroom'.

The Thompsons had two children, of whom the younger was my mother, Alice. The elder by a year was Elizabeth, who was to achieve remarkable success as a painter of military subjects. In my youth reproductions of 'The Roll Call' and 'Quatre Bras' were almost inevitable decorations for the waiting-rooms of doctors. 'The Roll Call' was the sensation of the Royal Academy of 1874; the hanging Committee welcomed it with three cheers and the Queen bought it. *Punch* had a cartoon of the face-lost pundits of the Royal Academy at their banquet. The President says: 'Shall we join the lady?'

Elizabeth married Sir William Butler,* an unusual professional soldier who often found himself sympathising with the Zulus and other 'natives' he was told to fight.

T. J. Thompson inherited £40,000 from his grandfather, which enabled him to live a life of ease and gave him liberty for his friendships, his club life, his reading and his travel. He made himself his children's dedicated tutor. Much of their young life was spent in travels abroad.

When the girls were seven and six, the Thompsons rented a villa at Sori, near Genoa. Every morning the girls underwent two hours' instruction from their father. From their neighbours they learnt a Genoese dialect and later a pure Italian. Dickens in 1853 visited them there and wrote in rather shocked terms to his wife:

* See *Remember Butler*, an excellent biography by Edward McCourt (Routledge 1967).

"I found them in a beautiful situation in a ruinous palace. Coming upon them unawares I found Thompson with a pointed beard, smoking a great German pipe, in a pair of slippers; the two little girls were very pale and faint from the climate, in a singularly untidy state. One (Heaven knows why!) without stockings, and both with their little short hair cropped in a manner never before beheld."

Here began my mother's love of Italy and things Italian. In later years she went to Italy whenever she could to visit her half-sister, who was married to d'Andrade and lived at the Castello di Pavone at Ivrea, or stay with friends such as the Thaws and their eldest daughter, who married Count Theodile and lived in Rome. In April 1906 she wrote to me:

"To think that I have not yet written to you from Rome! Not one day have you been out of my heart. Nor have I seen anything wonderful in this still glorious city and this 'divine climate'—so Shelley called it—without anticipating the joy of sharing it with you some day."

My grandmother painted, composed, played the piano, wrote poetry. 'We had lessons on the balcony in the summer', my aunt Elizabeth remembered, 'and our mother's piano sent bright melody out of the open windows of the drawing-room when she wasn't painting the mountains, the sea, the flowers. She had the semi-grand piano brought out on to the balcony one full-moon night and played Beethoven's Moonlight Sonata under those silver beams while the sea murmured its applause.'

In her old age my grandmother had the pleasing fantasy that after playing a Beethoven sonata she would find on the piano bouquets of flowers, placed there by the spirit of Beethoven himself. Alfred Noyes, as a young man, was a devoted visitor to her and he told me that in fact it was he who had placed the bouquets there, then silently leaving without my grandmother having seen him.

In 1864 the Thompsons went to stay at Bonchurch in the Isle of Wight and my mother and my aunt led the normal life of young ladies: croquet, dancing, riding, concerts. But before my mother was twenty her diary was full of woe because of a lost young love and, even more, because she had no career:

"Of all the crying evils in this depraved earth the greatest, judged by all the laws of God and humanity, is the miserable selfishness of men that keeps women from work. . . By work I mean work of the mind as well as of the body."

Nevertheless she was not idle. She studied economics, philosophy, Latin and Greek with her father; and made herself a master of Italian, German and French. But she believed that if she indulged her sense of poetry 'whatever I write will be melancholy and self-conscious'. Ruskin, a new friend of her parents, reproved her for her melancholy, but praised her poetry.

Her mother and sister became Roman Catholics, and soon afterwards my mother followed them—the third of quite separate conversions. For her, she told me, it was not so much a concession to the unseen and unknown as a conviction that the Catholic church alone offered effective moral guidance and control. Indeed she had speedy proof of this. The priest who had instructed her was forbidden by his superiors to see her again, and she wrote to him the sonnet 'Renouncement' by which she is too often represented in anthologies.

My father too was a young convert to Roman Catholicism, but his upbringing was very different. He had little schooling. Generous emotion took the place of learning in all his life. He came of Quaker ancestry on both sides of his family. When I was a child he told me that I should be proud of the fact that my great-great-great-grandfather was (as I heard it) William, Duke of York. I found the news of my royal descent surprising but not unpleasing. In fact, however, the significant word proved to be Tuke, not Duke; and the reference was to 'Tuke of York'—James Hack

Tuke, who in 1792 founded in York 'The Retreat', the first humane lunatic asylum, where the inmates were not manacled as was the custom elsewhere. Another Tuke, Samuel, was a friend of William Wilberforce and helped him in his campaign for the liberation of slaves. When I grew up I was even prouder of a still more remote ancestor—William Tuke, great-great-grandfather of my great-great-grandfather, who was imprisoned for his resistance to the Militia Act of 1668.

When he was eighteen my father came to London and worked among the poor of Holborn. He established there his life long habit of never passing a beggar (and there were many in London in those days) without making a small gift. His forefathers certainly worked in my father, who throughout his life made propaganda for the oppressed.

Our family name was originally the French Mesnil, and in various centuries went through such changes as Megnal, Maynil, Meynell and Mennell. My father was born a Mennell, so spelt, and he and two of his brothers reverted to Meynell. Was there a touch of snobbery in this reversion? I can only guess, but it is a fact that there was and doubtless is a rich and well-known 'county' family who use the 'y' spelling. The change has its inconveniences, since one has so often to explain its pronunciation or spelling. For instance, when my mother was lecturing in the United States in 1902—a rare thing then for a woman—the chairman at one of her lectures asked how to pronounce her name. 'The "y" is silent', she said, 'as in Reynolds.' So the chairman announced her as 'Mrs Meynolds'.

An anecdote my father told us concerned Sir James Simpson, the inventor of chloroform. On one of his journeys south to assist at a lying-in of Queen Victoria, Simpson stayed with my father's uncle in York and there prayed over my father, then in his early 'teens. 'I have made of pain an oblivion—it remains for you to make of it an ecstasy', he said. Noble words indeed. It is to me a pleasing coincidence that in 1956 my wife and I helped to defeat the proposal to ban the medical use of heroin—something near to Simpson's hope of 'ecstasy'—which Anthony Eden,* then Prime Minister, tried to impose on this country.

It was my father's early ambition to be a writer, a poet, a reformer, even one day to edit a magazine that would be radical as well as literary and religious. He habitually searched for new poetry, and was much moved by a sonnet quoted in a review of Alice Thompson's 'Preludes', her first book of poems. He contrived to be introduced to her, and they fell in love and were married. Together they made plans for their future livelihood, the founding of a magazine, *The Pen*. The marriage took place in 1877; *The Pen* appeared in 1880. The marriage lasted 45 years, until my mother's death; *The Pen* lasted for only seven weekly issues.

In 1881 Cardinal Manning, who had inherited the *Weekly Register* from William Wilberforce, made a present of it to my father—'The only man in England I would trust it to', he said. Two years later my parents revived their magazine project which had been virtually still-born some six years earlier. They felt they had learned from their hard-gained experience and now they transformed *The Pen* into a monthly and re-named it *Merry England*. My sister Viola has written:

"All the ardour of the new magazine was in support of the social revolution of the Young England Movement, the revival of the peasantry, the abolition of the wrongs of the poor, the spread of art and literature... The magazine appeared for twelve years... I remember that, when we children inquired of our parents what they were busy at, if it was the *Weekly Register* their answer had a desperate sound, if it was *Merry England* it had not."†

* Earl of Avon in 1960.
† *Alice Meynell, a Memoir*, by Viola Meynell (Jonathan Cape, 1929).

47 Palace Court. The London house designed for Wilfrid and
Alice Meynell by Leonard Stokes.

(*Above*) Family Group at Palace Court. From left to right: Madeline, Everard, Viola, Alice Meynell, Wilfrid Meynell, Olivia, F.M. (*Below, left*) Alice Meynell in middle age, by her son Everard, and (*right*) Wilfrid Meynell in old age, by his daughter Olivia.

Childhood

From the marriage of Wilfrid Meynell and Alice Thompson sprang the Clan Meynell. Unlike the rest of my family, I was proud of the fact that in 1914 Wyndham Lewis, in one of the two issues of his publication *Blast*, wrote: 'Blast Clan Meynell'. It is true we were—and through our descendants are—clannish. And we are quite a large clan.

I had two brothers and four sisters: Sebastian, Monica, Madeline, Everard, Viola and Olivia. Before Olivia there was Vivian, who died in infancy, and after Olivia came I, the youngest. The age-gap between my eldest brother and me was as big as the gap between me and my eldest nieces, so I felt that in a sense I bridged the generations.

One factor which helped to create the Clan Meynell and to maintain it was the country house, at Greatham in Sussex, which my parents bought in 1911. They continued to live in London, so Greatham was a weekend and summer-holiday home. I shall return to the subject of Greatham, but for the moment it is enough to establish its important part in our family life by saying that when my father left the property to my sister Olivia she and her husband generously established it as a family trust. Its upkeep has been aided by the sale from time to time of Alice Meynell and Francis Thompson manuscripts to American universities. Some of the family still live at Greatham the year round and it is the holiday home of many of my parents' descendants, who, with their husbands and wives, numbered ninety-seven at the last count a year ago.

I now turn to my childhood. I was born at 47 Palace Court, Bayswater, a house which my parents had built and where we lived until 1905, when I was fourteen. To build one's own house so close to the heart of London has long been an impossibility for all but millionaires, and my parents were of quite modest means. The site cost £1,300 and the building £2,500. The money came from a £10,000 settlement my grandfather Thompson had made upon my mother when she married.

My parents must have enjoyed themselves building their house: indulging their personal tastes and planning for their needs in the way of bedrooms for a family of six children and another, myself, to come. The house was well-proportioned, four windows wide and with five floors above the ground. The red brick and the small-paned windows made for character without ornamentation. This was early in London's 'Dutch' red-brick period, when the Georgian style was little cherished. The external appearance hasn't changed today except for the London County Council blue circular plaque which records that 'Alice Meynell, 1847–1922, Poet and Essayist, lived here'. (Inside, as I found to my surprised horror when I went there again after some sixty years, it has been transformed and mutilated for use as a students' club.)

On the ground floor, in our time, there were hall, cloakroom, morning-room, dining-room, and 'servery', and an ample staircase leading to landings as big as small rooms; on the first floor, library and drawing-room, then two floors of bedrooms and an attic floor; kitchen, scullery and pantry were in the basement, to which there was access from the street by way of the area. The lavatories were all secret rooms for secret use: never in all my time at Palace Court did I see my mother entering or leaving a lavatory. Such a sight she would have thought very embarrassing— probably a general attitude of the period.

The architect of our house was Leonard Stokes, and he did his work so well that Nikolaus Pevsner mentions it, and parties of architectural students are now sometimes seen studying it from the pavement opposite. As a child I was snobbishly proud of it.

I often used to wait outside until there was a passer-by to see me go into the porch.

It will be noted that I was born into a house which boasted a room called 'the library'. Every inch of its walls that wasn't window was covered with books: no pictures, no mirrors—nothing but books. There was a long work-table down the middle of the room and workman-like chairs round it. Under the window were lockers for pamphlets and papers that wouldn't go into the shelves. The house was an untidy one and the books overflowed into every other room, but at least there was order in the library shelves.

My earliest memory, from the age of four, is of the corner-cupboard in the night nursery. I had difficulty in going to sleep. Children do not 'go' to sleep; sleep has to come to them, often by a difficult road. When I was four years old my invocation of sleep was a loud shouting which kept me awake and annoyed my nurse. In the hope of frightening me to silence she told me that the corner cupboard held a Man with Two Heads who would be aroused by my noise. When my mother heard about this she knelt by my bed to reassure me, then opened the cupboard door to prove that it was empty. I howled with disappointment. The Man with Two Heads had become my favourite mind-toy.

I tend to remember events by the places of their happening: for example, the topmost flight of stairs that led to the nursery floor. I had been shouting a six-year-old's defiance at my French nurse. My mother, knowing that I would take more notice of my father's voice than of hers, attempted an imitation. 'Quiet up there, at once' she called in pseudo-masculine tones. I interrupted my howling and turned to my nurse with the confidential remark 'C'n'est pas Monsieur, c'est Madame'; then I resumed my howling. There was also trouble with my nurse at the low railing, perhaps fifteen inches high, which divided path from grass in Kensington Gardens. I was just big enough to step, or rather climb, over it. My nurse objected. There was a fracas; I was hurried home and my nurse reported to my mother that I had kicked her. 'It isn't true', I said. 'I only pushed her with my foot.' That was my first exercise in the nicety of words.

Why do I report trivial details of 'naughtiness'? By derivation that word should mean 'nothingness'. I am not sure that my acts meant nothing. Perhaps they were an indication of protests and politics to come.

Harriet Slark ('Hadah') was the family nurse and later, when we had French governesses, our cook. She had little use for my sisters—'you great girls'—but was devoted to my two brothers and to me. She read vastly to me; almost the whole of Walter Scott and Jules Verne. She had to do much 'skipping' of boring passages at my shouted insistence. She was tolerance itself, but she had her rules. My youngest sister and I sometimes had our baths together when we were six and five, but she made us wear bathing suits. It was with difficulty that I managed slyly to discern, and demonstrate, the most obvious difference between the male and female body.

In childhood, 'home' is really a whole locality. My 'home' in this sense was as large as the space bounded by Queen's Road (now Queensway) on the east, Westbourne Grove on the north, Notting Hill Gate Station on the west, the Royal Palace Hotel and the Carmelite church on the south; and Kensington Gardens at the top of our road, our daily playground. They were functional boundaries: the hotel because my mother's closest friend (and our beloved present-giver and treat-procurer) the American Agnes Tobin, for long lived there; the Carmelite church because that was where we heard Mass every Sunday morning; Notting Hill Gate because I was sent there post-haste almost every Sunday evening to buy a packet of cigarettes for offering to guests— 'Nestors', handsome fat Cyprus cigarettes, 10½d. for a packet of twenty, but sadly lacking pictures of cricketers such as 'Ogden's

Guinea Gold' contained. Once, because 10½d. was also the price of a box of soldiers, I had the thought, quickly rejected, of buying them instead of cigarettes and running away from home.

My childhood's London—the London of the turn of the century—was the greatest city in the world in terms of population and the riches of the upper crust. It was the London of horse-omnibuses and the black, smoky District Railway from which you could not hope to emerge as clean as you went in. (I thought it proper to go to watch cricket at the Oval in what started as white flannels.) The first tube, the 'Tuppenny Tube', ran from Shepherd's Bush to the Bank; twopence for any length of journey.

In our neighbourhood London was a quiet, peaceable sort of place. The loudest noise was of horses' hooves. In the hall of our house was the customary whistle; one blast summoned a four-wheeler, two a hansom cab. The long slope of the Bayswater Road between Queen's Road and Marble Arch was so empty in the early days of the century that I learned to ride a bicycle on it. An extra horse was hitched to the bus for the haul up Church Street from Kensington to Notting Hill Gate. One could stop a 'bus anywhere on its route with a lifted finger. The animal lovers had their say; on the backs of the top seats of the buses there was this notice: 'We speak for those who cannot speak for themselves. Refrain from stopping the bus on an incline.' Few then spoke for the multitude of *humans* who could not 'speak for themselves'— the beggars at every corner and the pathetic out-of-work, who would run all the way from Victoria Station to our house behind the 'four-wheeler' for the tip to be had for unloading the luggage. Crossing-sweepers were important on the muddy roads. Their livelihood was the tips from mud-saved pedestrians.

This too was the London of the Sunday muffin-man with his wooden tray of muffins under a cloth carried on his head; of the dairy cart with shiny zinc cans bound with brass; of caps and aprons for the maids; of the kitchen range feeding, as a second duty, the hot water to the bathroom upstairs; of the chamber-pot in every bedroom; of the lamplighter for the gas street lamps. Grown-ups always asked a child—as I suppose they still do—what he wanted to be when he grew up. My enthu-siastic answer was—'a lamplighter, but if I can't be that, then a poet'.

'Ladies' wore hats at lunch in their own homes and veils out of doors and were be-muffed in winter. Men—I mean 'gentlemen'—went out for a daily walk which was called their 'constitutional'. Women—I mean 'ladies'—rarely went out on foot and never un-accompanied. A 'gentleman' wore a top hat when he went out, and brought it and his gloves with him into the drawing-room when 'calling'—leaving them in the hall would imply that he was staying in the house.

Telephones were rare (we hadn't one) and communications between the then relatively small literate population was by six-penny telegram or by District Messenger—boys in uniform with jaunty caps on the sides of their heads, about whose future my parents used to worry because it was a dead-end occupation.

In Queen's Road I often saw the imposing, whiskered, top-hatted, frock-coated figure of William Whiteley, the 'Universal Provider' (as his famous shop claimed to be), standing on the opposite side of the street gazing at his windows as one surveying his world, the very spirit of universal provision. (The poor chap was soon to be murdered by a young man who believed himself to be his illegitimate son.) Queen's Road also sold ice-creams at twopence each (one sat at a table and was served for that!), and Moscow Road nearby offered farthing boxes of sherbet, in an un-known number of which (it was claimed) there was a threepenny bit as well as the sherbet; so we gambled, always unsuccessfully, right up to the limit of our threepence a week pocket-money.

Westbourne Grove held Stroud Son and Richard, where once I procured on credit a pair of trousers in the hope of getting out of the strictly defined knickerbocker age-group; but I was made to return them, unworn.

London at the beginning of the century had no fewer than seven evening papers: five 'pennies' and two 'halfpennies'. The 'pennies' didn't carry news so much as special articles and reviews of books and exhibitions and commentaries on sporting events. My mother used to write for one of the 'pennies'—the *Pall Mall Gazette*—and in those quieter days her articles were thought fit subjects for posters. 'Royal Academy: Mrs Meynell's first notice.' Next day, 'Royal Academy: Mrs Meynell's second notice'. When I was seven I got one of these posters and carried it round the house shouting 'We are well off for famousness now'.

When I was seven and my youngest sister Olivia was eight it was our habit to have a run-and-walk before breakfast up to Campden Hill. Once she stopped me and said, 'I want you to promise that you will never go into a public-house'. I gave the promise. That was over seventy years ago; I have seldom been into a pub for a drink during all those years, and when I have it has always been with a memory of the promise and even a little sense of shame.

Christmas for us never brought a Christmas tree. (My parents would have none of what was a new, foreign and Protestant cult.) But it had its habits: the Midnight Mass; the 'place' for presents that each of us had on the long window-seat in the drawing-room; the turkey given to us every year by the Little Sisters of Charity— a return to my father for a successful claim on their behalf for money from the estate of a deceased Duke of Norfolk; the pine-apple, the number of whose leaves we estimated competitively; and, shortly before Christmas, the mysterious rite performed by my father in the pantry. This was the making of Chartreuse for gifts in wood-cased bottles to his friends. I have my father's recipe, in my mother's writing:

Chartreuse (Green)

1¼ Quarts Spirits of Wine
1   Quart of water
3   lbs Sugar
1   (3 frcs) Bottle of Chartreuse Elixir
1   Bottle of Eau des Carmes.

With it is the circular put out by the monks of the Grande Chartreuse at Grenoble:

"Chartreuse affords certain relief in cases of serious Apoplexy, Fainting Fits, Asphyxia, Indigestion and also Exhaustion attendant on Laborious Confinement... It is a powerful febrifuge. In cases of Epilepsy it has proved an effectual remedy... It is also serviceable to save a valuable horse when attacked by colic."

Every Sunday evening at Palace Court my parents were 'at home'. Open house was kept for anyone interested in poetry and literature, but also for artists and other 'interesting' people. I know that Robert Browning was a visitor because my father once told me to look with reverence at our silver teapot, from which Robert Browning had been served. I must have been very young, for I remember that I had to ask who Robert Browning was.

At these evening parties there was endless poetry-reading, much singing (musical guests arrived always with their music), endless 'literary talk' by my mother's devoted admirers... No, not endless. There were two signals for their departure. The first gong, so to speak, was the arrival of the hot blackcurrant-jam drink. The second was my father unbuttoning, just a little ostentatiously, the top button of his boots.

In general we children were 'in' on everything. We were free not only to admire famous writers but also to ignore them in favour of such things as ping-pong played on the dining-room table, sometimes with my brother Everard's friend, the young painter William Orpen, the Irish champion of the game.

For me the most familiar visitor was my godfather, Francis Thompson—a visitor so constant as to be almost a member of the household. The story of how my father discovered and rescued him has been told before, so I will do not more than summarise what my father told me.

Thompson was the son of a Manchester doctor and was himself put to the study of medicine, but he failed his examinations as he had earlier failed in his half-hearted studies for the priesthood. He had become an opium-eater; and in 1885 he fled to London not to seek his fortune but in the hope of abandoning his misfortune. His only books were an Aeschylus and a Blake. He had no employment till a benevolent passer-by saw his distress and gave him a dogsbody job in his shoe-shop; but Thompson couldn't manage the shutters or tidy the floor. Sometimes he sold newspapers, sometimes matches. When he had a few pence he slept in doss-houses; when he hadn't, on the Embankment. After two years of this kind of life he sent an essay to *Merry England*. With the essay was a poem, 'The Passion of Mary', scrawled on blue sugar-wrapping paper. But it was six months before my father read the manuscript and then his reply to the given address—c/o Charing Cross Post Office—was returned 'unknown'. Thompson had ceased to call.

So in 1888 my father published the poem in *Merry England* as his only means of contacting the poet. It worked. Thompson wrote again, this time giving the address of a chemist's shop, and my father hastened there. He paid what the poet owed for opium, and was put in touch with him.

Francis Thompson became my father's lifelong devotion. In old age, when a stranger was to be introduced to him, my father's question was always—'Is he a sufficient Thompsonian?' Once after a wineless dinner my father invited a guest to come into the library for a rare treat, which the guest's thirst made him interpret hopefully. The treat proved to be a reading of a new poem by Francis Thompson.

We children were taught to overlook the poet's untied bootlaces, the overcoat often worn forgetfully through dinner, the collar much too big (or was it the neck much too thin?), the smoke issuing from a smouldering pipe in his pocket. In my early 'teens I had an easy companionship with him, sharing an interest in the stop-press cricket scores. More than thirty years his junior, I felt towards him as towards a younger brother—this misfit of a man, this jack-in-the-box whose comings and goings were always unexpected because he never knew the time, often not the day. Just as he was 'the Poet'—*the* Poet to us children in a household that knew more poets, I suppose, than it knew ordinary people, so to him we were *the* children. And so it was that many of his poems were addressed to us. Here are lines from the poem which he wrote for me, his godchild.

> And when, immortal mortal, droops your head,
> And you, the child of deathless song, are dead;
> Then, as you search with unaccustomed glance
> The ranks of Paradise for my countenance,
> Turn not your tread along the Uranian sod
> Among the bearded counsellors of God;
> For if in Eden as on earth are we,
> I sure shall keep a younger company.
> Pass where majestical the eternal peers,
> The stately choice of the great Saintdom, meet—
> A silvern segregation, globed complete
> In sandalled shadow of the Triune feet;
> Pass by where wait, young poet-wayfarer,
> Your cousined clusters, emulous to share

With you the roseal lightnings burning 'mid their hair;
Pass the crystalline sea, the Lampads seven:—
Look for me in the nurseries of Heaven.

One phrase of this poem pleased me even at my earliest reading age. He had called me 'young poet-wayfarer'. Naturally I didn't like the 'young' and didn't understand the 'wayfarer', but 'poet' —yes, that meant that I was like my mother. Many Thompson manuscripts have gone to the Roman Catholic Boston College in America, but this poem is still mine—in its rough early draft and in its finished manuscript. When I was old enough to become familiar with it, my political sense was pleased indeed that 'the eternal peers' were elected—'the stately choice'—not hereditary.

While we children were young, my parents had to be careful to make ends meet, despite inheritances. They had built a large house and had a large family. They helped to keep themselves and us by their writings and the owner-editorship of their magazines. My mother's many child-bearings were never allowed to be a hindrance to her work. (A letter written by the poet and editor W. E. Henley when I was born illustrates this. He congratulates her equally on 'the newcomer' and on an essay which she had lately sent to him.) My parents never gave up the habit of rigid personal economy, which they regarded as a social, and even religious, duty. This has often been mistaken, even by their own children, for evidence of lack of means. In fact it was evidence mainly of self-denial and partly of inattention. At Palace Court 'the servants' were a cook, a housemaid, and one nurse or sometimes two. Housekeeping was divided between my mother and my eldest sister, neither of them qualified or interested in the task. My mother's account books—she always kept accounts— show her expenditure: on clothes £8 this year, £11 that; with only one tiny outburst late in her life: 'Fur necklet £18', and then underlined, as an excuse for extravagance, 'to please Wilfrid'.

The correction of proofs was a daily occupation in which my parents' many literary friends joined. When I was a little boy I was allowed in the library, where they worked, only if I sat *under* the table. Mostly this was fun. I got to know my father's helpers as much by their feet as by their faces. And 'under the table' became my own kingdom, from which I could without shyness declaim Gray's 'Elegy' to the Sunday-night supper guests. But one memory survives which still carries pain with it: my mother suddenly going down on her knees, down to my level, before she hid herself in the dark drawing-room. She had just been told of the death of Coventry Patmore.

This was in 1896, when I was only five, so I never knew Patmore. But when I was older my mother talked to me of him. He was, next to my father, the greatest emotion of her mature life. She once told me: 'Your father is a man of wonderful character; Coventry Patmore was a man of wonderful intellect.' She explained that she had destroyed many of Patmore's letters to her because in them he expounded an unusual theory of love and sex. 'It could be misunderstood', she said. Her children owe gratitude to Patmore, for it was he who commissioned Sargent to make the drawing of my mother which has often been reproduced and is in the National Portrait Gallery.

Francis Thompson became a press-day helper, or rather would-be helper. On one occasion J. L. Garvin,* who could be almost as disturbing by his brilliant relevance as Thompson by his irrelevance, paid an unexpected call. Proofs were already overdue. 'The Poet' was sent by my father to entertain Garvin, perhaps the liveliest and most versatile talker of his day. Garvin was overwhelmed into silence by Thompson's dissertation—on what? On

* J. L. Garvin, then on the *Daily Telegraph*, later the famous editor of the *Observer*.

the relative merits of Lyons' and A.B.C. teashops. Thompson reported: 'Never have I known Garvin so brilliant.'

We children of magazine-producing parents inevitably produced a family magazine. A friend of my parents was Clement Shorter, who had just founded a weekly illustrated magazine, the *Sphere*. Asked by my father what had prompted him in this undertaking, Shorter, who suffered very much from adenoids, replied: 'It is a bere whib, a bere whib.' And so we called our magazine, our 'mere whim', the *Bere Whib*. It contained my first 'poem', written at the age of six:

> Agnes Tobin comes from America
> She is sweeter than angelica.

Of all the people who thronged my mother's life when I was young I was most attached to Agnes Tobin, daughter of a gold-rush pioneer who had settled in San Francisco. She was learned in music, poetry and languages; she translated Petrarch and wrote poetry. She came to London in the 1880s and became my mother's devoted admirer and friend. Thereafter, the greater part of Agnes's life was spent in England and France. She was a friend of Yeats and Arthur Symons, and Joseph Conrad dedicated *Under Western Eyes* to her.

In 1903 there befell a great estrangement between Agnes and my mother, exactly why I have never known. When I found that my schoolboy letters to Agnes were not answered I took my distress to my mother, who annihilated it by revealing her own greater sorrow. With juvenile arrogance I wrote to Agnes to tell her of my mother's grief and as a result they met again. But a reconciliation after such an estrangement obviously cannot obliterate it. Deep affection and friendship survived, but the fervour was gone.

My mother was acutely and tenderly conscious of all our nursery doings, but we younger ones found it hard to be parted from her at night. A bargain was struck. She was to visit us after we had gone to sleep, not waking us but leaving a 'sign'. It didn't matter what the sign was—a hat, an umbrella, an upturned chair or a sweet. What we wanted was a proof of her visit.

In those days I regarded anyone bearded as ancient, from my student brother Everard and my father to George Meredith. But Meredith was really old. His head was fearsomely like the picture in my nursery of God the Father. There was an excited yet reverential air among us children before his visits. It was a relief to me to observe that, ungodlike, he needed the support of a stick and that his deafness produced in his conversation what he called 'the frequent "eh?"' Every Christmas he sent to us children a handsome tip, by way of a cheque to our father. Once he signed his cheque 'George Meynell', a slip which the psychologists or trick-cyclists of today would doubtless think significant. He gave me a silver-gilt 'art-nouveau' mug engraved 'Francis Meredith Meynell from George Meredith', thus omitting my third name— my father's first—Wilfrid. Later my mother gave me one of her books of essays, similarly inscribed. My father chanced upon it and with a mixture of jealousy and affection, inserted 'Wilfrid, please'.

III

Schools

When I was six years old I was sent to my first school, the Convent of Our Lady of Sion in Bayswater, as a day-boy. At the end of each day's session Mother Gonzales required us to stand up and give ourselves marks in such 'subjects' as obedience, attention and neatness. I always gave myself the maximum of ten marks and I remember only one occasion when Mother Gonzales ventured to lower my mark. It was for 'neatness'. 'No, only five', she said with an embarrassed fleeting glance at my middle. I had forgotten to do up my fly-buttons.

When I was seven I had become too much of a nuisance at home and I was sent to the boarding-school of the Misses Lamprell at Hove. There were only seven or eight of us, all boarders. The staff, domestic and tutorial, were Miss Agnes, Miss Madge, their aunt old Mrs Travers, and one hired mistress. Every evening Miss Agnes brought out her mandolin and accompanied our going-to-bed hymn.

Clearly I remained an undisciplined child—so much so that Mrs Travers consulted a doctor about my behaviour and its cure. 'Cane him' was his specific, duly reported to my distressed mother. Mrs Travers, perhaps half-heartedly, attempted this. I snatched the cane from her and dealt her one unfeeling (and unfelt, because of her many petticoats) blow. Then, as so often, shame and tears followed victory. For this incident, I was sent home for a fortnight in the middle of term. My parents, whatever they felt, reproached me only with a look.

At school I had been taught the England-is-always-right attitude towards the Boer War. I bought a vulgar toy called 'one in the eye for Kruger'* in which an elastic-mounted button could be

* President of the Boer Republic in the Transvaal.

flicked against his portrait. This my mother confiscated. 'Traitor' I called her. Like many Liberals at the time, my parents were pro-Boer; my uncle William (Butler) had been sent home from South Africa, where he was Commander-in-Chief, because of his opposition to the war. I am moved by a self-picturing letter written at this time by my father to my mother during one of their rare partings. He is at work in the office of the *Tablet* and at 7 o'clock has missed the evening post:

" Dearest of Women: The *Tablet* office is no place to hymn in —but I did mean to get off a line thence before the clock struck seven. An incursion of the Cardinal [Vaughan] caused a diversion, however, and the clock struck. Did I tell you that I lunched with him on Saturday ? Among other things Bishop Brindley said: 'If I were Lord Methuen I would give the Boers no quarter.' I could not resist saying 'Perhaps he has read the Sermon on the Mount'. The eyes of two Monsignori, anti-war, glistened. The hatefulness of a bloody-minded Bishop made my hand tremble so much that I could not without betraying it cut my orange! So I left it. "

I have a childish memory of J. L. Garvin coming into the house shouting from the newspaper that he carried what I heard as 'robbers in the kitchen are going to escape'. I rushed down to the kitchen . . . they had already gone. Then what an anti-climax. I was told that what Garvin had reported was 'Roberts and Kitchener are going to the Cape'. But clearly I had some real feeling about the war. My mother told me that varying my usual phrase, 'have you heard the latest ?', which she said often referred to my own wrongs, I came to her in tears with the question, 'Have you heard the saddest ?' The saddest was a Boer War battle with many thousand killed.

Miss Agnes was one of the kindest of people but she also believed in those habits of order and discipline which were admired in those days. We had rice pudding for lunch every day of the week

"Lord and Lady Lytton's annual juvenile fancy-dress ball at Knebworth House. Left to right (back row): Mr Francis Meynell, Mr Edward Marsh, Mr Jasper Plowden. (Front row): Master Robert Lutyens, Miss Linnet Lafone, Lady Hermione Lytton, Miss Betty and Miss Barbara Lutyens, and Lord Knebworth." From the *Daily Graphic*. (*See page* 65.)

BLAST

The Post Office   Frank Brangwyn   Robertson Nicol

Rev. Pennyfeather   Galloway Kyle
(Bells)   (Cluster of Grapes)

Bishop of London and all his posterity

Galsworthy   Dean Inge   Croce   Matthews

Rev. Meyer   Seymour Hicks

Lionel Cust   C. B. Fry   Bergson   Abdul Bahai

Hawtrey   Edward Elgar   Sardlea

Filson Young   Marie Corelli   Geddes

Codliver Oil   St. Loe Strachey   Lyceum Club

Rhabindraneth Tagore   Lord Glenconner of Glen

Weiniger   Norman Angel   Ad. Mahon

Mr. and Mrs. Dearmer   Beecham   Ella
A. C. Benson   (Pills, Opera, Thomas)   Sydney Webb

British Academy   Messrs. Chapell

Countess of Warwick   George Edwards

Willie Ferraro   Captain Cook   R. J. Campbell

Clan Thesiger   Martin Harvey   William Archer

George Grossmith   R. H. Benson

Annie Besant   Chenil   Clan Meynell

Father Vaughan   Joseph Holbrooke   Clan Strachey

21

Wyndham Lewis's comprehensive list of 'blasts' 1914 (*see page 17*).

except Sunday, when there was a rather thin custard. This I ate with a fork in order to make it last longer. The rice pudding I would not eat. My hands were tied behind my back and the pudding was smeared over my mouth in the effort to make me eat it. I have never since been able to face rice pudding. Again, we were allowed only one glass of water at a meal because, we were told, more might induce the habit of drunkenness in later life.

Our religious teaching culminated in the assumption that we all longed to suffer martyrdom. Thus we were required to answer the question, 'Would you prefer to be burnt at the stake or frozen to death?' We all chose to be frozen—perhaps because the slower death would offer just a chance of rescue. When at the age of seven I made my first communion I was told by Miss Agnes that this was the happiest day of my life, a phrase which I duly used in a letter thanking my parents for their congratulations. My father in writing to me quoted a remarkable paradox of Cardinal Manning's: 'If we only knew how ready God was to forgive us, we should never offend Him'.

How remarkably things learnt by heart in childhood stay in one's memory! I can still rattle off the dates of all the kings of England and the multiplication tables up to nineteen-times, the learning of which became a gloat over my sisters, who had stopped at the more conventional twelve-times. The catechism and several prayers and litanies were other by-heart exercises. In the 'Hail Mary' comes the phrase 'Blessed be the fruit of thy womb'. This last word was an embarrassment to Miss Agnes, lest we should ask its meaning; so we were taught to say, 'Blessed be the fruit of thy-um'.

From Miss Lamprell's I went to St Anthony's, Eastbourne. It's owner and headmaster was Mr Patton and I got on very well with him until a parents and masters cricket match against the boys. Before my own innings I was umpiring while Mr Patton was bowling. I had never before seen finger-and-wrist spinning of the ball, and I thought it unfair. So I no-balled him. 'Why?' he demanded. 'For throwing' said I. I was removed from my place at the wicket.

George Hirst, the great Yorkshire cricketer, was my hero at this time and in 1904, when he had his benefit, I sent him a hard-saved half-crown, asking him how to make the ball swerve. His reply in his own round and careful hand was as follows:

"Dear Sir, [this alone was worth the money to a schoolboy] thank you for the 2/6. I cannot tell you how to make the ball swerve, hold the ball with the seam between the first two fingers. Yours faithfully, George Hirst."

But that was not the end. There was a gap of an inch and then magnanimously another 'George Hirst'—detachable for a swap.

M. Talibart, the French master, was a great reassurance. He did not despise the fluent but very juvenile French which I had learnt from my French *bonne* and he encouraged me in the reading of French poetry. I still have by heart poems of Victor Hugo and Alfred de Musset and Verlaine learnt from him in those days.

My mother kept some of my letters of this period, presumably the most communicative that I wrote. But, alas, they indicate nothing more than a conventional schoolboy. For instance:

"Darling Mother, Thank you so much for your letter and chocolates. I could not write before because as I play for the first eleven all my spare time has to go to the nets. Your devoted son."

And to a sister:

"Dearest Madeline, Thanks very much for the cakes and letters. I am improving in my batting. I wish you would send me a box of caramels. I did write to you and to mother but I suppose they got lost in the post."

How I wish I had kept my mother's letters to me! At this time she always finished them with 'your devoted mother, A.M.' That seemed to me too distant. I begged her to write 'Alice Meynell' in full, because I had such pride in her name. From then until she died she never failed to do as I had asked.

One of the delights of my days at St Anthony's was the receipt, regularly once a fortnight, of a long letter from my eldest sister's husband, Caleb Saleeby. He was a doctor of some note through his writing, and an early propagandist for clean air. His letters ran to six or eight foolscap pages, written in his own hand and presenting some scientific subject. He used also to take me to the Christmas Lectures for young people at the Royal Institution. Not with deliberation but because of his scientific approach to things, he caused in me the beginnings of doubt about my religion. When at confession I dared to ask whether a really good God would send people to Hell, my confessor said, 'My son, you are suffering from spiritual pride. Say ten "Hail Marys" as a penance'. I was eleven.

I repeated the question to my mother. Although a convert to Catholicism, she kept her own mind and interpretation of its dogmas. 'If there is a Hell,' she told me, 'God would not allow anyone to stay there for eternity.' Letters still exist which show that in the 1880s my mother had been in anxious communication on this subject with her friend St George Mivart, the biologist, who had become a convert to the Catholic church early in life but who was excommunicated shortly before his death in 1900. He reinforced my mother's repudiation of Hell. One of his letters ends as follows: 'Let Hell and damnation be entirely banished from your thoughts... Most certainly, taken the way they are commonly understood, they do not and cannot exist.'

Sometimes my mother took me to see my grandmother, by then a widow but still a great character. She lived in Turnham Green with her piano and many cats. On one of these visits my grandmother studied my appearance and said, 'Ah, the face and figure of a Roman Emperor...' I was exalted for a moment, until she added 'of the decadent period'.

When I was fourteen I went to Downside, the Benedictine

school in Somerset. At the beginning of my first term, in homesick misery, I begged Dom Leander Ramsey, the headmaster, to allow me to go home. He was so kindly persuasive that I agreed to stay. Years later, when I was in the sixth form and in some mild trouble, he reminded me of what I had said at that first interview: 'All right, sir, I will give Downside another chance.' He had hidden this piece of arrogance in his mind and now used it against me with an upturned eyebrow.

He was a remarkable man: he had virtually abolished caning—something quite revolutionary in those days. Only once was I caned. Valentine Browne (later the journalist Lord Castlerosse) and another boy called French (we despised him a little because his name didn't begin with ff) and I were held to have much general aptitude but to be very backward at Latin. We were given special coaching by a young master in the headmaster's study. We found that if we fidgeted with anything we were told to throw it out of the window. One day we arrived early and filled our pockets with all the headmaster's small belongings that we found on his desk. Then we began our great fidget. 'Out of the window!' shouted the young master, and joyfully we obeyed. Pens, pencils, ruler—one thing after another. There was inevitably an hour of reckoning when the headmaster re-occupied his desk. This time he did use the cane, but mildly, not because of the inconvenience we had caused him but because of our abuse of the special privilege of working in his study.

And what an open mind that man had! I went to him once to point out that at evening prayers everyone in the school had to say, 'I desire to be dissolved and to be with Christ.' 'Not one of us really desires that', I said. All Dom Leander said in reply was, 'That is enough'. But next term I found that the prayer book had been reprinted without the offending phrase.

I cannot say that I was very much interested in learning at Downside. I had the wits to get by and that was enough for me.

But I enjoyed essay writing, and I reported to my mother, 'I have just finished a sixteen page essay on, or rather against, the House of Lords, and last week I did one of fifteen pages on "The beautiful is as useful as the useful or more so".' One prize, one only, came my way. It was the poems of Byron. My mother, fearing I suppose the effect of Don Juan on my morals, returned it with a protest to the headmaster. A dreary book by A. C. Benson was the replacement.

Proudly, I became editor of the school magazine, *The Raven*. This made a distraction from school studies, but my letters home justified it as useful training 'if I take up journalism, as I hope to, in later days as my career . . .' I persuaded my mother to write an essay for it. It was a comparison of English and Irish landscapes. Never can *The Raven* have had so good, and so irrelevant, a contribution.

My other interests were well balanced between poetry and games. I have a letter in which I avow my youthful preferences in poetry:

"I think Victor Hugo one of the very greatest of poets. I should be content I think, or nearly so, if the literature accessible to me consisted entirely of Victor Hugo, Wordsworth and Francis Thompson. I do not think I should miss Shelley a bit! Is that a very fearful thing to write?"

I made the first eleven in cricket, football (Downside was then a soccer school) and hockey. There was a habit of the school 'giving' a bat to anyone who scored fifty in a school match. The first time this happened to me, my father discovered, when he received the school bill, that he was charged for the bat. Never a games player himself, he certainly hoped I would never get my fifty at Downside again.

Sex. Yes, for me it was powerful but private. I never had a word about the 'facts of life' from my parents or nurses or teachers. My keyhole efforts to overhear my mother's instruction to my eldest sister when she became engaged were unsuccessful. 'Babies come through their mother's belly-button' an elder boy had told me at Miss Lamprell's. (He was soon to go into a seminary on his way to priesthood, so maybe he never learnt any more or better!)

At Downside one could deduce that masturbation was fairly common from the number of boys who chose Dom Dominic, out of a dozen on offer, as their confessor. He was ill and permanently confined to his room in the monastery. There he heard confessions, and thus we avoided the embarrassed out-of-confessional meetings which we would have had to face with any other confessor. The polite formula that we all used was 'I have sinned against Holy Purity'. What a nonsense! Already I held the view, now I believe widely accepted by sociologists, that there is nothing wrong in private masturbation. It is certainly as healthy an outlet as nature's 'wet dreams', and less self-involving, as well as less dangerous to others, than too early or too casual homosexual or heterosexual experience.

At Downside I had my first paid commission. The publishing firm of Burns & Oates, which was managed by my father, paid me two guineas for bringing up to date a little book called *A Short Catechism of English History*. The old edition ended about the 1870s; my additions gave me one of my first political opportunities. One of my questions ran thus:

"*Q.* What great statesman attempted to do justice to Ireland in 1885?

A. William Gladstone."

The publishers did not spot this until the book was printed. Then outraged Unionists, as the majority of its directors and clients were, secured the book's withdrawal and amendment.

My politics were active at school. I reported to my mother that I had managed to persuade the committee of the senior library to replace *The Times* by the cheaper *Morning Post* and—the real achievement—*The Tribune*, the new Liberal daily. I also persuaded one of the 'cupboard Johns', as the kitchen employees at Downside were called, to lend me secretly *Reynolds Weekly*, then a propagandist republican paper; and in the senior debating society in 1906 I proposed a resolution that 'we welcome with joy the election of the first Labour M.P.s'. I found a seconder—but not a single other supporter. My father kept the 'speech' I wrote for this occasion. I wince now at its verbosity, and while I confess to a little pride in its sentiments I was soon to find all I wanted to say in these lines of Chesterton:

It may be we shall rise the last as Frenchmen rose the first,
Our wrath come after Russia's wrath and our wrath
                                        be the worst.
We are the people of England; and we have not spoken yet.
Smile at us, pay us, pass us. But do not quite forget.

This passage I have used in many a speech and I caused the whole poem to be printed in the *Daily Herald* in 1917.

I was able to nourish my political interest in the school holidays by visits to the *Tribune* Rendezvous, in which political lectures were given. There I first heard and met Philip Morrell. He argued the case for the Single Tax—a land and property tax. He was handsome, eloquent and (in the economic situation of that era) seemingly cogent. Later I was to know him well as Lady Ottoline Morrell's husband, and as a fellow member of the Savile Club. He kept his handsome presence to the end of his life.

I made long-standing friendships with two masters at Downside. With Dom Bruno Hicks, who later became Abbot, the first link was cricket; he was an admirable bat and became vice-president of the Somerset County Cricket Club. He gave me lessons in astronomy, using the telescope on the roof of the monastery. There he even allowed me to smoke a cigarette on the understanding that I never let anyone at school or monastery know. In 1948 he told me that he was coming to London and I begged him to come and see me. I waited for his ring at the bell with some anxiety. Would I even recognise him? At Downside he seemed already an old man, as did any master—though in fact, as I calculate, he was only thirteen years my senior. I hurried to open the door and there he was, no less handsome and scarcely older-looking than when I had last seen him nearly forty years before.

With W. E. Campbell, another master, I was also still in correspondence at this time. Then he told me that recently a boy in parting from him before leaving Downside said: 'Goodbye, sir. You're a very young old man'. True enough. Campbell helped my rebel side at school. *Tono-Bungay* by H. G. Wells was then running in the *English Review* and it was thought to be bawdy and irreligious and anti-establishment, and so the magazine was banned from the school library. Campbell conveyed it to me secretly month by month. To my mother he wrote in 1907:

"I see a good deal of Francis. Things, or rather I should say *thoughts*, go so hardly with him and he has yet to learn that one can only suffer for the many by suspending judgement and trying to understand . . . trying to compassionate with others. . . ."

While I was at school, I saw relatively little of my sisters and brothers. In London holidays I joined them in the mixed hockey and cricket games of their 'Posset Club'—my sister Madeline was a good over-arm bowler. We went then and later to many dances together, including Slade School balls since my brother Everard and my sister Olivia were both students there.

At Downside was laid the foundation of a friendship which was momentous for me—and all through an error of identification in the Abbey. One day we were invited to 'pray for the soul of Robert Cryan'. This I took to mean a form mate of that name and, much distressed, I went to the Head for details. 'No,' he said, 'this prayer was not for your friend but for his father,' the anniversary of whose death it was. My form mate told this to his mother and she began a new chapter in my life. Happy? Yes. Miserable? Yes. Shaping? Yes, I think so.

Mrs Cryan was in her early forties. I was what was considered a mature seventeen. We became very fond of each other. Was it a curious falling in love on both parts? It had its mild, almost modest, physical aspect. For me, I suppose it was combined with a sense of growing up, even a first step, a discovering but hesitant step, away from the domination of home. She had two teenage daughters, but at first I was little aware of them.

Mrs Cryan invited me to make a holiday visit to her house in Merrion Square, the smartest square in Dublin. And a little later, in 1909, she took me with her children to Rome to be present at the beatification of Joan of Arc in St Peters, a moving spectacle presided over by Pope Pius X. But when I returned home I was glib about it at a party in the Smith Square house of Reginald and Pamela McKenna. Lord Riddell was there. When he had heard my description he asked if I would care to repeat it in the *News of the World*, which he owned. I was elated and said 'Yes, indeed'. He asked me what I would call my article. I thought that I must play down to his paper's standard, so I gave him what I still think a good—at any rate for a just seventeen-year-oldster—journalistic reply. 'Hullo Halo,' I said. He was shocked, and that was the end of that.

IV

College

At the beginning of the 1900s my father's fortunes had prospered. After eighteen years of hard work on it, he had sold the *Weekly Register* for £840 and he had become first the reader to Burns & Oates, then its general manager at a salary of £500. Here he showed so profitable a competence that he was made a partner and was given a third of the company's shares by its two proprietors, which brought his earnings to not less than £1,500 a year. He had also his earnings as a journalist. Money was coming in too from my mother's poems and essays and also from Francis Thompson's poems after his death in 1907, a recompense to my parents of truly poetic justice. So, with inheritances, the family was comfortably off by the time I was growing up.

My father began to find his daily bus journeys to and from his work too time-wasting. With the efficiency which was perhaps a result of his Quaker origins he decided to make into a flat the top storey of the Burns & Oates premises at the corner of Orchard Street and Granville Place and in 1905 we moved into this. The Palace Court house was let.

I was now due to leave Downside and my parents planned for me a university career at Oxford. In those days there was no difficulty about getting in if one's parents could afford it, as mine could. I tried for a scholarship at Balliol. I did well enough in the written papers to get to the interview stage for the top candidates. Then, in a room of awesome vastness with a phalanx of dons at the distant end of it, I was mum-chance. Asked what Latin books of reference I had studied, I could think only of Smith's Smaller Classical Dictionary. The Master in dismissing me made me feel that he wondered a little how I had got that far.

[42]

To my parents I pointed out that Modern English Literature at Oxford began with Beowulf and 'Old English' and proceeded through 'Middle English' before arriving at Chaucer, whereas at Trinity College, Dublin, English Literature began with Chaucer. To this I added the very practical argument that Mrs Cryan had offered me hospitality in her house, which would relieve my father of much expense. So to Trinity College, Dublin, I went in 1909. In a careful letter to my father I detailed all the costs:

"There is an entrance fee of £15 followed by half-yearly payments of £8. . . . One has to join a society or club and these fees and one's book bill and the requirements of one's tutor total about £12. As to sports subscriptions and dress allowance I was told variously that £30 or £40 was necessary. The last figure is of course absurdly high. There is one more item to make the list comprehensive—£9 for three return fares between Dublin and London annually. The total thus amounts to just under £69—a large sum, dearest father, but very happily, only about half the amount you spend on me at Downside. . ."

I cannot pretend that my studies at T.C.D. occupied a large or indeed a sufficient part of my mind. My concern was with the family with whom I lived and with their friends—chief among them Maurice Healy, nephew of Tim Healy, the famous and rebellious Irish political leader. Maurice was later well known in his own right as Q.C., broadcaster and wine expert.

I visited Tim Healy one day and he flattered me by being most entertaining throughout a long afternoon. Maurice later told me that almost invariably he shook hands and then sat in complete and masterly silence until he rushed from the room, not to appear again until his guest had departed.

Maurice, then a law student, and I were members of the Society of St Vincent de Paul. The poverty in Dublin was horrible, and it was our duty to visit the poor and dispense platitudes of religious comfort along with totally inadequate gifts of money or food or medicine. Our visits did not take us far afield—some of the worst slums were at the back of the houses in the two rich squares, where stables had been turned into monstrously overcrowded tenements.

My uncle William (Sir William Butler) died at Bansha Castle, his Irish home, in June 1910. I did not go to the funeral, but to my father I reported that I had sent a fine wreath as instructed; that the Irish press paid unanimous tribute to Uncle William; that Queen Alexandra's message of sympathy was kind, though ungrammatical; and that the wreath had cost £2 10s.

My Dublin friends included the poets Padraic Colum, Thomas MacDonagh, St John Gogarty and, less closely, George Russell ('Æ'). We used to meet in a house in Merrion Street where poetry and politics had an equal and passionate rating.

Irish, but settled in London, was Katharine Tynan (to us and all her close friends 'K.T.'). W. B. Yeats had made a selection of her poems, and this was beautifully printed by his sister, Elizabeth Yeats, at her Dun Emer Press, where I was an admiring visitor. I was not wholly content with Yeats's selection, since it did not include my favourite *The Quiet Nights*, but my need was satisfied by K.T. herself; she wrote the poem for me in my copy of the book.

Alfred Noyes, the first English poet I knew beyond the immediate family circle, came to Dublin in 1908 for the production of a play of his, and invited me to the first night. This was the beginning of a long friendship. Like so many at that time I had been moved by his narrative poem of child-adventure, *The Forest of Wild Thyme*, in which the children were lost and at last found, so I wrote sentimental lines to him. (One of them, one only, isn't so bad. I leave you to find it.)

> O Alfred Noyes, yours is the gleam,
> You have the nursery rhymes by heart

You dream as young-eyed children dream
And yet your dream is all apart . . .
Oh, do not light the lamp I pray,
I pray you, narrow not the bars,
For in closed doors we are all astray
And a lighted lamp puts out the stars.
Book-lore is nought to fairy toys
So, go on playing, Alfred Noyes . . .

His reply neatly and very properly rebuked me:

Worse than hemlock, worse than fennell,
Worse than nightshade, Francis Meynell.

I went often to the Abbey Theatre, then in its heyday, and once
to a concert of which the star was Caruso. Besides Caruso's incred-
ibly beautiful singing there were piano pieces played by a young
woman called Hilda Saxe. Hers was a performance I cherished
in memory not much less than Caruso's, and the enthusiasm of
the music critics justified my feeling. I did not meet her then.
Maurice Healy became my comforter in the desperate situation
which was soon to arise. I fell in love with Edith, one of Mrs
Cryan's daughters. We were all sleeping out one hot summer
night at Mrs Cryan's holiday house in Killiney and Edith came and
lay down beside me. We kissed, no more, but that was enough:
we pledged ourselves to each other. I reported my new involvement to her mother and showed her something I had been im-
pelled to write:

Spirit of smiles and tears, you came to me in the night
The quartered moon aglow in your hair and the lessened light
Of an army of stars in your eyes, weary of truant sleep.
Little self-skilled you were, who thought you came to weep.

My bitter reward was that her mother decided I must leave the house; and heartsick I transferred to 13 Botany Bay, within Trinity College. I was not allowed thereafter to see or to correspond with Edith or her sister. Even in my sorrow I enjoyed the excited pleasure of having published in the *New Age* a poem of mine addressed to Edith, my first signed appearance in print.

Only scraps of memory of Trinity days come back to me at this long distance in time. As when, in a Dramatic Society play, I performed at the Gaiety Theatre, playing second male lead to W. F. Casey, and so beginning a friendship which was resumed twenty-five years later when he was editor of *The Times*. Or when my rooms were due to be redecorated and to the astonishment of the Dean I chose a brown wrapping paper for the walls and hung upon it a number of Steinlen prints. This was very avant-garde and Slade-Schoolish. Then there was the solace, in my Botany Bay rooms, of the pianola and piano which I hired. Because the man responsible for the promotion of pianolas in England was a friend of my family he let me have my pianola for 8s. 6d. a year.

I was sometimes invited by the Aberdeens to the Vice-Regal Lodge—initially a tribute to my mother, whose poems they both admired, and afterwards because I joined in some of Lady Aberdeen's 'good works'. I served occasionally as a waiter in a sort of tea-club which she ran with the laudable but wholly unrealistic purpose of providing a get-together place for English and Irish middle-class people. The Aberdeens, being Liberals and suspected of favouring Home Rule, were not popular among English residents in Ireland.

Oliver St John Gogarty, who possessed one of the few private motor cars in Dublin at that time, once drove my tutor and me out to Dalkey to visit Provost Mahaffy of Trinity.

It was a great occasion for a freshman to be taken, and by such companions, to call on the Provost so famous for his wit. The wit didn't shine, but the sun did, and the harbour of Dalkey looked entrancing. So did the grand half-circle, as I remember it, of the elegant eighteenth-century houses of Sorrento Terrace where he lived. But perhaps my memory was affected by the glamour of the whole occasion, for when I revisited Sorrento Terrace nearly sixty years later it was no more than a half-dozen small houses without much character.

Why so long for a revisit? I could not face a return to Ireland till my old age. Grief does in the end die, though shame only slumbers. It took me long years to come at last to a historic rather than a personal view of the wanton and cold-blooded execution by my country of the leaders of the Easter Week rising in 1916, some of them my friends: most of all Thomas MacDonagh, the poet, and Jim Connolly, the Labour leader.

My life at T.C.D. had become far from happy. The combination of closeness to and utter division from my young love, Edith, was hard to bear, and early in my third college year, before I was able to sit for a degree, I left T.C.D. and returned home. I did not see Edith again. She died four years later scarcely out of her 'teens. My ever-considerate father welcomed me to a job he invented for me, and my mother to her comforting embrace. And this is what I wrote of Ireland:

> You who gave at my first demand
> A love to my lips, a friend to my hand,
> A company I could admire
> Of men hot with the poet's fire:
> You who gave me more in a year
> Than many such would bring me here,
> Ireland, take, if your proud heart can,
> The homage of an Englishman.
>
> And first those friends—the poets who
> As much as songs had men in mind:

[47]

MacDonagh and Pearse of the rebel kind;
Gogarty, Colum, Stephens too,
Who with loud angers used to meet
At the mild house in Merrion Street,
Holding me, stranger, as their own
Because I was a poet's son.

Quick-known, quick-loved, quick-lost. I prize
The rhetoric of your sunset skies;
The patchwork fields; the low-winged cloud,
The voices rich and not too loud
That take some cadence from the birds
And music make of our Saxon words;
A stillness in the to-and-froing,
A purpose greater than the doing,
Politics broken at the seams—
A people wakened to their dreams.

Ireland gave me more in a year
Than many such would bring me here—
A love, a grief, a gaiety,
And a little of hating, it may be
(May that, and more, be forgiven me).
And she never gave grief but she gave me a friend.

And so I pray, will it be at the end.

Yes, there is still some sad sense as well as some emotion here.

V

Family

While I was at school and university my parents' busy life in a world of which I was only an observer continued in all its variety. In addition to her work on their magazines, my mother also wrote essays, first for Henley's *Fortnightly Review* and then, anonymously, for the *Pall Mall Gazette*. These last made a stir, a commotion, in the smaller and sensitive reading world of the 'nineties. When her first collected essays were brought out by John Lane at the Bodley Head, Max Beerbohm wrote that while he was 'still trying to work his way in at the back door she sprang, like Minerva, full-grown from the Bodley Head'. In another article he wrote: 'Enthusiasm for the Queen is easy to understand. She is our monarch and she has reigned for sixty years, and so we love her. But who made Mrs Meynell a ruler over us? She is in danger of becoming a substitute for the English Sabbath'.

The literary personalities of that day discovered my mother first as a name, then as an acquaintance and, in the case of George Meredith, finally as his 'dearest friend', his 'dearest Portia', as he named her because of her power in making a point. The painter John Sargent, a reserved man, was among those who were watchful for her weekly essays: 'I shall be reckless tonight and give you thanks', he wrote to her, 'for many a delight brought home, or for the slight push that sends a doubtful idol toppling. I don't know which I enjoy most'.

My father was a never-ceasing journalist with such things as paragraphs in the *Daily Chronicle*, reviews in the *Athenaeum*, a weekly page in the *Tablet*. When Shane Leslie had to be absent from his editorship of the *Dublin Review* (published, despite its name, in London) my father agreed to take his place for a while. A letter from my mother describes the ensuing disorder: 'The drawing-room is in a state of chaos quite indescribable, since the *Dublin Review* is edited on the writing-table, on the piano and the chairs and the floor, and in the fender'.

In the last ten years of her life my mother became a poet again and a new generation of readers, led by a new generation of critics—J. C. Squire (planning the *London Mercury*), Drinkwater, Chesterton, Garvin—found her a new fame. In 1913 she was among those proposed as Poet Laureate. The *Star*, the *Pall Mall Gazette* and the *Daily Mail* favoured her and a plebiscite in *T.P.'s Weekly* placed her next to Kipling, with Masefield, Hardy, Robert Bridges and Yeats behind her. Another kind of laureateship was hers when in 1940, eighteen years after her death, an edition of her poems was included in the *Oxford Editions of Standard Authors*, and reprinted in 1941, 1942 and 1947. It is a sign of the utter change of taste in poetry that after this not a single edition of her poems was in print until I made my own selection and published it, as the only Nonesuch Press paperback, in 1966.

My mother was not only a poet herself, she was a cause of poetry in others. Meredith wrote sonnets to her—not very good ones; Francis Thompson, John Drinkwater, George Rostrevor Hamilton, Katharine Tynan and Vita Sackville-West all addressed poems to her or to her memory. Jack Squire made this prose portrait of her which seems to me exact as well as kind:

"I, one of many who were honoured by her kindness and benefited by her wisdom, shall carry her gracious memory to the grave. There, in her London flat or in the ample library room of her country cottage, she would sit in her corner; a woman with unwhitened hair, very upright and calm. She still gave an impression of youth and beauty . . . a saint and a sibyl smoking a cigarette."

To her children as they grew up, and always to her husband, my mother was someone to be protected—from household duties, from bores, from undertaking works of mercy beyond her strength. We had our jokes about her, untrue but plausible—for example that she had spent an hour in a cabman's shelter in the belief that it was a slow-to-start tramcar.

I think now that she was over-protected, even a little constrained by our care. Our view of her—the family view—was that she was complete: completely just, good and happy. But does complete happiness reside in such a poem as this, in which she addressed the spirit of sleep?

> Come and release me; bring
> My irresponsible mind; come in thy hours.
> Draw from my soul the sting
> Of wit that trembles, consciousness that cowers.
>
> For if night come without thee
> She is more cruel than day. But thou, fulfil
> Thy work, thy gifts about thee—
> Liberty, liberty from this weight of will.

The 'weight of will' was heavy on her through all her life. Long after her enforced parting from the priest who inducted her into Catholicism she had another no less painful parting from Patmore, at her husband's urgent wish.

There were also, thank goodness, a few little vanities: her hiding of her age, her intense pleasure in praise—'recognition' as it was then called. But she kept her head. In a letter to Patmore about the praise given to one of her essays she said, 'You are always to remember that I am *not* a goose'.

My mother maintained a close reticence about her inner feelings. Even her devoted letters to my father on her rare absences from home were, I think, as much responses to his expectations as they were her own voluntaries. A like reticence she allowed to her children; though well aware of their plentiful romances, she did not ask about them.

A vital part of our family life was the house at Greatham in Sussex. The original farmhouse and eighty acres of wood and pasture were bought by my parents in 1911 for £1,600 plus £600 for the timber. My parents added a library to the farmhouse, converted the cowshed into a cottage for Viola to live in, and built a house and bungalow close at hand, thus establishing the family— or Clan Meynell—'colony'. After the first war, I was to build myself a cottage on a far point of the estate; no disloyalty to Clan Meynell, but thus I preserved my freedom.

My father's concern was with the out-of-doors. On one occasion he found a neighbour moving his fence to our side of a ditch. 'In Sussex,' said the neighbour, 'one may claim as far as a deer may leap on the other side of one's fence.' 'May not a deer leap either way?' asked my father.

To Greatham came some of the writers who were my parents' London visitors—Wilfrid Blunt, Ralph Hodgson, Shane Leslie*, Hilaire Belloc, Jack Squire, George Rostrevor Hamilton, E. V. Lucas, the gay essayist and anthologist. Padraic Colum, the Irish poet, spent his honeymoon there; their bedroom (Padraic told Eddie Marsh, who told me) was embarrassingly un-sound-proof. Others who came were David ('Bunny') Garnett, Harold Hobson, son of J. A. Hobson, and Herbert ('Bertie') and Eleanor Farjeon. All four became my close friends.

Writing to me in 1958, Shane Leslie cast his mind and mine back to those Greatham days:

"I have been reading books about and by the Bloomsbury Group. I suppose when I had the coterie fever I fell in with your father and became exposed to the Greatham Group, which sounds more mellifluous than the Bloomsberries. I wish

* Sir Shane Leslie, cousin of Winston Churchill, poet and inveterate Irishman who wears the Irish kilt.

as much were written about visitors to Greatham and the happy days they passed in the Meynell Constellation. Wishing you all the blessings for Pentecost or the Derby, whichever be the feast on the arrival of this letter."

My father had a special love for my eldest sister Monica. After her marriage broke down he installed her in the new house he had built close to his own at Greatham. (I did not care for its architecture, and nicknamed it 'Regreatham'.) He also put at her disposal the rarity of a car and a gardener-chauffeur. The car was an early French affair that he had bought from his friend Lady Hosier*, who had complained to him of the noise it made. My father told her that the greater the noise the safer it was for pedestrians.

Before this my father had had a White Steamer, the paraffin in which had to be alight for a good quarter of an hour before the car could be started. It had a peculiarity, dangerous even at the mild speed of which it was capable: it accelerated slightly when it was steered to the right, slowed when it was steered to the left.

My brother Everard was an artist manqué, a journalist, and finally a bookshop-keeper, where he specialised in seventeenth-century poets and sold prints by Eric Gill and Lovat Fraser. He married the lovely contralto singer Grazia Carbone, who was of south Italian parentage but born and brought up in the United States. They had four children to care for, and this inevitably diverted the parents from their arts. Everard wrote pleasing books about Corot and about Bellini and also the definitive *Life of Francis Thompson*. In the second year of the 1914 war, after much doubt and cogitation, he enlisted in the Artists' Rifles. He was never sent abroad and 'rose, but only very slowly'—as it pleased him to emphasise—to the rank of corporal. E. V. Lucas remarked that Everard was probably the only corporal in the British Army to have written a life of Francis Thompson.

* She became the mother-in-law of Winston Churchill.

After my brother's discharge from the army at the end of the war he developed tuberculosis and went with his family to the U.S.A., where it was thought he might find effective treatment. My mother sold jewels given to her by Coventry Patmore to tide him over, and later assigned to him all the royalties on her last book of essays. Hospital treatment near Buffalo (Grazia's childhood home) was unsuccessful and he went to Genoa. I visited him there, but left a few days before he died in 1926. I pencilled lines in the train on my way home. I print them here not as poetry but as evidence of my love for him and of my sense of shame in leaving him when he was at the door of death.

> All that I see and hear in the Genoa train
> Has an equal rhythm of mind, eye, ear:
> The trochee, trochee, trochee of the train.
> These sights and sounds are curvatures of my heart.
> (He'll die, he'll die, he'll die an iambic death.)
> Now as we slow to go over the station points
> I see and hear the dactyl with the trochee
> (Uomini ... Donne ... *Everard* ... *Meynell*).
> All one is my journey's beginning and middle and end;
> For the train never pauses in its death lullaby.
> This were a better place for my brother to die,
> A crash and the bright burnt moment.
> No parody of life, like the still-growing
> Nails and hair of the tomb ...

It was Christmas, and Vera (my second wife) was spending it with Bertrand and Dora Russell and Clifford and Joan Allen in Devon. I picked up our car in London and drove through snow, the dreariest drive of my life, as far as Lynmouth, my destination. It was not a happy Christmas. There was some strain between Vera and me, and my thought of Everard was sadly constant.

My sister Viola was made close to me by her writings. She was a talented novelist and short-story writer, and author of two family records.* I count some of her poems as at least the equal of my mother's. Viola was always humble, and her first novel† was anonymously published lest it might earn more notice than it merited because she was her mother's daughter.

My youngest sister Olivia was a Slade School student and as a painter had a ready talent. Only recently I have seen the scrap-books she kept long ago and they make me realise now, as I had failed to do before, how closely she followed my doings. All my early poems are there, cut from the papers which printed them. But more surprisingly there are innumerable cuttings from the *Daily Herald* of the period when I worked for it.

My mother died in 1922 when she was 75. I visited her on her death-bed at Granville Place. She turned her ravaged face away from me. Viola said that this was a sign that she 'still defended her personal dignity'; my simpler view is that she did it so that I should see less of her pain. Putting out her fragile arm towards me she said, 'Here are "my bluest veins to kiss".' How wonderful that Shakespeare could give her such apt words! And then, her last words to me, 'This is not tragic. I am happy'.

I mixed my early and my last memory of my mother in this sonnet:

> Time is not mocked. Did you when you were five
> Play ring-a-roses round the slow-foot second?
> Go distant journeys 'twixt the tick and tock?
> Perceive your mother, between beck and beckoned,
> Age, sicken, die—and come again alive
> (Oh wonderful) with the rustle of her frock?

* *Alice Meynell* (Cape, 1929) and *Francis Thompson and Wilfrid Meynell* (Hollis & Carter, 1952).
† *Martha Vine* (Herbert & Daniel, 1910).

If I slipped sideways, breathbound, swift and supple
I could pass between the clock-beats to the closet
Not scraping either second of its bloom;
Then from their pegs, like clothes, new lives uncouple,
And try them on, 'gainst my own shape's deposit.
I was the He, the Hunter. Time was the stay-at-home.

My mother died when I was grown a man.
Eternity was ended. Time began.

I was not so close to my father until his old age—until I could
'father' him. Only once in my early grown-up years did he speak
intimately to me, and moving I found his words: 'I have given
my shoulder for many a sad woman to weep on', he told me, 'and
I think that you will have similar opportunities. Do not abuse
them'. Indeed I was to have those opportunities—and, in his
terms, I did abuse them. Despite all the many ways in which I
defected from his judgements and feelings—in religion, in politics,
in morals—he never showed anger, never even argued.

My father did much verse writing, chiefly based on puns, of
which this is a sample:

> Men fall in love yet scale the skies
> From earth's profoundest prison.
> Oh change the word as there it *lies*:
> Not *fallen* in love, but *risen*.

He loved any sort of play on words. Once he argued in print with
Sir Thomas Massy-Massy, who had objected publicly to the
Catholic syllable in the word 'Christmas', claiming that it should
be changed to 'Christ-tide'. My father said that reform should
begin at home, and addressed him as 'Sir Totide Tidy-Tidy'.

My father survived my mother by a quarter of a century. He
was devotedly looked after by his daughters, mostly at Greatham.

In 1948 Viola and I were asked to broadcast together in the BBC series 'Return Journey', organised by Stephen Potter, about our young days together. I went to Greatham to rehearse it with Viola. We sat in the library. My father, then ninety-six, stayed with us, declaring that he was too deaf to hear a word that we said but would like our company. At the end of perhaps three-quarters of an hour of rehearsing he announced that we were wrong on five points, and supplied the corrections *seriatim*. Deaf ? Only when he did not want to hear.

My father died in that same year. The *Manchester Guardian* obituary was, my sisters and I thought, by far the best. I was deputed to write to the editor and inquire who had written it so that one of the family might express our thanks. The editor replied, 'It is *you* that *we* have to thank! You wrote it for us five years ago'. I couldn't believe it until my secretary produced the draft. I must have felt that by writing the obituary I was committing a kind of patricide, and therefore I managed to wipe out the memory of it. The psychologists would have a name for this.

Most surprising among the letters of condolence was one from Ezra Pound (who had alienated his English and American friends by Fascist broadcasts from Italy during the war) written from a 'hospital' in Washington. Its last line is a tribute to the tolerance of my father.

"Dear F.M., News of your father's death recalls far distant past. I send these regards to you as I don't know your sisters' present names.

He at least would be willing to be remembered.
Yours E. Pound."

Here is the epitaph my father wrote for himself:

When my last fires of life burn low
(I who have loved all fire-light so),

When hence you bear my load of dust
To the grave's pit as bear you must,
Remember that naught perisheth
In all God's universe but Death.
Weep not, though tears be holy water,
Tears of a wife, a son, a daughter.
Think of me only when you laugh;
And if you write my epitaph,
No name or date be there, but rather
'Here lies her husband and their father.'

VI

Early Work,
Early Play, Early Protest

I have felt bound to pursue the theme of my parents and family and their doings at the expense of chronology, but now I must return to my personal story as an emergent young man facing the necessity of making his way in life.

When I left Trinity College Dublin my father planned to employ me at Burns & Oates. I thought it would be well to learn a little about the book trade first, partly, I suppose, to give me a modicum of independence from my father. I proposed myself as an apprentice to Arthur Waugh (father of Alec and Evelyn), who was head of Chapman & Hall. He told me that I should need a year to study the less interesting beginnings: first I must learn to store and pack books; then to invoice them; then to travel them to the book-sellers.

'What about money?' I asked.

'Three hundred pounds', said he.

I exclaimed, 'Surely that is a lot to pay an ignorant learner'.

His surprised reply: 'My dear boy, that is not what I would pay you, it is what you would pay me'.

That was the end of that.

My first job at Burns & Oates could not have been more mundane. I was sent to collect from Ernest Oldmeadow, a Soho wine merchant, a small sum long owing for an advertisement in the *Catholic Directory*, a Burns & Oates publication. Oldmeadow said he was about to taste some Vieuxpré (note the name) champagnes: would I join him? I said a somewhat eager 'Yes'—I had never before in my nineteen years of life tasted champagne.

He took me up to his office, sat me beside him before a sink, explained that I was to taste first at the front of the mouth, then at the back, and then spit out. Was I to waste good champagne in that fashion? Not on your life! Bottle after bottle was opened; I tasted and swallowed. Two hours later I was returned in a hansom to Burns & Oates, clutching my wine-glass so firmly that it could not be freed from my hand—and without having collected the sum owing. Apart from this, in my long life I have never been the worse for liquor, and often the better.

My father appointed me as his assistant in the design of Burns & Oates books and a year later—when, I hope, I had proved myself—to be in effective charge of design and production. We enlarged the firm's programme to include the works of my mother and of Francis Thompson, which my father withdrew from John Lane, an admirable publisher fallen from his graces, I am sorry to say, because of Lane's publication of *The Yellow Book*, which harboured works considered by my parents to be 'shocking'.

The *Collected Works* of Francis Thompson was published three years after I joined the firm. Then I had a very personal lesson in detail, for when it was printed my father discovered that several commas had broken away from the ends of the lines and that a number of kerns (top loops) of the letter 'f' had broken off. Day after day piles of imperfect volumes were massed in our flat above Burns & Oates. My father established a sort of fire-bucket drill. One of my sisters would find the pages, my father would dab in the commas and kerns, another sister would apply the blotting paper, I would restack the volumes. Some hundreds of corrections were thus made.*

* Thompson's *Works* were in three volumes, but somewhat audaciously I caused 25 copies to be printed on very thin India paper, which allowed the three volumes to be bound up together as one. The title-pages carried the declaration 'Printed for F. M. W. M. May 1913'. The copy I still have was bound in limp vellum. To whom the other 24 were given and how they were bound I cannot remember.

My father entrusted the printing of a number of Burns & Oates books to Bernard Newdigate at the Arden Press, Letchworth. There I went often, thus becoming both humble pupil and proud patron of that notable typographer.

But the most important friendship and technical association that I formed at Burns & Oates was with Stanley Morison. In 1912 he was, not happily, a clerk in a bank. My cousin Gerard Meynell was founder, co-editor, publisher and printer of *The Imprint*, a short-lived but influential magazine of printing and the arts; he advertised for an editorial dogsbody and Morison got the job. When *The Imprint* folded, my father, impressed by Morison's writings and his recent conversion to Catholicism (as well as his need of a job), engaged him to be my assistant in book production at Burns & Oates.

Morison was twenty-four, I was twenty-two. We shared a devotion to religion, to socialist politics, to the seventeenth-century Fell types, and to cricket. We also observed a style, but a difference, of dress. All heads were covered in those days; working men wore caps, shopkeepers wore bowlers, the gentry and pro-fessionals wore toppers. But we, like priests, wore large slouch hats—Morison's the more priest-like because his was black. He made his hat more practical by boring a hole through its crown so that he could safely peg it on the hat-stand of any teashop.

Together at Burns & Oates we planned and designed many books, chief among them an *Ordo Administrandi Sacramenta** in Latin and English (with rubrics properly in red) printed in Fell types by Frederick Hall at the Oxford University Press. This was the first book in which I let myself go, even to the extent of having

---

* This book was included in the Fell Exhibition in 1967 to celebrate the publication of the great book on Bishop Fell and his types in which Morison and Harry Carter collaborated. At the invitation of the Oxford University Press I opened this exhibition proudly though sadly a day after Morison's death.

a few copies printed on 'real' (mulberry-leaf) Japanese vellum paper. I engaged Eric Gill to cut in wood the letters of the top line of the title page because there wasn't a suitable size of the Fell types.

I tried but failed to persuade Edward Johnston to design a new type for Burns & Oates, but he happily agreed to inscribe by hand the ten initial letters of each of the fifty copies of my mother's 'Ten Poems' which I myself set and printed in 1915. He was one of the great men and great letterists of his time. His own handiwork, his teaching and his book *Writing, Illuminating and Lettering* set afoot the world-wide revival of interest in penmanship. (As Ruari McLean wrote in 1959: 'Practically all lettering in Europe today is being taught by people taught by people taught by Johnston'.) His work and influence alone do not make a man truly 'great': he must have a great personality. Johnston showed it in his way of life and in his way of speech. Both had to be exact. The notice that he put outside his door when he was engaged in strokes of the pen or in thought was 'Preoccupied'. Noel Rooke, his friend and pupil, reported an occasion when he entered the master's studio without knocking. Johnston, surprised, let a pencil fall from his sloping scribe's desk, and muttered 'Damn'. Then he pulled himself together: 'I must apologise first to God, then to you and finally to the pencil itself; for if a round object did not fall from an inclined plane we should have no right to expect it to stay still upon a flat one'.

Other Burns & Oates books of this time were a book of short stories, *The Goddess of Ghosts*, by C. C. Martindale, which had on its title-page a border of printer's flowers (or 'fleurons')— a style of decoration that became almost a signature of Morison's and my early typographic work—and pretty editions of poems by Katharine Tynan and G. K. Chesterton, both friends of my parents. Once when Chesterton was lunching with us I asked him to autograph my copy of *The Wild Knight*, his earliest book of poems. He wrote in it what seemed to me a phrase both pleasing and exact: 'To Francis Meynell this book was not given by his friend G. K. Chesterton'. Many years later when I was asked by book collectors in New York to autograph their copies of Nonesuch books and I used Chesterton's phrase, I found that I left behind me a trail of offended people. To them the phrase proclaimed that I was not, in fact, friend enough to have given the book.

In 1913 I organised and edited *Eyes of Youth*—an odd enough book containing some unpublished early poems of Francis Thompson's and verses by Padraic Colum, Shane Leslie, Ruth Lindsay, Maurice Healy, Judith Lytton, and by me and three of my sisters. It had an introduction by Chesterton. To this collection (or part of it) George Moore reacted with this passage*:

"I turned over in bed, and must have dozed a little while for I suddenly found myself thinking of a tall sallow girl [my mother] with brown eyes and a receding chin, who used to show me her poems in manuscript ages ago. I thought them very beautiful at the time, and of this early appreciation I need not be ashamed. . . Unfortunately these poems preluded nothing but a great deal of Catholic journalism, a Catholic husband who once read me a chaplet of sixty sonnets which he had written to his wife, and a numerous Catholic progeny who have published their love of God in a collection of verse entitled *Eyes of Youth*. . . The volume concludes with the poems of Francis Meynell; but I think he lacks the piety of his sisters. We will assume that the ladies go to confession once a week, and the gentleman once a month."

His view of our poems was reasonable enough, but he scarcely did justice either to my mother's appearance or to her writing; her skin was fair, she was generally held to be beautiful and much of her poetry and the major part of her prose dealt with life, not with religion. My father's 'chaplet of sixty sonnets'? Impossibly

* From George Moore's *Salve*, p. 162.

[63]

out of character, both the writing of them and even more the reading of them to any acquaintance.

Life for me in those days was as much play as work. My father liked 'society', but he was too busy, and perhaps also too puritanical, to allow himself much indulgence in it. He had also another reason: he wanted to make opportunities for me. So he adopted the remarkable policy of accepting invitations and then sending me to fulfil them. I ought to have drawn back in embarrassment, but thank goodness I didn't.

What proved to be the opening of many doors in my young social life was the transfer to me of an invitation to a dinner-party given by Mrs Sybil Hart-Davis in 1910. There I met Lady Tree, Lady Diana Manners and Duff Cooper (they were not yet married), and far more significantly Eddie Marsh, civil servant, man of culture, man of the world.

It was Eddie Marsh who introduced me into the society of the rich, fashionable intelligentsia of the time and to much more; to a new look at, even a new discernment of, painting. He added too to my uncertain scepticism, which was important for someone brought up as I was. He once said to me: 'There may be a God, but I cannot be at all sure that he is a good one'.

Eddie was an every-weekend guest at great houses and often he arranged that I should be invited too. Thus I made close friends with the Lyttons at Knebworth, where a favourite after-dinner game was the recitation of poetry. One chose one's piece, and the recital was checked against the printed text. I discovered how frequently one got a word wrong. I did pretty well but Pamela Lytton did best of all.

There were also weekends at Nevill Holt, Lady Cunard's country palace, where Eddie had introduced me as 'the poet': an exaggeration pleasing to me though scarcely justified by perhaps a dozen of my poems which had been printed by the current intellectual journals. I found myself a little shocked by Thomas

Beecham, an invariable guest, who seemed to be offering love to Lady Cunard even when he was playing the piano, with her reserved and seemingly uninterested husband's back turned upon them.

Eddie had to drill me in manners for these occasions. In our poetry-readings together he corrected my French accent, and even my English, because I used the short 'a' which we had all learnt from our north-country father. Eddie also taught me to tie my evening tie—I had previously worn made-up ones, a despicable sign of ungentility...

In 1911 Nijinsky came to London with the Russian Ballet. I went often with Viola and Olivia to see him and Karsavina. We could afford no better than gallery seats (benches rather) at Covent Garden. I am apt to be height-sick, but I could manage so long as I kept my eyes shut during the intervals. The dancers were such an absorption that I forgot my trouble during the performances. The Russian Ballet under Diaghileff became a general obsession, and there was nothing odd in my procuring a Nijinsky costume for wearing at fancy-dress parties. In a picture in the *Graphic* showing a group at a 'Juvenile Ball' at the Lyttons when I was twenty, I see that I am dressed as Nijinsky; next to me, and looking pretty well as young, stands Eddie, who was in fact nineteen years older than I was.

Eddie, with his lifted eyebrow, bright eye, high voice and monocle, was a good-looking man, almost dandyish in the precision of his dress. Some people today might assume that my relationship with him was a homosexual one. Was he in love with me? He never showed it physically, and I didn't even know that there was such a thing as sodomy.

At the height of our friendship, in 1911, I made a fantastic demand of Eddie. I visited him at the Home Office, when Winston Churchill was Home Secretary, with Eddie as always his Principal Private Secretary. The Home Secretary's room was empty and

Eddie rather abashedly allowed me to sit in Churchill's chair. Then I said: 'If ever I am sentenced to death for high treason or murder, will you see that I am offered a reprieve if, but only if, I ask for it?' Eddie went from one leg to another in embarrassment, half-turned, gazed at me over his shoulder, and finally jerked out the promise. Why should I have made such a silly demand? A trial of Eddie's devotion to me?

The walls of Eddie's rooms were covered with contemporary paintings and more were stacked against the sofa. To explain this overflowing picture gallery he told me, with surprising shyness, that his great-grandfather was Spencer Perceval, the Prime Minister who was assassinated in the Lobby of the House of Commons; that his family had been awarded a large sum in compensation, part of which had come to Eddie; and that the income from this 'blood money', as he called it, he used to help young artists.

In my evenings with him, poetry was non-stop. Proudly I introduced him to my mother's work. 'Her essays', he said, 'made English prose as exciting for me as Latin prosody.' He told me that before we met his interest in English poetry had virtually stopped with Milton. I brought to his notice, not always for admiration, the work of contemporary poets—William Watson, John Davidson and of course Francis Thompson; whereupon Eddie made and chanted to me this delightful jingle addressed to the Muses:

> Ye nine, behold, among your pastures romp
> The sons of Wat, of David, and of Thomp.

Eddie now determined to devote his 'blood money' to poets rather than painters. I introduced him to Harold Monro, himself a poet, who controlled and financed the Poetry Bookshop in Theobald's Road and published the *Poetry Review*. One does not foresee the long consequence of a small action. 'This was an

important moment for Eddie', Christopher Hassall wrote to me
when he was preparing his biography. What ensued was the publication by Monro of the five volumes of *Georgian Poetry*, edited,
and at the outset financed, by Eddie and bringing to a much wider
public the poems of Ralph Hodgson, W. J. Turner, Rupert
Brooke, J. E. Flecker, W. H. Davies, James Stephens, Robert
Graves, J. C. Squire, Edmund Blunden and others. For me
Harold Monro had a triple appeal: his own poetry, the many
poetry readings he arranged—in some of which I joined—and
cricket. We were only cricket watchers together in pre-war days,
but in the 'twenties he was the most fluent batsman in my 'Long
Primers' team—named after a small type-face.

Early in 1911 my father received a letter from his friend Charles
Fitzpatrick, Chief Justice of Canada, who was then presiding at
the Hague over an Arbitration Court to settle a dispute between
Newfoundland and the United States about certain fishing rights.
He invited my father to help him to draft his report. His reason?
In his letter of invitation he wrote: 'Between you and I, I am not
much of a hand at grammar'. My father accepted—but sent
me, aged nineteen, in his place. Working in his study at The Hague
I corrected Fitzpatrick's grammar and healed his split infinitives,
but when, as often happened, there were visits from participants
in the dispute, I was hastily hidden in his bedroom. As a reward he
invited me to visit Canada at his expense. To my delight he added
Maurice Healy to his invitation. We travelled on a tidy small
liner, the s.s. *Virginian* of the Allen Line.

While we were on the Atlantic the Wilfrid Laurier government
had fallen. This lessened Fitzpatrick's power of patronage, which
would have procured free tickets for our journey to Vancouver; but
'Fitz' kept to his bargain.

Somewhat to his displeasure I determined to visit the United
States before I returned to England. To my parents I reported
that a lecture agent had arranged for me to give poetry readings in

Buffalo, Rochester, New Haven, New York and Derby, Connecticut. These went easily enough and made me feel that I had come from a pleasant provincialism in Canada to a highly sophisticated country.

In England friends of my own making were Reginald and Pamela McKenna. Pamela was much younger than Reginald, and they had not an easy sharing of tastes. She was a good pianist, up to professional standards. She made their houses in London and Somerset party-centres more for young artists and writers than for the smart world of politicians. Reggie's political interests had to be served, but for Pamela this was duty more than interest. Her aunt was the famous gardener Gertrude Jekyll of Munstead, whose gardening boots William Nicholson made into a full-scale picture. Of Reggie I was a little awe-struck: he was the first Cabinet Minister I had met. A minus was the fact that as Home Secretary he was responsible for the 'cat-and-mouse' act against the Suffragettes,* a plus that he was strongly opposed to conscription.

My awe was tempered by the fact that he had been a Cambridge rowing Blue. When he was sitting he looked as if he must be a very tall man; when he stood up he became short, so disproportionately long was his body in relation to his legs.

My social life included many dances, and as I was on the hostesses' list of 'eligible' young men, I went often to dances given by people I didn't know and who didn't know me; but there was always good music for the waltz and two-step of those days, good food, champagne (not that I was a drinker) and charming partners. One politely inquired of one's partner in the waltz, 'Do you reverse?' The Ritz, expanded under marquees, was a favourite site for these dances, and so also was 13 Grosvenor Gardens—a house people would not live in because of the unlucky number,

* Women were let out of prison when their hunger-strikes made it dangerous to their lives to keep them any longer; a little later they were re-arrested.

though they were quite willing to hire it for coming-out dances.

I often went with my sisters to more intimate dances, such as H. G. Wells gave in Church Row, Hampstead. There we had the fun of seeing Henry James surveying the scene from the sidelines—stout, formal and with his sentences prepared for the intervals but often cut short in mid-utterance by the resumption of the music. Once he stooped to restore a fan dropped by my sister Olivia. 'An elephant striving to pick up a pea', said H.G.

How embarrassed any accident or error made me! Once at dinner at the d'Erlangers the stud from the front of my highly starched dress-shirt fell into my soup. Today a young man—if he indeed wore a dress-shirt—would surely make light of such a happening. Not I, not in those days. Covertly I scooped the stud into my soup-spoon and thence with the soup into my mouth; then a polite cough into my handkerchief and I had my stud again.

At poetry readings at my parents' flat a companion was Ezra Pound. I am sure my parents were not 'with' his poetry, and it is a sign of their broadminded kindness that they welcomed this unknown and iconoclastic stranger from the United States. I was young enough and conventional enough to enjoy teasing an innovator. Once I was walking with Ezra on a lovely night. 'Behold,' I said, 'the full moon, an egg in the dark frying pan of night.' 'A fine image', he said to my amused surprise. 'I will remember it.'

Some six years later Ezra went often to the Kensington studio of the lovely Phyllis Reid and Stella Bowen, who soon became the 'common law' wife of Ford Madox Ford—what a disagreeable term for the brave and delightful Stella! These were close friends of mine. With them and me Ezra hopped at dances and preached defiance of the conventions and poetic standards of the day. Margaret Postgate, one of the group, aptly described him as a 'bearded faun'.

To Margaret, Ezra read Eliot's 'The Love-Song of J. Alfred Prufrock'; and well do I remember her reading of this poem to me. Ezra was shrilly eloquent and politically aligned with a Sinn Fein circle in London, which was a link between us.

Another occasion of my father's pushing me forward in his place had a happy outcome. George Rostrevor Hamilton, then a brilliant young civil servant lately down from Oxford, had become enamoured of Francis Thompson's poetry and hoped to write a book about him. He sought an interview with my father, who referred him to me. I was won by his charm and by the precision of his mind and I was later to find myself drawn by much of his own poetry.* He became a friend of all our family. My friendship with him grew until his death in 1965. His earliest book of poems, about 1911, is the subject of a letter to him from my father:

"Willie Yeats was here yesterday and chanted your 'Unattainable', saying 'How beautiful, how imaginative!' Then he asked if you were dead. When I replied alive and young his enthusiasm seemed to be a little damped."

Again, when Charles Morgan was very young and in doubt about his capacity to write, he presented a letter of introduction to my father. He too was referred to me; so at the mature age of twenty-two I discussed with young Morgan the future of the novel in English literature and his possible place in it. Satisfied with his attitude and aptitude, I went so far as to encourage him to become a novelist...We did not meet again for many years, when we were both elderly and both members of the Saintsbury Club. We grinned together about my precocious patronage.

William Andrew McKenzie was a poetical-political influence for me. He was at one time a street-wanderer and a Rowton

* Despite his notable career in the Civil Service, for which he was knighted, he was able to publish eighteen books of poems and seven prose works. His *Collected Poems* were published by Heinemann in 1958 with a devoted dedication to his wife Marion 'after 40 years'.

House* lodger, and so appealed to my parents' sense of pity. One
of his verses stays in my mind:

> In mighty Rome when Nero ruled
> The simple-minded plebs he fooled,
> Fooled them with royal grace and ease
> By scattering bread and circuses.

> Today in Britain Demos rules,
> And we, some forty million fools,
> By pomps and Parliaments are fed:
> We've got the circus; where's the bread?

> I hear a rumour thunder-low—
> Soon shrieking to the stars 'twill go:
> 'Let us have loaves upon our shelves,
> We'll make the circus for ourselves.'

A few years ago I happened to refer to McKenzie in a poetry
lecture at Colchester. There were some nuns in the audience.
One of them surprised, even shocked me after the lecture. She
said: 'I am a daughter of William Andrew McKenzie; he is dead
and it may interest you to know that he is being considered for
beatification by the Holy Office'.

My parents were strongly in favour of woman suffrage.
Supporters of this campaign were divided between the consti-
tutionalists (the Suffragists) and the militants (the Suffragettes).
Inevitably I inclined towards the militants. My mother and sisters
were Suffragists. Both Suffragettes and Suffragists joined in the
great marches which ended in mass meetings in London at the
Albert Hall. My mother, well beyond sixty, and my sisters took

---

* At that time Rowton House provided a homeless man's London
lodging-place for a few pence a night. McKenzie's book was called
Rowton House Rhymes (Blackwood, 1912).

part in a number of these. Olivia sold Suffrage papers in the London streets. The repressive measures against the Suffragettes became more and more severe: they were imprisoned and when they hunger-struck they were forcibly fed.

In November 1911 there was a Suffrage meeting in forbidden territory just outside the House of Lords. It was at this meeting that I first heard and met that great fighter for great causes, Lord Pethick-Lawrence. H. W. Nevinson, known as the 'Grand Duke' to his friends and the most famed radical journalist of his day, was the principal speaker, and for his speech he mounted the plinth of the Richard Coeur-de-Lion statue. A policeman seized his ankles and tipped him off, then mounted the plinth to guard it. So I seized the policeman's ankles and tipped *him* off. I was arrested and frog-marched to Scotland Yard. On the way I shouted to sympathetic onlookers that I was a friend of Reginald McKenna, the new Home Secretary, thinking somehow to alleviate my painful journey. But I failed, and the next day I was fined £5—a large sum in those days.

In March 1912 I wrote to my father about a Suffrage meeting at the Albert Hall:

"Last night's meeting is beyond description. At dinner we heard that the Pethick-Lawrences were let out on bail. Then the Albert Hall—a box near the platform. Mr and Mrs Pethick-Lawrence enter from the opposite end of the Hall and pass down the central gangway with Mrs Besant, Israel Zangwill,* Nevinson. The first rows do not recognise the prisoners: only a score of people had heard the news of their bail. Then a wild cry of recognition goes up—and it *is* 'up' in the Albert Hall, lined from floor to ceiling with a militant multitude. It is a thing to remember and to be thankful for: Mrs Lawrence, round-faced, rosy, smiling: he with never a tremor or change of expression upon a grave, sad, ill-looking

* Philanthropist, Suffragist and author of *Children of the Ghetto*.

countenance. Oh what a cheering! And then Mrs Besant! and then Zangwill—a glorious speech! And then money, more money—£10,500. The meeting made me feel entirely militant. The movement is irresistible."

In the same month, some militants having set fire to the letterboxes of shops in Oxford Street, a meeting was held by West End traders in the Queen's Hall to call upon the Government to make much more dire the punishment of militants. I decided to attend this meeting and my brother Everard came with me to control and perhaps protect me. As each resolution was put to the meeting I rose and opposed it. One of the resolutions demanded that the offending women should have their heads shaved. I was the only speaker against the ruthless resolutions and finally the chairman insisted on knowing what firm I represented. When I answered 'Burns & Oates', a contemptibly unimportant concern to that audience, there were howls of derision.

My performance was commented on in the evening papers. This put me in an embarrassing position, since I had no authority whatever to claim to be the mouthpiece of my firm, of which the majority of shareholders-cum-directors was high Tory. Next day, however, while I awaited the likely disciplinary summons, two ladies arrived at Burns & Oates. They asked for me and one of them said, 'I am Mary Dodge. I used to know your parents well. We were in the gallery at the Queen's Hall last night. I have come to give you £500 in acknowledgement of your firm's brave stand, and I want you to spend this on your firm's books for any poor Catholic communities that may need them'. Never had Burns & Oates had an order of this magnitude. My provocative action was overlooked. To me she gave a gold watch. Soon, alas, I pawned it so that I might take Phyllis Reid to dances. I was never able to redeem it.

The other woman with Mary Dodge was Muriel, Lady De La Warr. Both were socialists as well as Suffragists and believed in the equal distribution of wealth. Mary Dodge, an American millionairess, occupied Warwick House on a lease which had to have the approval of Buckingham Palace itself. What was good in her eyes, such as harbouring Mrs Pankhurst when she was being sought by the police, would not have appealed to authority. Therefore she remained as anonymous as possible and she made Lady De La Warr her public 'front' in many causes. The most important of these were the Suffrage movement and George Lansbury's struggling paper, the *Daily Herald*.*

Not all the two ladies' enterprises were productive. Just before the war they were behind—well behind—a body called the National Political League. There was a conviction then, particularly among the women of the Suffrage movement, that there existed in London a highly organised trade in 'vice' (which word always meant sexual vice) and that some of the police were bribed to overlook it. In utmost secrecy the League planned an investigation, and early in 1914 I was asked by Lady De La Warr if I would help in that part of the inquiry which was to expose the provision of sexual 'exhibitions'. Lady De La Warr advised me to tell Hilda Saxe about it in strict confidence (we were beginning to think of marriage then), since it might possibly involve me in some public scandal. Hilda's permission obtained, I was introduced to Miss Broadhurst, the president of the League.

Miss Broadhurst's plan was that I should first be introduced to a 'private eye' known only as 'Miss C', and then to Miss C's two middle-aged male investigators. They took me and another young man of their choice (on one occasion he was my friend Shane Leslie) to houses where two women gave sexual performances, sometimes together and sometimes with small girls. The professional 'investigators' made us believe for a time that we were under the dangerous surveillance of the White Slave traffickers, who, we were told, supplied the wretched women performers.

* Mary Dodge helped also in the arts. In 1910 she financed the first production at Covent Garden of Ethel Smyth's opera *The Wreckers*.

I made half a dozen such visits to 'exhibitions' arranged expressly for me and my companion, the two 'investigators' posing as pimps involved in the traffic. I gradually became uneasy about the honesty of these investigations. After studying Miss Broadhurst's draft report, which confirmed my doubts, I put them in writing to Lady De La Warr; whereupon further investigations were abandoned and the report suppressed.

This was a high time for my early, very sentimental and usually religious poetry writing; verses of mine appeared in the *Westminster Gazette*, the *Evening Standard*, the *English Review* (an honour this) and the *Oxford and Cambridge Review*. I was also a formal reader of poetry at Warwick House, close by St James's Palace, where Mary Dodge was hostess to assemblies of her friends, and also to sessions of young ladies at their fashionable school in Queen's Gate. These occasions demanded an attire of morning-tail-suit, lapelled grey waistcoat, patent leather shoes, and throttle-type collar with a top hat and gloves in not-too-distant sight. So dressed I declaimed Keats and Browning and Francis Thompson and Alice Meynell and Yeats. And nobody laughed.

Then and now, and during a long in-between of poetry reading for the BBC, I have been insistent on showing the metrical and rhyming shape of a poem as well as in making clear the meaning of the sentence. That is seldom done today, and yet to someone whose heart and mind are in the poem this combination is perfectly feasible. I went so far as to have words about this with Charles Laughton. I had seen him play Macbeth at the Old Vic in the 'thirties and a few days later I protested that he had sacrificed metre to meaning instead of combining them by appropriate intonation and pause. I even declaimed a few of his lines to justify my thesis. He gave me the raised eyebrow combined with the downcast eye and mouth which he used so effectively, and said: 'Perhaps, dear Francis, you think yourself qualified to rehearse me in all my parts?'

In those early grown-up years I talked politics constantly, and no doubt boringly, with my mother, who delighted me by saying that she believed in communism because she thought it accorded with the teaching of Christ; with my brother-in-law Percy Lucas, who opposed my views so strongly that on one shameful occasion I slapped his face (my tearful apologies followed almost instantaneously and he forgave me); with Maurice Healy, whose early ardour for Irish Home Rule seemed to me sadly waning; with my agreeing sisters Olivia and Viola; with Stanley Morison, whose political theories were like mine but much better founded. There were many public meetings. On one of these I heard Cunninghame Graham (a romantic-looking man, tall, old and handsome, a character out of William Morris's *News from Nowhere*), who recited his socialist doctrine as if it were metaphysical poetry.

Adrian Fortescue, a priest, handsome and mannered, with a learned love of fine printing, taxed me with being a rebel and warned me of the possible danger to my faith. Curiously, that made me decide to write an irreligious 'poem'. I was just twenty-one. I never ventured to show it to anyone—and 'anyone' meant chiefly my mother. As poetry she would have tut-tutted it, as blasphemy she would have been hurt by it. Truly it was no more blasphemy than a hiccup with a hand in front of the mouth. It revives my memory of Oxford Circus when it was for the most part still a circle of stucco Regency buildings, and the 'Madame L' line calls to my mind 'Madame Louise' herself, wide in stature and easy to see through the door of her hat shop.

Street Lamps and Sky Signs
(Oxford Circus 1912)

Cohort and squadron, line on line,
A gleaming army, mute and strong,

They stand and shine, they stand and shine,
Challenge the stars the whole night long.

Mild angels of the flaming sword,
They have my soul exparadised—
How may I turn my eyes abroad
From these to the pale stars of Christ?

And look! the signs, the signs in colour,
Egyptian Palmistes and Pale Ale,
Pianos and Pills, the Broad-brimmed Bowler,
And Madame L's Rebuilding Sale—

A thousand thousand tethered stars,
A myriad fireflies on a frame.
Look, Saturn, to your rings, and Mars
To the red rumour of your name. . .

This clash of yellow, pink, and blue—
This democratic roar of red—
I too shall shake and shout! Like you
Put out my tongue, and wag my head.

And, when my life-flare flickers down,
If fall I must as Lucifer fell,
I'll thank the God who let me clown
For the bright lights—the lights of Hell.

I read Tom Paine and Edward Carpenter and William Morris.
But what prompted my passionate feelings was not theory: it
was the sight of the distress of extreme poverty and the knowledge
that this was generally accepted as a normal social phenomenon.
I had seen it close in Dublin; one did not have to look far for it in
London. The 'East End' was a horror term. I went once to a small
metal-working factory where the employees, mainly girls, had

attempted what would now be called a sit-in. They looked half-starved—their wages were a few shillings for an almost endless week. The sight of them stayed in my sleeping as well as my waking mind.

There was still a general belief in 'progress'. My ambition was to help to hurry hurry hurry it on. I was fired by such things as my mother's experience one night. She was awakened by screams, a woman's screams, which dwindled away down the street. She hastened to report this incident at the police station. And the reply? 'No need to worry, *lady*; that wasn't a *woman*, that was only a *female*' (i.e. a prostitute). The class distinctions that I abhorred could not have been better summarised.

Now that they had found me, Mary Dodge and Lady de la Warr thought I might be helpful in other ways, so in 1913 I was invited to meet George Lansbury at Lady De La Warr's flat in the Adelphi. That meeting was a turning-point in my life. It was the beginning of a close friendship and association with that great man which lasted for many years. It proved to be, despite some misdemeanours, the least selfish chapter of my life.

How can one describe personality? The shape of a head, the expression of a face, the colour of the eyes, the stance, even the clothes?—all these would apply just as well to a figure at Madame Tussaud's as to a human being. George Lansbury was the most dominating man of all my life. But 'dominating' is in itself a misleading word. His was a persuasiveness that I found irresistible from the moment of our first meeting. His handshake was all brotherliness and his long gaze into my eyes revealed much more than it could have seen.

'G.L.' (as he was to nearly all who knew him, but to me he allowed the closer 'George') influenced me the more profoundly because it was thought and conviction, and not just sentiment, that made him a rebel. My own politics were and remained mainly emotional. Here was a man whose brain could lead and feed my

[78]

ignorant and disorganised but, I think, sensitive and eager political views.

The *Daily Herald*, which was to be my main link with Lansbury, had begun as a propaganda sheet for the London Society of Compositors during their strike in 1911 for a 48-hour week. Early in 1912 it aspired to become a national daily newspaper, under the aegis of Ben Tillett, the dockers' leader, T. E. Naylor of the London Society of Compositors, and Lansbury. It had a capital of £300, the price was a ha'penny, the average circulation a few score thousand. Charles Lapworth was the editor, sitting under the sometimes anxious eyes of Lansbury, the Chairman. 'To get into its columns a writer had only to be a rebel; he had to be an enemy of the existing capitalist system, and what he was in favour of mattered less.'*

In 1913 the paper went bankrupt and Lansbury bought it from the Official Receiver—chiefly with money guided by Lady de la Warr from Mary Dodge's benevolent riches. This was my entry into the paper's affairs; through them, I was made a director of the new company, with Lansbury and Lapworth. I confess to being at this stage little more than a stooge, the earliest of 'Lansbury's Lambs' as the group of helpful and hopeful young devotees— Harold Laski, Gerald Gould, W. N. Ewer, Douglas Cole, William Mellor—were later to be called.

There was soon a crisis: George Lansbury decided that he could no longer tolerate Lapworth's 'hate' attitudes towards political opponents. 'I can hate conditions with the best or the worst of men', Lansbury wrote later, 'but I have never felt hatred of anybody'. So a meeting of the three of us was called, and G.L. and I voted two to one to oust Lapworth. He was given what— considering the paper's circumstances—could now be called a golden handshake. By whom? Nominally by me. I have the endorsed cheque: 'Jan. 3. 1914. Pay Charles Lapworth two hundred

* Raymond Postgate: *The Life of George Lansbury* (Longmans, 1951).

pounds'. Of course it wasn't my money: it was put into my meagre account by Lady de la Warr.

Horatio Bottomley's scurrilous weekly, *John Bull*, had a quick reaction. It suggested that Lapworth's dismissal and my appearance as a director were part of a Roman Catholic conspiracy to divert left-wing politics. It asked 'whether the policy of the paper is to be changed to conform more closely to the personal ideas of Mr Francis Meynell, the head of the Catholic Publishing Company'. (It meant Burns & Oates, of which my father, not I, was the head.)

George Lansbury did me more than justice when he wrote in his story of these affairs, *The Miracle of Fleet Street*, that he 'left Francis Meynell to manage the business side of things'. The production of a daily newspaper, even on the scale of the *Daily Herald*, was no simple matter. I had no experience of 'management', I was twenty-two years old and fully employed by Burns & Oates. My weekly 'management' meetings amounted to little more than assenting to G.L.'s plans—except in one respect: I began to be concerned with the paper's style of printing, beginning with the revision of its headpiece.

In the autumn of 1913 the *Daily Herald* devoted most of its space and emphasis to the desperate strike in Dublin, where the employers required that every labourer should sign an undertaking never to join a trade union. James Connolly and Jim Larkin were the men's leaders, and the conditions of a labourer's life were a working week of 70 hours for wages ranging between 12s. and 15s. a week. The *Daily Herald* failed in its effort to get a sympathetic strike started in England, but it did collect money for shiploads of food to be sent to the Dublin strikers by the Co-operative Wholesale Society.

The *Daily Herald* organised a great meeting at the Albert Hall. Larkin was to be the chief speaker, but he was arrested and imprisoned in Dublin. This made the militant Labour movement in

England all the more angry and excited. The Albert Hall meeting was a wildly enthusiastic one and we arranged a second. My memories of the poverty in Dublin and my admiration for James Connolly, whom I had met there, made me an eager helper in the organisation of these meetings. Larkin, now released from prison (for which he thanked the *Daily Herald*), came to the second. Vast crowds assembled to greet him. Edgar Lansbury (G.L.'s son and my close friend) and I were in charge of the stewards. No easy task, for there were thousands of supporters unable to get into the over-crowded hall and there were also some scores of university students who had managed to force their way in, hoping to break up the meeting. (Yes, the students then were on the side of the Establishment.) Edgar and I swung down from one tier to another of the Albert Hall (a thing I couldn't do in cold blood) as the quickest way of dealing with troublemakers below.

Meanwhile thousands of voices sang 'The Red Flag' and Edward Carpenter's 'England Arise'.* The whole hall throbbed to the words and tunes and to Lansbury's thunder and Larkin's lightning. So did my heart.

My devotion to the songs we socialists knew by heart and sang at all our many meetings had a happy climax for me a few years later when I designed and the *Daily Herald* published *The March of the Workers and Other Songs*. I chose the songs and Pamela McKenna edited the music. One poem of my choice, 'The Voice of Toil', by William Morris, had no tune, so Pamela herself composed one for it. Now, nearly sixty years later, I cannot read the words or hum the tunes of this collection without a break in my voice. Sentimentalist I was and sentimentalist I remain.

* Edward Carpenter (1844–1929), ex-fellow of Trinity Hall, Cambridge, ex-parson, ex-socialite, socialist, poet and handicraft worker in the manner of William Morris.

VII

Conscientious Objector

On August 4, 1914, the War. To me it was the confrontation of two equally culpable imperialisms at the expense of the common man on both sides; but to my parents, accepting the propaganda phrase of the time, it was 'the war to end war'. One all-important solace I had in this painful conflict of views—the staunch support of Hilda Saxe.

I have told how I greatly admired her when she played the piano at the Caruso concert in Dublin. To my surprise and delight I found that my sisters knew her. By 1913 we were constant companions, at concerts, at political meetings and as dancing partners. We were in love. In the very month of the outbreak of war we were married. Hilda was five years older than I was, but was not my mother five years older than my father? Hilda was brought up and remained an agnostic. I was then still a Roman Catholic. In my piety and interest for her salvation I effected a surprise baptism of her with a dash of water on her head and the saying of the magic words before she could recover from her astonishment. This meant nothing to her, but she realised that it gave me much comfort.

Bertrand Russell and E. D. Morel founded an anti-war body called the Union of Democratic Control. I joined it, but it was too gentlemanly and intellectual in its ways to deflect me from the proletarian activities of the *Herald*.

Two months after the declaration of war I lunched with Reginald and Pamela McKenna. War and politics were the only topics of conversation: our host was Home Secretary, and the other guests were C. F. G. Masterman, also in the Cabinet, George Lansbury, and Violet Markham brightly planning the organisation of women on the home front. Surprisingly, we were almost equally divided on the war issue: Reggie McKenna and Violet Markham were pro-war; Pamela and Masterman were neutral and questioning; Lansbury and I decisively anti.

A few days later I made my first signed contribution to the *Herald*. It has been said that this was the first vehement anti-war article to be published in England.* Its title, 'The War's a Crime', was a ridiculous understatement. The war was not a crime but a billion crimes. What moved me to anger and adjectives was a phrase by Edmund Gosse† in the *Edinburgh Review*: 'The red stream of blood', he wrote, 'is the Condy's Fluid, the sovereign disinfectant, for us all.' I labelled this a 'reptilious doctrine' and concluded: 'The lands are clotted with blood and the seas are swallowing their dead, and the clean sweet rivers are full of mangled corpses—amen, amen, it is all a tonic for Mr Gosse'. I record this not in pride of the terms of my denunciation but because Gosse's phrase represents a 'patriotic' attitude inconceivable in World War II, yet needing, alas, to be remembered and feared today.

Hilda and I settled at 67 Romney Street, Westminster—a little Georgian house with panelled walls and a wooden spiral staircase. It was the first of a row of decayed houses to be refurbished, and our rent and rates, because the rest of the street was still a slum, was a just-manageable £80 a year. I was still working for Burns & Oates; Hilda was still giving piano-recitals; and in April 1915 I was able, oddly enough, in spite of the stresses of war-time, to start a tiny venture, the Romney Street Press, at one end of our dining-room. For a number of reasons it did not last long. One of them was the constant fear that the printers' ink would get into the soup.

The poet Ralph Hodgson was one of our frequent and most

* *Those Foreigners*, by Raymond Postgate and Aylmer Vallance (Harrap, 1937).

† Sir Edmund Gosse (1849–1928), librarian to the House of Lords and later literary pundit of the *Sunday Times*.

happily received guests. His arrival was often an excitement, because he had a skill and a wish to collect any stray dog (there were plenty in those parts and days) and to bring it in with him. Siegfried Sassoon and Walter Turner (whose poem 'Chimborazo Cotopaxi' resounded in its time), who shared a near-by house, were friends both politically and poetically. Turner dedicated to me his first book of poems,* and Siegfried began the charming habit of giving me an inscribed copy of all his books of poetry as they appeared. With his ginger hair Siegfried was a very startling sight. I remember him as wearing sandy-coloured tweeds, a yellow waistcoat and a pink shirt. Henry Nevinson and the novelist Evelyn Sharp were guests whom we entertained with a touch of awe, dissipated by their knowledgeable and enthusiastic praise of Hilda's playing.

Uninvited to our doorstep was a gang of local youths. They were not violent or destructive, but saw no reason to allow us or our guests an easy passage in and out of the house. I happened to tell George Lansbury about this. He said, 'All you have to do is to ask for the Captain.' This I did. One of the boys jumped up from the step and I asked him politely to move the boys away. He showed his authority instantly, and they never bothered us again.

We were most happy, and happily produced a daughter in Lady De La Warr's country house at Winslow, which she lent for the lying-in—a house more comfortable, more servanted than anything we were accustomed to. This is the letter that I wrote in October 1915, within hours of Cynthia's birth, to Mary Dodge, who had so often unofficially godmothered me:

Sand Hill, Winslow, Bucks.

> Dearest of Friends:
> How can I say
> In the old customary way
> My purpose on this natal day?

* *The Hunter and Other Poems* (Sidgwick & Jackson, 1916).

[84]

This form I use, for want of better;
A letter but a rhyming letter.

Then came many, too many, lines of emotional and pietistic verse before I got to the point:

Now to be brief, if that I can:
'Cynthia Mary Marian'
Are the fore-names our babe will bear.
PLEASE WILL YOU BE HER GODMOTHER?
Our true address this letter lacks.
To set right any wrongful fancies
Know that it comes from Hilda Saxe
And Francis.

The tenderness of my mother's letter to me did not silence her preoccupation with words and metres:

"I was filled with joy and thankfulness when your wire came; all blessings on little Cynthia. It is a lovely name, although as you know I like a dactyl to precede the trochee Meynell— Monica, Madeline, Viola, Everard. You had to be a trochee on account of Francis Thompson. I call Cynthia a trochee . . ."

I summoned the local priest to perform the christening; he came, but was somewhat indignant when he found that he was not attending nobility, as our address implied. Only the titled, he told us, were normally christened in their own houses and not in church.

Hilda now took Cynthia for a safety-stay at Greatham. I went often at weekends, taking my bicycle on the train for the four-mile ride at the end of the railway journey. There were many rumours in town and country that German spies were using lights to signal the Zeppelins; so it was not surprising that after one night-arrival on my bicycle a police sergeant should appear and question the use of my bicycle lamp. Thereafter I had to ride without a light—not too difficult since there were no cars on the roads.

In the spring of 1915 my sister Viola lent her Greatham cottage to D. H. Lawrence and his wife Frieda, and there they stayed for six months. Viola, a determined admirer of Lawrence's early writing, had moved into the parental house next door, and she overlooked and underheard the battles between Lawrence and Frieda that resounded every now and then in her cottage. When I was there and I saw the Lawrences working up to one of their rows I would try to slink away. Lawrence would shout at me, 'Sit still, can't you, and listen'. Usually this was a prelude to silence, so I had nothing to listen to.

I was not important enough for full-scale attack, but I received many direct though somewhat trivial rebukes: Why did I sing jeering songs against war-lords? Why did I favour (why indeed!) the rebuilding of Regent Street when stucco was so valuable as a sun reflector? How dare I giggle over *Irene Iddesleigh*, that unintentionally comic novel by Amanda Ros, which Lawrence affected to admire? Was it possible that I was really ignorant of the song 'Mr McKinley he ain't done no wrong', which Lawrence and Frieda were fond of singing?

But Lawrence was far from being all negatives. He spent three and a half hours every day giving lessons to my ten-year-old niece Mary Saleeby to prepare her for her entry to St Paul's. He usefully made bookshelves for Viola's cottage, and planned to make her a herbaceous border. He was the first person in all my life to persuade me to 'go for a walk' of some miles. As a pointer-out of birds, trees and flowers to this ignorant cockney he was a revealing companion. Sometimes Lawrence wanted to open my inner sight as well as my outer. Nearly all marriages, he said, were frauds and failures. Why had I married so young? Was it because I was afraid of myself? Was it to escape from my family? The answer that one was in love he regarded as sentimentally evasive.

On the last of our walks Lawrence shocked me by his contemptuous references to people who admired and helped him: Lady Ottoline, Lady Cynthia (scornful emphasis on the 'Lady') were trying to climb to fame on his back; Eddie Marsh was a vain nonentity—'he ought to have his bottom kicked'. Was it shameful of me to report this to Eddie, who was feeding money and opportunities to Lawrence? Questioning oneself may be easily rhetorical or may show a genuine doubt. In my life there have been a few vales of tears but inevitably many veils of years: looking back through them I am not ashamed in this case of 'telling tales'. Eddie was a friend, Lawrence a mysterious acquaintance.

Lawrence's biting-the-hand-that-fed-him attitude was soon applied to my family. In his story *England, My England* Lawrence used personalities and environment from real life—my father, my sister Madeline, her husband Percy Lucas and their daughter Sylvia, and the Greatham scene—as a basis for his story. In it the principal character Egbert (Percy) is made an unhappy, stilted, empty and impecunious man, rebelling against his dependence on his father-in-law and driven to the war by the unhappiness of his marriage.

In truth, Madeline and Percy were a devoted couple; he had a small but sufficient private income, enhanced by some earnings from his genealogical studies; and there was nothing embarrassing to him about the gifts from my father. He went to the 1914 war at its very beginning with the ardour of so many who believed it to be the 'war to end war'. In all-too-real life Sylvia, six years old, had fallen on a sickle and irreparably crippled herself. Lawrence describes this and attributes it, falsely and cruelly, to the carelessness of her father. In fact the sickle was dropped in long grass by a friend. Percy was abroad at the time of the accident.

Authors must, I suppose, use incidents in the lives of their friends on which to build elements of their stories. Compton Mackenzie put Lawrence into one of his stories and Lawrence put most of his erstwhile friends into his. But does this justify the recognisable, and indeed admitted, presentation in detail of a group of people and their setting when it is mixed up with horrid inventions of their behaviour and motives—a mixture which cannot be separated by the ordinary reader into truth and fiction? No reader could tell what was circumambient truth, what cruel invention.

Was the family fear of identification with the characters exaggerated? By no means. In a letter to Lady Cynthia Asquith (Sept. 5, 1915)* Lawrence himself admitted:

"You will find in the *English Review* for next month a story about the Lucases. You remember we passed by their cottage and went into the garden at Greatham with Herbert Asquith and John. The story is the story of most men and women who are married today—of most men at war, and wives at home."

For some forty years editors and commentators refrained from naming the Lucases and Meynells, and there are those in 'Clan Meynell' whose main objection is to the editors of Lawrence who have recently blazoned forth the identification. They certainly might be quieter about it, but can they justly ignore it when Lawrence himself named his prototypes in letters of the period? I find *England, My England* far too lush for re-reading and re-assessment now. At the time I charged Lawrence with a libellous intent and put what was doubtless an undue emphasis on his breach of hospitality. He made no direct reply to me, but I like to think that there is a hint of one in a letter to a friend of his and of ours: 'I don't want to see the Meynells ever again, any of them'.

There was one real-life incident which I cannot forget and which Lawrence would have considered too sentimental to purloin. Sylvia's mother was kept waiting in an anteroom of the

* *The Collected Letters of D. H. Lawrence*, edited by Harry T. Moore (Heinemann, 1962).

hospital while treatment so painful was being given to the little girl's leg that her cries rent the air and her mother's heart. When her mother was at length allowed access, Sylvia said, 'Oh, Mummy, did you hear me *pretending* to scream?'

By now, a year after the war began, the appeals for more and more recruits were not producing all the Government wanted; so conscription loomed. In face of this, a number of pacifists formed the No-Conscription Fellowship. Its first manifesto, dated September 1915, was signed by Clifford Allen and Fenner Brockway* as Chairman and Hon. Secretary. Soon it was to have the active support of Bertrand Russell. I joined it, and became chairman of the very busy London branch. All three that I have named became my friends, Clifford Allen the most intimately. I had an early accolade, as I took it, from Bertrand Russell: 'I like you, Meynell, because in spite of your spats there is much of the guttersnipe about you'.

Inevitably I had become a little notorious for my anti-war activities and I looked for an opportunity to spare my father the embarrassment of my presence at Burns & Oates. Here again Mary Dodge and Lady De La Warr were my rescuers. They agreed to my suggestion that there was an opportunity for a new printing press of high quality to serve socialist ends. They were theosophists as well as socialists. They and their friend Mrs Besant awaited a new gospel from a young man called Krishnamurti, whom they expected to be a second coming-to-earth of God. He was in fact a reasonable and unpretentious young man and soon decisively abdicated from the godhead.

While he was still in the running, he and I played tennis against each other at the begardened old manor house on Wimbledon Common to which Mary Dodge had moved. He baffled me by using the 'American reverse service', a dazzling novelty of the

* Both were many times imprisoned and both many years later were made Lords: a tribute to their political capacities and devotion.

time. I suggested to him that this extension of his godlike powers was perhaps just a little unfair.*

The ladies' first object was to prepare the way for the Lord; I wanted to prepare it for the Socialist International. In 1916 they provided the money for me to start the Pelican Press, and I left Burns & Oates to organise it. In those early days I had plenty of time to spare for kindred work, typographical and sub-editorial, at the *Herald*. Stanley Morison was promoted to my place at Burns & Oates until he was imprisoned at Wakefield as a conscientious objector. An early task of the Pelican Press was the production of the *C.O.'s Hansard*, a weekly report of parliamentary questions and debates about conscientious objectors. I made therein the first use in England of the beautiful Forum type of F. W. Goudy.

Because Morison and I were both Catholics, socialists and conscientious objectors, it was a harmonious thing for us to found together in 1916 the 'Guild of the Pope's Peace'. This was an anti-war propaganda group, and I doubt whether propaganda has ever had such fine printing and so little effect. The Guild had a committee of seven, including two priests, and this was the limit of its membership; I was the honorary secretary and designer of its documents and its 'office' was our house. Its aim was to publicise Pope Benedict XV's appeals to both sides to stop the fighting. He was as outspoken as even I could wish in condemning the slaughter, which, in his Easter 1916 message, he described as 'dishonouring Europe and humanity'. We published a small book of *Prayers for Peace* which the Oxford University Press printed in seventeenth-

---

* Ian Coster recounted this episode in his book *Friends in Aspic* and added a companion story: 'Mrs Besant was interviewing the President of Magdalen College with a view to entering Krishnamurti. "You will remember that he is the son of God?" said Mrs Besant. "Madam," replied the President, "have no fear. We have sons of many distinguished persons at Magdalen".'

century Fell type. Even here I could not resist having a few copies printed on linen-rag paper and bound in limp vellum.

When, in August 1917, the Pope produced his 'terms for a just peace'—disarmament, freedom of the seas, restitution of all territories and international arbitration 'in substitution for armies'—we put them in an eight-page quarto pamphlet which we distributed free. The English Catholic hierarchy was against the Pope's 'stop the war' stand and our tiny Guild was denounced in the *Tablet*. During these years I gradually veered towards what I like to think of as conscientious agnosticism, which has by no means lessened my admiration for such a revolutionary programme as the Sermon on the Mount.

Now came the proud tragedy of the Easter Week Rising in Dublin—a great cause, from its outset hopelessly forlorn and bloodily repressed. Certain of my acquaintances, who in this tragic context became my heroes, were among those executed. There was the poet Thomas MacDonagh, dear to me in poems and person when I was at Trinity, and the Labour leader James Connolly, known through the *Herald*; and there was Sir Roger Casement. It is not digressive for me to write here about the Easter Rising because my attitude to the war was undoubtedly connected emotionally with my love of Ireland from my Trinity days and my reaction to Easter Week and Casement's execution.

It was by chance that I had met Casement in 1913 when he was held in high repute for his exposures of monstrous cruelties inflicted on the native populations in the Belgian Congo and by the Peruvian Amazon Company (a British enterprise) in the Putumayo district of Peru. Hilda and I were making a modest return of hospitalities to Pamela McKenna and Eddie Marsh by giving them lunch at a family-favoured Italian restaurant when Casement, bearded and singularly handsome, came to a nearby table. Eddie introduced us and I invited him to join us for coffee.

We wanted to hear him talk of his brave and lonely investigations. 'No, no,' he said with a hand over his eyes, 'I still have horrible nightmares about what I saw.'

Carson and F. E. Smith (later Lord Birkenhead) and the rebellious English officers at the Curragh had resisted Asquith's pre-war plan for Home Rule for all Ireland. Now Casement, a devoted Home Ruler, saw the war as Ireland's opportunity. From Germany he took ship to Ireland, was caught and put on trial for treason. In his speech at his trial he gloried in the charge of treason to England because, he said, it proved his patriotism to Ireland. He made biting fun of the fact that he was charged under a wholly English law passed 565 years before. He was hanged for high treason in August 1916, and his memory was defiled by the leakage, through carefully chosen public voices in the United States, in Ireland and in England, of homosexual passages in what were alleged to be his diaries. The motive for this shameful policy appears in an official document by the legal adviser to the Home Office: 'to prevent Casement attaining martyrdom'.

Like many others, I felt deeply and tragically about the use of the diaries, doubting their authenticity and shocked by the utter irrelevance of their use. The politely named 'Intelligence Branch' of Scotland Yard chose the poet Alfred Noyes as its main public voice in the United States. I knew him well: a man of devoted simplicity, with a touch of humour in his poetic stance, but politically innocent even by my standards. I scolded him for allowing himself to be used in this fashion and a coolness came between us, resolved many years later by his book *The Accusing Ghost—Justice for Casement*,* in which he tells of his slow-growing doubts and final disbelief in the authenticity of the diaries. On the other hand a recent impartial inquirer has come to the conclusion that the diaries were genuine.†

* Gollancz, 1957.
† *Roger Casement*, by H. Montgomery Hyde (Penguin Books, 1964).

Sir Basil Thomson was the 'discoverer' and disseminator of the diaries. If they were forgeries, was he the likelier to have made them because of propensities of his own? A few years later, when he had been knighted and was Assistant Commissioner at Scotland Yard, Thomson was convicted of acts of indecency in Hyde Park and was dismissed from the service. One thing about which there can be no doubt is the impropriety and irrelevance of the use that was made of the diaries. It silenced the widespread call for mercy and led a wavering Cabinet to approve the hanging of Casement.

When Clifford Allen was arrested as a conscientious objector and brought before the tribunal in the Town Hall at Battersea I was among the sympathetic admirers of his brilliant but unreported exposition of the case for absolute, i.e. unconditional, exemption. Tribunals before which conscientious objectors came had the legal power to grant this, but many of them were unaware of it, and those who were aware ignored it. Instead, if they were convinced of the applicant's honesty, they gave relief from military service only on condition that he undertook work of 'national importance'. To many this was acceptable, but not to the band of us who were known as 'absolutists'. C.A. made his point in vain. Prison sentence after sentence followed, inducing the frail health that affected him all the rest of his life. In the brief interval between his imprisonments I asked him how he occupied his mind in solitary confinement since he was allowed no books. He told me that his chief comfort and companion was a knot in the plank of wood that formed his bed. He said 'It was my point of concentration and meditation'.

My call-up came later than Clifford Allen's because I was married. I was called before the local (Marylebone) tribunal in August 1916. My conscientious objection was in part emotional, a horror of killing and inflicting pain: I still had in me something of the small boy who wept tears about the killed in the Boer War.

[93]

Partly my attitude was religious. I was still a Roman Catholic and Pope Benedict XV denounced the war. No doubt I over-emphasised religion at my tribunal because it was one of the accepted reasons for conscientious objection. But in the main my reason was my political conviction that there was nothing to choose between the social systems here and in Germany, that the war was a war between two imperialisms. Only for what I considered overwhelmingly good ends—and that for me then would have meant social revolution—would I have supported war and killing.

C.A.'s expository and courteous manner at his tribunal hearings had taught me to abandon, for my hearings, my habitually somewhat provocative demeanour. I have the report of the proceedings before my first tribunal and I quote here a verbatim extract because it gives a glimpse of how these hearings were conducted.

THE CLERK: This is the appeal of Mr F. M. W. Meynell, 25 years of age, publisher's manager.

THE CHAIRMAN: Have you anything you wish to say? Please be as brief as you can. Our time is very valuable.

MR MEYNELL: I shall be as brief as I can, Sir. The point I want to try and establish is that my objection is largely political, but none the less for that conscientious within the meaning of the Act.

First, I cannot in conscience kill men who are perfectly innocent. In the German army and the belligerent armies generally there are a great number of volunteers who are there only out of the highest motives, though they have been fed upon many lies. The greatest class of all are men who are there simply as conscripts. These men cannot be called guilty of the war.

Secondly, I feel that I cannot surrender my conscience, my right of judgement, to anybody else's keeping. It is, in the common phrase, the soldiers duty 'to do and die and not to reason why'. Well, Sir, if I were a soldier and told 'to do' such a thing as sink the Lusitania or shoot so-called rebels in Ireland, or take part in the starvation of a population, or drop bombs on civilians, I should refuse.

Then, Sir, as a Catholic I pay some heed to what the Pope says even on a political matter. From his central position, and because of his spiritual interest in all countries, he is well able to survey the war and its causes and tendencies. He has said that it is a war which is 'dishonouring humanity'. He has appealed to all the belligerents to take other means to settle the dispute. He has told them over and over that the war is not the way in which these tremendous problems can ever be solved. He has begged them to have a truce and a conference and to make a declaration of conciliatory peace terms.

Roman Catholics have a definite system of moral theology, which you may grudge us, but which enables us to look up any point and find what must be considered an authoritative answer. I will quote from two books, each of which is a standard moral theology text-book for priests.

Gury-Ballerine says: 'A man not yet enlisted is bound in conscience to examine the justice of a war, nor can he in conscience enlist while in doubt concerning its justice'. Lehmkuhl says: 'Those who fall under the law of conscription may take part in the fighting as long as they are not satisfied that the war is plainly unjust'.

Thus my religious grounds lead me directly into politics.

THE CHAIRMAN: Have you considered the position of a great many million Roman Catholics, subjects in the German and Austrian armies?

MR MEYNELL: Yes, I have indeed. I should say they are, the vast number, satisfied as to the justice of the war (whether through the spoon-feeding of the German Press or not I cannot tell) just as I am satisfied that the tens of thousands of Roman Catholics in the English Army are in it because they consider it to be a just war. My case is different. I am very sorry, but I do not consider it a just war.

THE CHAIRMAN: So you put your private judgement against the authority of so many million fellow religionists?

MR MEYNELL: I do not put my private judgement against all of them. You have one set of Catholics fighting for the Allies, and their private judgement is set one way; and you have the private judgement of the people on the other side, set another way. That shows you can get millions of people perfectly honestly coming to totally different conclusions.

THE CHAIRMAN: I do not think it fair to bring up the authority of the Pope, because all Christians deplore the war. Have not Popes waged war themselves?

MR MEYNELL: Have I not made myself clear? I was referring to this particular war. The Pope's utterances have been about this war. I would be equally loth to judge papal action in the past as in the future.

I would now like to produce some written evidence that I am truly a 'conscientious objector'.

THE CHAIRMAN: You have now kept us a long time.

[I was allowed to read the letters. They were from James Douglas (editor of the London evening newspaper, the *Star*), Charles Masterman (lately a junior minister in the Government) and Eddie Marsh (the principal private secretary to Mr Asquith).]

THE CHAIRMAN: I do not see how you can get over the law, 'Render unto Caesar the things which are Caesar's', Caesar being the law.

MR MEYNELL: I am willing to render to Caesar every mortal thing he can lay claim to, but the whole basis of my claim is that the services to which he lays claim do not belong to him but to God. If I have not made you feel that I have absolutely failed.

THE CHAIRMAN: You are a soldier at the present time under the Act. Read what one of your own quotations says about that.

MR MEYNELL (referring to the Lehmkuhl quotation): I may fight 'so long as I am not satisfied that the war is plainly unjust'. But I *am* satisfied that the war is plainly unjust.

THE CHAIRMAN: You are setting up your private judgement against the judgement of the lawful authority.

MR MEYNELL: Certainly, as every martyr has set his up. Please do not think I want to make a personal analogy! Every Catholic who refused to take the oath to Elizabeth set up his private judgement against the State.

THE CHAIRMAN: You have no objection to undertaking non-combatant service?

MR MEYNELL: I have as profound an objection to that as to any other.

THE CHAIRMAN: Have you an objection to working on the land?

MR MEYNELL: Most certainly if I am compelled thereto by the Military Service Act. I am not planning simply to get out of dangerous service by coming here. I have come before this Tribunal, not expecting to get the exemption which I claim, but because I think I am doing something to spread the idea of pacifism. That must govern all my decisions in this matter.

THE CHAIRMAN: I think our opinion is that you have made at least a case against fighting, but I do not see how possibly you can object to non-combatant service.

MR MEYNELL: May I say a word about that. The Act does empower you to give absolute exemption.

THE CHAIRMAN: Yes, but I do not think we shall. I do not see why we should.

MR MEYNELL: If the Act empowers it, is there any conceivable case which a conscientious objector can put before you which would persuade you to do that?

THE CHAIRMAN: I have not considered that. I cannot conceive how any man can object to working in a hospital for the wounded.

MR MEYNELL: You do not think my objection is sincere?

THE CHAIRMAN: No, I think it is sincere, but I think it is erroneous.

MR MEYNELL: But, Sir, you are not asked to agree with my opinions only to say that they are sincere.

THE CHAIRMAN: I cannot conceive anybody objecting to what I have suggested. Therefore however wrong it may be, the Tribunal exempt you from combatant service. But you will have to serve as a non-combatant. You may appeal against it.

MR MEYNELL: That means you are offering me a place out of danger, but compelling me to help other men to fight.

THE CHAIRMAN: To alleviate suffering.

MR MEYNELL: The non-combatant corps has got nothing to do with the alleviation of suffering, and no non-combatant gets near the firing line.

THE CHAIRMAN: Supposing you are in the R.A.M.C.?

MR MEYNELL: That is not the same as the non-combatant corps. But in any case, I should refuse any part in service arising out of the war.

THE CHAIRMAN: We cannot exempt you from non-combatant service.

MR MEYNELL: You are putting me in the unfortunate position of having to go through the military machine, of resisting and being sentenced to hard labour, and—quite possibly— even to the death penalty, like those thirty-four other noncombatants in France.* I am perfectly willing, because it may be the most effectual way of making my protest.

My appeal from the local to the national tribunal was heard in September 1916. I added two other letters to those I had produced to the first tribunal. These were from H. G. Wells and from Lord Lytton (a one-time Tory Minister). These letters all said that they profoundly disagreed with my views but that I was undoubtedly honest and a fine etc. etc. fellow. When he gave me his letter H.G. told me that he would rather that both his sons died than that they would grow up to share my views. In fact he didn't long maintain his support of the demand for 'unconditional surrender' by the Germans, and in August 1917 he argued publicly for a negotiated peace. I reproduced his *A Reasonable Man's Peace* as a leaflet at the Pelican Press.†

The Appeal Tribunal again granted me exemption from combatant service only. I surrendered myself to the military authorities on January 29, 1917.

I decided upon a thirst as well as a hunger strike. The Suffragettes had proved that a hunger strike led to forcible feeding, temporary release and re-arrest; whereas in any army guardroom with other prisoners my not eating and not drinking might be hidden from the authorities until I was too far gone to be forcibly fed. They would have to give me my unconditional discharge or let me die.

If I should be discovered too early or be unable to stick it out I

* They were later reprieved.
† The first page of the leaflet is reproduced for its typographic effect in Holbrook Jackson's *The Printing of Books* (Cassell, 1938).

would be sent to prison where, I was told, one would be allowed one's Bible but no other book. I possessed a Douai Bible in three quarto volumes, printed in 1635. For these I caused to be made bindings of magnificent old vellum, in the boards of which, back and front, there were hidden cavities. There I was able to secrete much thin paper and many pencils. I took this multi-volume Bible with me to the guardroom and I still possess it. In the event I was not to need its hidden treasure.

I began my hunger and thirst strike two days before my arrest to test my ability to undertake it. Once the charge of being an absentee (undefended, of course) had been heard by a magistrate I was handed over to a military escort and taken to Hounslow Barracks. There I was brought before a sergeant-major whose remarks were short and ripe. If he had his way he'd bloody well like to . . . But when that was over we talked and I explained why I had refused alternative service.

'So you *are* a fighter', he said. Then he generously called in Hilda, who had been waiting in the street, and left us alone in his office for half an hour to say our goodbyes.

All that remained was for me to refuse the order to don uniform and then, with another C.O., I was given three blankets and marched off to the guardroom. It was just before lights-out and we found ourselves in a room lit by one candle, half the floor space filled by a sloping platform on which six or seven soldiers were lying wrapped in their blankets. They made room for us. It was so bitterly cold we even kept our soft hats on.

The morning was occupied with ritual, both formal and burlesque; we were marched to and from company commanders and commanding officers, and our offences recited and repeated. At midday we were told we were going to a guardroom inhabited by 'your friends'—and indeed those other C.O.s made us welcome. A boy took me aside and fixed absorbed eyes on mine. 'Are you enlisted in the army of Christ?' he asked.

For nine days this guardroom was my home. It was large and light, but very cold. There was ample food—for the others. The guards were friendly. We had half an hour's outdoor exercise morning and afternoon. We were allowed visitors and Hilda came to see me every day. My resolution was also fortified by an approving letter from my hero George Lansbury and by news from my mother (to whom I had reported my hunger—but not my thirst—strike) that my father was persuading himself into a less critical view of my doings.

I had no temptation to eat or drink. I had made my decision before my arrest and my body now loyally accepted it. But by the end of a week my mouth, tongue and throat were parched and painful. To assuage this I put my face in a basin and sucked in water then expelled it. At night I did this every hour or so, making possible some little patches of sleep.

But then I had a terrible doubt. Was I absorbing some of the water? On the eighth day a medical friend—Quaker and socialist—came to see me and told me my fear was justified. He found me amazingly well and thought I was unlikely to collapse for another two or three days unless I made use of the cold and increased my exercise to reduce my bodily strength.

For the next two days I went all out. Fast marching at morning and afternoon exercise; indoors I marched again, following a curved diagonal path which gave me the longest available course. Out of doors there was a biting wind. I wore no jacket or overcoat. I rubbed snow over my head and when we came in I lay down in a sort of ecstasy of shivering. My heart seemed to enjoy jumping from the pit of my stomach into my mouth. Like one of Jack London's characters, I seemed to chew it and swallow it down.

On my ninth night the desire to sleep was greater than ever before. I had a tiny tube of morphia tablets—an extreme stand-by which I had hoped not to use. I took two tablets from the tube but I could not swallow them. I slowly chewed them into a bitter powder. I sank into sleep. I awoke dizzy but contented, though my tongue was so hard, dry and shrunken that it seemed inanimate, like a limb asleep. As usual, I splashed myself with icy water to my waist; as usual the guard, amused, inquired if the water wasn't too hot.

Exercise was now more difficult. I knew that, joyfully, in the first hundred paces. But I lasted it out. The difficulty was to walk straight and evenly back to the guardroom. When I went to see my wife in the visitors' room I could not speak because of my stiff tongue, but I scribbled that I was becoming excellently weak.

That night we were offered baths. Here was unexpected help. The bath was deep, the water very hot. I lay in it a long time, so arranging my head that if I fainted it would, I hoped, dangle over the edge. Then I emptied the bath and filled it with water so cold as to be scarcely fluid. When I was numb, I managed to get out and dress. Leaving my shirt open, I walked back to the guardroom through thinly falling snow. I did not sleep, but nothing was unendurable: I knew tomorrow would be my climax.

In the morning of that twelfth day I collapsed at Hilda's feet when she came to visit me. I was taken to the military hospital. I was not wholly conscious, but I knew that Hilda would not allow me unknowingly to agree to anything that would compromise my resistance to military authority. I tried to tell the doctor about my strike, but my tongue cracked, and bled a little. 'I can see you're starving', he said. I was carried into a small private room. I had no anxiety, because I knew that I was too far gone for forcible feeding. I was told that if I would take nourishment I would be discharged from the army unconditionally. I nodded and accepted the sweetest drink of my life—a spoonful of peptonised milk. Peace came upon me as dusk used to come to my childish eyes, soft wave upon wave.

Three weeks later, on February 11 1917, I received my promised discharge from the army as 'unlikely to become an efficient soldier'. And a little later came, to my amusement, a notice that my application (never made) for a pension had been refused.

While I was convalescing in the military hospital I began to make plans—editorial and typographical—for the *Herald* against the time when it was to become a daily again, at the war's end. This freed me from my self-centred obsession, and after a recuperative holiday in Cornwall with Hilda and Edgar and Minnie Lansbury, I went back to my work at the Pelican Press and on the Board of the *Herald*, and to a continuing but less personal protest against the war.

In May 1917 Siegfried Sassoon made the most rousing of all anti-war personal demonstrations. He was a young officer known for his valour in the trenches; he was accepted by the aristocracy as a proper huntin' man; he was admired by the intellectuals who had read his anti-war poems. Now he refused to rejoin his regiment at the front. With Bertrand Russell he came to see me at the Pelican Press, bringing a careful typescript of his reasons for his act of mutiny. This I printed and circulated till the police seized the copies. Two years later, when the *Daily Herald* was re-established, Siegfried was, at my suggestion, appointed literary editor.

VIII

In the Red

In March 1917 came the first Russian Revolution. The overthrow of the Czar and his cruel and corrupt government thrilled the whole Labour movement, and many outside it. George Lansbury tells of our reaction at the *Herald*.

"Seated at lunch one day, Francis Meynell, Robert Williams, Harry Hease, W. H. Harford and myself formed ourselves into the Anglo-Russian Democratic Alliance, and invited Robert Smillie, W. C. Anderson and others to join us. We were severely criticised by friends for our audacity."*

Audacious we were. The Alliance, which was mainly the *Herald*, organised a 'Russia Free' meeting at the Albert Hall on March 31 and nearly 20,000 tickets were asked for whereas 12,000 was our limit. The meeting became the first great public expression of the demand for peace, and it moved hitherto silent people all over the country to call for an end to the war.

Hilda was on concert-platform terms with Clara Butt, and persuaded that great singer to sing 'Give to us Peace in our Time, O Lord' at the meeting. When I was preparing the printed programme I was warned by a kindly Jew from the East End that there would be trouble from the many Russian–Jewish exiles certain to come to the meeting if we did not explain the English use of the tune, since it was also the tune of the Czarist National

---

* *The Miracle of Fleet Street*, by George Lansbury, p. 113. Robert Williams was second-in-command of the Transport Workers' Union; Hease was an old personal friend of G.L. (I doubted his socialism). Harford was the *Herald*'s general manager. Robert Smillie was the devoted President of the Miners' Federation. Anderson was a leftist Labour M.P.

Anthem. 'You must print an explanation in Yiddish,' he said. That seemed sense and since I had no appropriate type I asked him to have a setting made. This he did; but before I printed it in the programme I thought it wise to check the wording. A Jewish friend translated it for me. 'I, so-and-so, the best and cheapest tailor in all the East End, wish to inform you and my comrades and likely customers that' etc. I was just in time to trim the notice.

Alone of all the press, H. W. Massingham* in his weekly *Nation* gave the meeting a fair report: 'Miss Butt sang alternate verses with the meeting and the effect was one of profound feeling', he wrote; and he emphasised the enthusiasm aroused by every speaker's call for peace. The orators included Lansbury as chairman, H. W. Nevinson, Israel Zangwill and Josiah Wedgwood, that very independent radical M.P. who had left the Liberals for Labour. I shared an aesthetic as well as a political enthusiasm with Josiah Wedgwood. He had been taught at Clifton College by T. E. Brown, one of my favourite poets. We agreed that Brown's usual representation in anthologies by a poem which began with the line 'A garden is a lovesome thing, God wot' utterly maligned his poetic achievement. (In later years I was able to give him a fairer representation in *The Week-End Book* and in a BBC radio talk.)

In June 1917 the Anglo-Russian Alliance and the I.L.P. organised a conference at Leeds.† It was attended by 1,200 Labour and trade union delegates, who passed a resolution calling for the setting up in England of Workers' and Soldiers' Councils

---

* Editor of the *Nation* 1907–23. Resigned editorship of *Daily Chronicle* because of his opposition to the Boer War in 1899.

† In his book *The Revolutionary Movement in Britain 1900–1921* (Weidenfeld & Nicolson, 1969) Walter Kendall reports fairly the organisation and resolutions of this meeting, but shows an unhistorical bias by referring to it as 'the Soviet Convention', thus giving the impression that it was a Russian affair.

on the Russian pattern. This was not quite as unrealistic then as it seems in retrospect. There was a widespread and passionate hope that this might be the moment both for peace and for peaceful revolution. Ramsay MacDonald of the Labour Party, Philip Snowden of the Independent Labour Party and Albert Inkpin of the British Socialist Party all joined in acclaiming the Russians as models to be followed.

Unity on a platform did not, alas, mean unity in action. Lansbury might have been able to hold these divergent groups to a common purpose, but he was ill and unable to attend the conference. Nothing came of it all save one or two ineffective local meetings. One of these was at the Brotherhood Church in Southgate Road, London, and it was broken up by people who had been led to believe that we were signalling to the Germans. Bertrand Russell was there and he describes in his *Autobiography** how most of us believed resistance to be useless or unwise, but how I was among the few who attempted it and returned 'with his face streaming with blood'. My wife and one of her sisters, like many others, had their clothes torn by viragos. My 'attempted resistance' was a violent effort to slam and bolt a gate of the yard that gave entry to the church. I failed, was hit over the head with a board and staggered for cover into the meeting. Not quite pacifist and totally ineffective.

We at the *Herald* carried on our battle for social revolution with the 'Charter for the Workers' which had been accepted by the Leeds conference. One of its sensational proposals was 'A Pound a Day is the Workers' Pay'. (In 1917 miners got 8s. a day, bricklayers and carpenters 1s. 1d. an hour, engineering fitters 51s. for a 60-hour week.) Another realistic proposal in the Charter was for a Public Health Ministry; and one that has never been realised was for the payment of wives and other houseworkers.

In November 1917 the out-with-the-Czar political aims of

* Unwin, 1968, vol. 2.

Kerensky and the makers of the March revolution had been over-taken by the Bolsheviks with Lenin at their head. Lenin was realistically determined to stop his country's war with Germany and less realistically determined to establish a wholly Marxist economic system. For me and the rest of 'Lansbury's Lambs' Lenin's was a most hopeful programme—the beginning of a new Socialist International. We did not foresee its slow degradation by Stalin after Lenin's death in 1924.

For the first three years of the war our Government took no action to deal with the fast-growing shortage of food except to appeal for 'voluntary' rationing. Sugar, bread and meat were the scarcest items. But were they scarce in the restaurants of the rich? I arranged with G.L. that I should go to the Ritz (then the smartest of all) to find the facts. To make my mission plausible I had to have a smart female companion. I took with me Gladys Lecoque, a beautiful young nurse who had attended Hilda in her lying-in. We dressed in our best and tried to adopt the regular patrons' attitude to the hotel staff.

After a large hors d'œuvres, taken mainly to reassure the maître d'hôtel that we were both bona-fide gourmands, I ordered tomato soup, complained that it was not rich enough and had it enriched by a jug of cream. Our next, and delicious, course was sole and lobster mated by a cream and white wine sauce. The fourth course was chicken, half a fowl for the two of us. Eating had now become a little difficult despite the fact that we had both prepared by abstinence for our feast. Nevertheless, I felt that my journalistic task was not yet done. Our waiter did not raise an eyebrow when I ordered one of the scarcest of popular foods—bacon and tomatoes. We were served three rashers apiece. Gladys managed to wrap hers in a handkerchief and put it in her handbag.

All through the meal I had been demanding rolls. Three proved to be my, not the Ritz's, limit. Fruit salad was our sweet course. I just couldn't bring myself to ask for sugar because the muscat grapes and the maraschino already over-sweetened it. Finally, coffee with cream. As we were bowed to the door we saw three old women in rags, huddled up for the night under the arches at the front of the hotel. Gladys gave them each a rasher of bacon. I walked with Gladys to the nurses' hostel in the Charing Cross Road and then betook myself home, glad of the air and the exercise. I ate very little the next day.

My article, in which I described our dinner in detail and reproduced a copy of the Ritz menu, was given the whole back page of the *Herald* with the streamer headline 'HOW THEY STARVE AT THE RITZ'. It was larded with some would-be satirical comments such as 'If prices are high and food is short down your way, why not pig it at the Ritz?' It was not without effect. There was a public uproar and questioning of Ministers, and the article was credited with helping to induce the food rationing which began two months later.

In February 1918 the *Herald* published a manifesto, 'To Workers at Home and Abroad'. I had little to do with the writing but everything to do with the printing. The terms of the manifesto were eloquently rugged, but I set its double-page 'spread' within a frame of seventeenth-century printers' flowers, with a fifteenth-century eight-line decorated initial and fourteen two-line initials. Of only one of its adjurations was I the author: 'Workers of the World, we believe in Internationalism—in Mother Earth as well as in Fatherland', a word-contrast which I pinched from a poem by G. K. Chesterton. In its own florid fashion—already my typographical fashion—it was a very successful eye-catcher.

In May 1918 the *Manchester Guardian* and the *Herald* published the Secret Treaties which the Bolsheviks had found in the Czar's archives. There had been suspicion before (I had voiced it in my article 'The War's a Crime'), but here was proof that the Allies had pledged themselves to the same policy of 'annexations' as they had charged against Germany. By secret agreements signed by Sir Edward Grey, our Foreign Secretary, in 1915 and 1916, all the Allies were to be aggrandised—Czarist Russia to have Constantinople, the Dardanelles and 'influence' over part of neutral Persia; Italy to have Trieste and south Tyrol from Austria; and France, Italy and Britain to have large slabs of Asiatic Turkey.

The sale of the *Herald* was quadrupled by its 'Secret Treaties' number to a quarter of a million, proving at least some solidarity among us divided socialists; but unhappily these revelations had no effect on war policy. Soviet Russia now planned an international socialist conference at Stockholm, which German as well as Russian socialists were ready to attend. Our Trade Union Conference voted only by a narrow majority for attendance at Stockholm, and Lloyd George, faced by the divided Labour movement, felt that he could refuse passports, which he did.

In November, the Armistice. I shall never forget our own emotion at that news. Civilians and soldiers and sailors now danced together in Trafalgar Square. Hilda and I joined a joyful Buck De La Warr, who was wearing his able seaman's uniform—he had refused to fight but served afloat on a minesweeper as a noncombatant. Emotion has no single way of showing itself. There were many with tears upon their faces as well as many singing 'Tipperary' and 'Knees up, Mother Brown'. I found it impossible that night to think of anything but the cessation of killing: I could not speculate on the positive peace that might or might not come.

What followed World War I was wholly different from what followed the anti-Hitler-war—as different as were the purpose and justice of the two wars. In 1918 demobilisation was ill-organised, there was much unemployment and poverty and prices rocketed. Unrest about the pace of demobilisation was so great that thousands of soldiers mutinied and refused to return to France and thousands more demonstrated all over the country and in Whitehall. Hilda and I typed a dozen copies of my own brief manifesto for distribution to the lorry-loads of soldiers expected to demonstrate at Westminster. I went to the Embankment, where the soldiers were to assemble. Only two lorries arrived: the others had been halted at their barracks. So ended my one-man contribution to the mutinies.

The voting registers were outdated and few serving soldiers had a chance to vote in Lloyd George's 'coupon' election in December 1918. As 'the man who won the war', Lloyd George—in his earlier days a fine fighter for the underdog—now routed both the moderates and the Left. To my sorrow, Lansbury was one of the many Labour leaders who lost their seats.

My consolation and distraction was my part in helping to prepare for the transformation of the *Herald* into a daily newspaper, due to happen in March 1919. A first step was to be an announcement of this project at an Albert Hall meeting which we organised a fortnight after the Armistice. The hall was booked and paid for. Without warning, the manager cancelled the letting and returned the money. Our response was 'direct action'. The Electrical Trades Union cut off the light from the hall and other unions made threats. A concert was due there on the very day of 'lights out', but, much more important, a few days later there was to be a lavish Victory Ball. Fuses can easily be replaced, but the Government reckoned that they could not send units of the armed forces to perform that simple job because this might well produce a refusal to obey orders. They therefore persuaded the Albert Hall management to restore our leasing of the hall.

It was three o'clock in the afternoon when we heard of the surrender, and lights had to be restored—that was our part of the bargain—in time for the evening concert. G.L. chased the Electrical Trades Union's head-office officials, and made it my duty to reach the union men who planned to stop the trains serving stations near the hall. This took us between two and three hours, after which G.L. and I had a happy and exciting rendezvous with a workman at the critical manhole in the street outside the Albert Hall, and watched, with some emotion, the simple process of restoring the light. A victory indeed.

Inevitably the meeting itself was packed. I was among the many speakers but I remember not a word of my few sentences. What I do remember is the instruction to aim my voice at a particular point in the topmost gallery. If I got a response sign from there, I could be sure that I 'carried' to the whole hall. There were no microphones in those days. I had a penetrating (too penetrating) voice and all was well, in that respect at least.

Public meetings were of great importance because there was then a desperate need for communication, which is a two-way affair. One achieved it by going to a meeting or ignoring it, by applause or silence. We of the Labour movement were apt to feel lonely—cut off as we were not only from our many friends outside the movement but also by the divisions within it. A crowded meeting, the voices of our political heroes, the singing together of the fine socialist songs, all made us feel that we were not solitary but in the great accord of the brotherhood of mankind. Political broadcasts on radio and television—still far in the future—do not 'communicate' in the same way; they merely announce, and they have almost wiped out great political meetings.*

The first day of publication of the *Daily Herald* on March 31 1919 was thrilling for me. I had committed the Pelican Press to the more than safe hands of Stanley Morison and become assistant editor to George Lansbury, the editor, and Gerald Gould, the associate editor. Langdon Everard was chief sub-editor and the paper's funny man. If Gerald Gould was G.L.'s right-hand man,

---

* Challenging occasions can still revive the old enthusiasm. In 1956 at the time of the shameful Suez policy of the Eden Government there were vast and effective protest meetings on the old pattern in Trafalgar Square and the Albert Hall. We even sang the 'Red Flag', led by Hugh Gaitskell.

I think I could be described as his left-hand man. I felt that Gerald's desire to be absolutely fair prevented him from being an ideal leader-writer (one of his chief functions) for a controversial paper like the *Herald*. I often disputed with him over his political judgements. Nevertheless we were close friends, particularly as rivals on the tennis court. He was on the heavily built side, though without rotundity, his head large and square, with thick prematurely grey hair through which he habitually ran his fingers while reflecting on his next leading-article.

George Slocombe was our news editor. He was a timid and anxious man until, inspired by a character in an Aldous Huxley novel, he grew a beard to hide his receding chin. The change was immediate and remarkable: he became master of his scene and staff. William Mellor was industrial editor and W. N. Ewer foreign editor. They were the two handsomest men on the staff and were greatly admired by the room nicknamed the 'Convent', where congregated the female staff, including Irene Clephane, Gerald Gould's secretary and my life-long friend.

The functions of the senior staff were far more free than our titles suggest; anyone of us could intervene in any department because we were friends and enthusiasts. In typographical matters the decisions were mine. I had planned the paper's headline: Henry Ball drew it in a kind of Johnstonian script, with a crowing cock, herald of the day, drawn by Lovat Fraser. Siegfried Sassoon as literary editor* brought to the paper a galaxy of reviewers, such as Arthur Waugh, David Garnett, H. J. Massingham, my sister Viola, Edward Garnett, Havelock Ellis and Leonard Woolf. W. J. Turner was music critic, Herbert Farjeon theatre critic. Everyone was underpaid—Herbert Farjeon indeed, when the *Herald* was still a weekly in 1918, had written to me offering his services without any payment at all.

* W. J. Turner took his place as literary editor in 1920 and made E. M. Forster his holiday substitute.

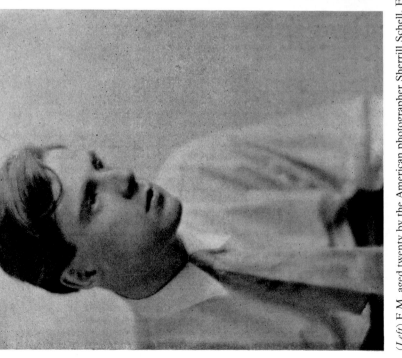

(*Left*) F.M. aged twenty by the American photographer Sherrill Schell. F.M. introduced him to Rupert Brooke, whose well-known profile portrait Schell made. (*Right*) Hilda Saxe displaying her Venetian dress by Fortuny, circa 1914.

THE C.O.'S HANSARD

A WEEKLY REPRINT FROM THE OFFICIAL PARLIAMENTARY REPORTS · PUBLISHED BY THE NO-CONSCRIPTION FELLOWSHIP 5 YORK BUILDINGS, ADELPHI, W.C.

No. 24   MAR. 29, 1917   1d.

COVERING THE WEEKS BEGINNING MAR. 12 & 19

HOUSE OF COMMONS

ROSSENDALE AND THE KNOCK-OUT BLOW

Friday, 16th March, 1917

Sir W. BYLES: Some reference has been made in this Debate to the startling news received from Russia this morning. If Kings and Governments will make playthings of their people, and set them up to shoot and to starve one another, they must expect that their thrones will be shaken. I want to suggest to the Government—and I am rather sorry that the Leader of the House has just gone out—a different way of winning the war. We have been two and a half years striving to overcome our enemies by physical force. I think that a better method would be to try to arrange with them by reason. I believe that we could get a satisfactory settlement and a durable and honourable

PRICE THREEPENCE

RUSSIA FREE!
TEN SPEECHES

DELIVERED AT THE ROYAL ALBERT HALL LONDON

On 31 March 1917   Authorised Report

SPEAKERS

George Lansbury   Maude Royden
H.W. Nevinson   Jos. Wedgwood, M.P.
Robert Smillie   Albert Bellamy
Robert Williams   Arthur Lynch, M.P.
Israel Zangwill   W.C. Anderson, M.P.

1917
LONDON
THE HERALD OFFICE
21 TUDOR STREET
FLEET STREET
E.C.

MEDITATIONS FROM THE NOTE BOOK OF MARY CAREY 1649–1657

printed & sold by
FRANCIS MEYNELL
67 ROMNEY STREET
WESTMINSTER
1917

(*Left*) Title-page of one of the two books printed at the Romney Street Press. It was dedicated to F.M.'s cousin Robert, in prison as a conscientious objector. Thirty-two copies were printed. Stanley Morison helped F.M. in the composition. Page size 5½ × 3¼ inches. (*Centre and right*) Examples of F.M.'s fanciful political printing at the Pelican Press. Page sizes 9⅜ × 6¼ and 8⅛ × 5¼ inches.

I always saw the first edition 'to bed'. This meant attending the composing room and seeing the last stage of the proofs with the night editor, W. P. Ryan, who was a perfectionist, particularly when anything concerning Ireland was at issue. One evening I found a crisis developing. The vans were waiting to take the early edition to the trains for distant distribution. There was a sudden blowing of horns, a signal that we were in danger of missing the trains. I dashed up to the composing room and found that Ryan had stopped the printing so that the spelling of the word 'galore' on the front page could be changed; he insisted that it was of Gaelic origin and must be spelt 'go lohr'. I intervened. The trains were just caught.

In 1918 and 1919 England was waging an undeclared war against the Russian Revolution. In what follows here I must be critical of Winston Churchill, who was Lloyd George's War Minister. I would like to have passed over this because I share with the rest of my generation a deep gratitude for what he did to guide and inspire the country in the war against Hitler. Churchill's achievements in that war are far too great and memorable to require a suppression of the truth about his acts against the Russian Revolution in the days when it might have been helped and guided to moderation and amity. There was the blockade of the Soviet ports, the Archangel and Vladivostok expeditions, and a vast supply of men, munitions and money to Kolchak, Deniken, Wrangel and other 'White' Russian counter-revolutionaries. We at the *Daily Herald* called this 'Churchill's war'. It would have remained an obscure campaign but for our exposure of it.

Churchill came at last into the open with a press conference which I attended. I put a number of biassed but pertinent and embarrassing questions to him. At the end of the meeting he observed Eddie Marsh speaking to me. He approached us, gripped my hand and asked Eddie who I was. Eddie, feeling awkward at knowing me, answered: 'He is the son of Alice

Meynell, the poet'. 'What is he doing here?' said Churchill, still holding my hand. 'Sir, I represent the *Daily Herald*', I told him. He threw my hand back at my chest as if it were a hand-grenade, and strode away with an even more embarrassed Eddie.

On July 8 1919 our paper had a dramatic 'scoop'. By some means unknown to me there came into our possession an Army Headquarters instruction to commanding officers in the occupied Rhine districts:

Confidential

To all units.

Bundles containing copies of the *Daily Herald* newspaper are being received at railhead. If addressed to units under your command will you please ensure that no copies are issued to the troops, and give instructions for them to be collected and burnt at your Brigade Post Office under the supervision of an officer.

It is important that the collecting and burning of these papers involve as little publicity as possible.

A fortnight later Osbert Sitwell submitted a blank-verse poem of 124 lines entitled 'A Certain Statesman'. By direct implication it credited (or discredited) Churchill with the instruction. At my suggestion, joyfully accepted by my colleagues, we printed this as a leading-article on July 22 1919. This made a paragraph in journalistic history.* It occupied more than a column. I quote enough to show its topic and temper:

* In 1944 the *Star* published a leading-article in verse and *World's Press News* remarked that this made editorial tradition 'rock on her heels'. I reminded them that the *Daily Herald* had been the first with this innovation. Fifty years after the Osbert Sitwell leader, *The Sun*, a bastard but then admirable descendant of the *Daily Herald*, also ran a leading-article in verse. The editor told me that he was well aware of our precedent.

The DAILY HERALD
Is unkind.
It has been horrid
About my nice new war.
I shall burn the DAILY HERALD.

I think, myself,
That my new war
Is one of the nicest we've had;
It is not a war really,
It is only a training for the next one,
And saves the expense
Of Army Manœuvres.
Besides, we have not declared war;
We are merely restoring order—
As the Germans did in Belgium,
And as I hope to do later
In Ireland.
. . . . . .
When Kolchak
Murders and mutilates
His enemies,
It is justice pure and simple;
Whereas we all know
That the Bolsheviks
Commit atrocities.
I shall burn the DAILY HERALD.
. . . . . .
Whatever I do
The DAILY HERALD grumbles:
. . . . . . I *shall* burn the DAILY HERALD.*

* This and two more of Sitwell's satires were reprinted in a pamphlet,

In August 1919 I took a quasi-holiday by joining a number of other invited journalists in a goodwill tour of Denmark. It was organised by Christian Aagaard, press attaché at the Danish Embassy in London, who was able to offer us the hospitality of the Danish King's yacht. His purpose was to win a sympathetic attitude in English newspapers to the Danish claims on Schleswig-Holstein. My own motive was to make inquiries about the possibility of arranging supplies of newsprint for the *Daily Herald.*

I was the youngest and least experienced of the English journalists and represented the only left-wing paper; my colleagues in general did not disguise their surprise that I should have been included in their senior and conventional ranks. Two among them were more friendly; one was Cecil Roberts, who was my senior by only a year; the other, surprisingly, the representative of the *Morning Post,* the most extreme of the Tory journals. I felt so separate from the rest that in some of our long hours at sea I pretended to feel seasick, however calm the water, and kept to my cabin.

The yacht was our home, but we landed at all the main towns and show-places of the various islands; we were greeted by the local mayor and dignitaries, whose speeches were always in excellent English, shown the local sights, given parties, lunches, dinners. We made a rota of answering speech-makers. We had little to say, but we made a game of trying to alter our terms and tones, not for the sake of those we were addressing (they, lucky fellows, hadn't heard us at our previous landings) but to mitigate our own boredom. I didn't do too badly when my turn came; I threw in a lot of Hamlet and Elsinore. Our visit to Copenhagen gave me an acquaintance with that city which I was to put to

---

The Winstonburg Line, published in September 1919 by Henderson's (known as the Bomb Shop) in Charing Cross Road.

good-and-ill use a few months later. My newsprint inquiries were unbusinesslike and fruitless.

Three months after my return from Denmark we at the *Daily Herald* thought it a good plan that I should try to be the first English journalist to get into Bolshevik Russia. The only possible route was by way of Sweden and Estonia. I had to carry some assurance of my political bona fides, and this I got in Stockholm from Höglund, chief of the Swedish Left (socialist) Party. He gave me a card certifying that I was a representative of the party's press bureau. He asked me to convey to Lenin, who was seriously ill, a supply of medicines. Nothing could have thrilled me more. I made an unpleasant crossing in a small ship to Reval (now Tallinn). I had been inoculated in Stockholm against half a dozen diseases and these made me painfully ill. In my rough night-voyage to Reval I took a sleeping pill. I half-woke in the night and dazedly swallowed several more. When the time came to land I was so deeply dormant that I had to be carried ashore. Later in the day I was able to find my way to the political woman who had been given notice of my mission. She had a secret means of communication with the Bolsheviks in Petrograd. My hope was to get to the border with Russia and there to be safeguarded across. Meanwhile I lodged in a sad little hotel, where I found Arthur Ransome, the story-writer and journalist, who had two motives for getting to Petrograd: his journalism and the fact that his Russian wife was there. Our food was pitiable and warm water so scarce that he, I and a young American journalist had to share the same shallow bath, changing our order of entry day by day. This proved to be a fruitless wait for me. Nothing came of the contacts made on my behalf with Litvinoff in Petrograd, for there was a White Russian force operating cruelly between Reval and the Russian border. I could not wait indefinitely. Ransome waited until the Reds routed the Whites, then in he went.

I felt defeated in my journalistic job and, at the time, defeated also as a bearer of medicine to Lenin. I left the parcel with my mystery friend in Reval, and I was told later by Höglund, to my delight, that it reached Lenin eventually.

I knew and admired Maxim Litvinoff, who became Soviet representative in London—a friendship unabated over many years, an admiration enhanced by his liberal policies within the Soviet, as Foreign Minister and, after 1934, at the League of Nations, where he led the movement for disarmament. He was married to Ivy Low, a close friend of my sister Viola and so too of mine. Ivy wrote poetry which was sometimes printed in the *Herald*. In the summer of 1920 Maxim was in Copenhagen negotiating with Jim O'Grady (the British representative) the exchange of prisoners taken in the undeclared war between the two countries; he was understandably enraged because the British Government would not allow his English wife to join him. The more serious but unavowed aim of the negotiations was the ending of that war.

I decided to go to Copenhagen partly as a news-gathering journalist, partly again in search of newsprint from Russia, which had been, pre-war, a main source of supply. Difficulty in buying paper had long been a major problem for us at the *Herald*. Apart from swiftly rising prices, there were some wholesalers who boycotted us. Lansbury himself had seen Litvinoff without effect; but I thought vaingloriously that my personal friendship with him might have better results.

I said Lansbury's effort was 'without effect'. I meant 'without success', for it had plenty of effects. The Secret Service obtained copies of telegrams passed between Litvinoff in Copenhagen and Chicherin in Russia. Into the reality of these telegrams was inserted the fiction that Lansbury had received Russian money—6,000 francs' worth of 'Chinese Bonds'. The method of circulating this 'revelation' to the Press was as mean as might be. First it was offered to a news agency on condition that it was to be reported as the agency's own discovery. The agency honourably refused. Then the Admiralty released the story—but not to the *Daily Herald*! But for the courtesy of the *Manchester Guardian*, who passed the handout to us, we would have been the only paper in the land to appear next day without this front-page story. 'Not a bond, not a franc, not a rouble' was our streamer headline. Lansbury fortified the denial by giving a list of the people who had helped the paper with gifts or 'investments' of money.

When I reached Copenhagen I telephoned Litvinoff in his hotel and was bidden to visit him. He left his sitting-room door open when I arrived, saying loudly that he always did this when he had visitors. He wanted to reassure the window-cleaner and the bannister-polisher on the landing (who, oddly enough, always arrived at the same time as the visitors) that no funny business was afoot.

I said, 'Here, dear Maxim, is a present from Ivy', and gave him a carefully parcelled new tie in which was sewn a note from Rothstein, who was substituting for Litvinoff in London. Maxim thanked me with an understanding glance and went into his bedroom. In a few minutes he returned, wearing the new tie. When we were seated and chatting, the door open all the time, he said, 'You English are great pipe-smokers. Here is some Russian tobacco to try', and he tossed me a tobacco pouch. I knew that he knew that I never smoked a pipe, so I guessed that the pouch contained an answer to Rothstein. It did—a practical one; for when I got back to my hotel I opened the pouch and found two strings of pearls.

My problem was how to get them back to England without being discovered. I was not doing anything illegal (jewels were not subject to customs duties), but I was a director of the *Daily Herald* and their discovery would mean a political sensation, particularly in view of the recent false statement about Lansbury. I wandered around Copenhagen with the pouch of pearls. In a shop window I saw cards with strings of toy pearls on them, priced at one kröner. I bought two of these. Back in my room I took the toy pearls off their cards and replaced them with the real ones. No, they didn't look in the least like a mere kröner's worth. So out I went again. Now I saw displayed fancy jars of Danish butter. I bought one and sank the pearls deep into the butter. I brought the jar safely back to England and delivered it to Rothstein.

A little later Litvinoff wanted to put more funds at the disposal of the newly established Russian Trade Mission in London. Since he had no currency resources he used me several times as a carrier of jewels, sometimes from Denmark, sometimes from Sweden, once from Finland. A willing carrier I was: international socialism seemed the hope of the world to all of us on the Left.

All these trips were made in search of paper for the *Herald*. While on one of them I received word from 'Trilby' Ewer that he had reason to believe that I would be searched at Scotland Yard on my return. In Copenhagen I bought a large box of expensive chocolate creams and in my hotel room removed the top layer on its cardboard tray; then into every chocolate of the two layers below I inserted a single pearl or diamond. I restored the top layer and ate one or two of the chocolates from it.

I thought it would disarm suspicion if I left the box with its lid open while I went for a stroll. I had already seen a man coming out of my room who, on being challenged, said he had gone in by mistake. One of Sir Basil Thomson's sleuths? After wandering about for perhaps an hour, I suddenly had a thought which made me wilt. Might not the chambermaid decide to help herself to a chocolate and take it from a lower layer so that its absence would not be noticed? I hurried back to the hotel and with infinite relief saw that the jewel-bearing layers were intact. I wrapped up the box and took it to the post office, but with my pen poised to write a name and address I was flummoxed. I could think of several safe recipients, but in every case some detail of address escaped me: the number of the road or the name of the district. It was the amnesia of anxiety. Then one sure and complete address came to mind: Cyril Joad's. But a trouble remained: he was a greedy eater and good chocolates were scarce in England. That meant that I must leave for England at once and so arrive before the parcel post.

Back in England I was indeed taken to Scotland Yard to be searched. They were civil enough, found nothing and apologised. Then I went to Cyril and told him that a parcel was due, perhaps the next day, from Denmark, addressed to him but really for me. All went well. Two days later I resumed possession and Hilda and I spent a sickly hour sucking the chocolates and so retrieving the jewels.

On another of my jewel-trips I was stopped on landing and my baggage was searched. The sleuths were helpful in repacking, but I found it difficult to thank them and at the same time prevent three large diamonds in my mouth from rattling.

Having failed to get paper from Russia, I thought it was time to get help for the *Herald* by other means. Why not money? This would enable us to outmanœuvre the English merchants' near-embargo on our paper supplies. The money must, of course, be an unconditional gift: a recognition of the fact that the *Herald* was the one paper in England that both reported and supported the Revolution. The 'Chinese bonds' affair and our newspaper rivals' reactions ought to have been a danger signal to me. On the contrary, I argued to myself that Lansbury's repudiation had been of fact not of principle: as an internationalist I, and surely he, would see no objection to the *Daily Herald* having help from Russia.

So on my next visit to Copenhagen I put our plight to Litvinoff: unless we could have help in paper or money we would have to raise the price from 1*d.* to 2*d.* This might be a deadly blow to circulation, since our public was suffering from the post-war slump and many were unemployed. Litvinoff agreed to put my plea to Moscow. It was successful, and I was offered £75,000 worth of jewels, with no strings attached.

My plan was to turn the jewels into money and then come to G.L. with the offer. If he said no, then no harm would have been done; if yes, he would decide how to publish the fact. But first I had to solve the problem of how to sell the jewels. I bought a book about jewels in the vain hope I would learn about values and so be a more informed seller. My close friends Edgar Lansbury and his wife Minnie lived in the East End and could make easy contact with unorthodox but honest jewel brokers with Hatton Garden connexions. Through them I sold all the jewels. We thought our transaction was secret. What folly! Neither we nor the Russians realised that diamonds normally on the English market were all cut in Amsterdam in a certain fashion, whereas Russian diamonds were cut in a style of their own. Inevitably the word went round in the trade, and thereafter to Sir Basil Thomson's Special Branch, that this flood of diamonds on the market came from Russia. Edgar was told by one of the now alarmed buyers that the police had visited him. Worse, we learned from the *Manchester Guardian* that telegrams from Lenin to the Trade Delegation had been decoded, that these referred to the offer of money to the *Herald* and that the story was being given to all newspapers except the *Herald*.

What was to be done? We had desperately compromised George Lansbury. We must tell him at once so that he could break the story before its official release. We sought him out at a committee meeting in a distant part of London and made our confession. He was hurt, forgiving and even understanding. His reproaches were not in his words but in the look on his face. In his *Life of George Lansbury* Raymond Postgate gives a merciful verdict: 'There was nothing in this that was wrong, but plenty that was unwise. Was not Meynell a director of the paper? Was not Edgar's name Lansbury?'

It was decided to tell the story of the offer at once and to invite the views of our readers, our staff and fellow directors* about its acceptance. So the next day's *Herald* splashed the story under the heading SHALL WE TAKE THE £75,000 OF RUSSIAN MONEY?

"The only reason against that we consider valid is that it seems pitiable that we should have to accept help from a country which, *because of British action*, is so impoverished.

On the other hand the offer is a magnificent demonstration of real working-class solidarity."

This was acceptable to most of the readers who answered the *Herald*'s question, but my fellow directors agreed in a unanimous 'No'. So, inevitably, I resigned from my directorship and my editorial post; undoubtedly I would have been sacked had I not offered to go.

George Lansbury in the *Daily Herald* of September 15 1920 reported my departure under a heading set in obituary 'black-letter' type. This made me smile, but I still find moving the over-generous text in which G.L. expressed appreciation of my eight years of service: 'In all that he has done or left undone I know he has been actuated by one motive only, that of service to the cause of international solidarity and goodwill.' He wrote to my parents with an equal generosity and an understanding of their unhappy concern. This I knew to be so great that I even doubted whether I should be welcome—probably chased by reporters—at Great-ham. To Stanley Morison I confided my sad doubts, and he wrote to my father: 'I assure you that it is a realisation of your feelings which keeps Francis from obeying his first impulse—to seek your roof'. My father made it plain to me that my fears were groundless.

* Ernest Bevin, Frank Hodges, Ben Turner—all trade union leaders —had become co-directors with Lansbury, Robert Williams and me.

The reaction of the daily and weekly press was quite fantastic. The *Evening Standard* gave the story a front page double-column heading and a leading article; the *Morning Post*'s four columns were titled 'Mr Lansbury Owns Up'; the *Daily Express* wrote of the 'Meynell Hunt'; the *Daily Mail* was quieter with a single column; the *National News* shouted 'Red Plot to Capture Europe' over its five columns; the *Daily News*, a Liberal newspaper, was content with two-and-a-half comparatively moderate columns. That was the first day's reaction—but the furore continued every day for a fortnight. The *Morning Post* was gently satirical in a personal piece about me—well removed in space and in tone from its political denunciation. This described me as 'an ardent idealist' and credited (if that is the word) me with 'the zeal, indeed the fanaticism, of the Englishman who finds himself in a minority and seems ready to embrace any cause as long as it possesses the saving grace of being abjured by the vast majority of his fellow-countrymen'. The *Post* writer went on flatteringly to stress how 'invaluable' to George Lansbury and my other colleagues had been my 'debonair and finished effrontery' and noted, with charming irrelevance if not inaccuracy, my accomplishment as a ballroom dancer.

However, more seriously, the question was being thundered at me: 'What have you done with the jewel money?' This I could not answer with any precision or candour, for in fact I had handed it over to Klishko at the Russian Trade Delegation, and to associate them with 'the jewel scandal' would almost certainly have produced a Government order to quit. I was told, and had no reason to doubt, that negotiable currency was desperately needed for the importation into Russia of utter necessities.

In his book *The Revolutionary Movement in Britain 1900–21** Mr Walter Kendall refers to my account of the importation of the jewels as 'romantic' and my disposition of the money as 'un-

* Weidenfeld and Nicolson, 1969.

[124]

likely'. Unsupported judgements like these are surprising in a book chockfull of exact and factual research. Nowadays my efforts look romantic and amateurish, but they were effective in the 'innocent' days of the 'twenties. I am rather proud of Ian Coster's reference to me as 'a man who could have gone through the amateur's gate of international intrigue'.*

The newspaper hubbub came to its climax with the sudden return to Moscow of Kameneff, who had been conducting negotiations for the resumption of Anglo-Russian trade. The press saw a chance to associate his departure with the jewel story; according to *The Times* the British Government had required Kameneff to make an explanation of 'this double dealing'.

Krassin was left in England with Klishko as his assistant to run the Trade Delegation. They had an office above a bank in New Bond Street. Klishko, whose English wife was a constant dancing partner of mine, called me to his office. 'There is danger', he told me, 'that we shall be expelled. We have here a large quantity of platinum. We do not want to take it with us. Will you guard it for us till our return?' I agreed, and struggled down the stairs with a barely portable suitcase in each hand. In the street I hailed a taxi. The first suitcase went safely in. When I lifted the second its handle came off and several wrapped bars of platinum fell on the pavement. A policeman helped me to lift them on to the taxi's floor. 'Heavy, ain't they?' he said. The taxi took me to our house in Romney Street. I managed to carry the suitcases to the drawing-room, on the first floor. Then I lettered a notice and put it at the foot of the stairs. It said: 'To the platinum bars, the property of the Russian Trade Delegation, behind the sofa above'. I wanted no charge of 'secreting' the platinum if it was traced to me. My friends thought that my notice was a joke. I didn't undeceive them. The Trade Delegation was not in fact expelled, and in due course I restored the platinum to them.

* *Friends in Aspic* (John Miles, 1939).

I had kept a foot in the door of the Pelican Press through all my adventures and misadventures with the *Herald* and to it I now returned full-time. It meant asking Stanley Morison to relinquish his position as my substitute, which he easily did, for he had other offers.

On November 11 1920 the body of the Unknown Warrior was buried in Westminster Abbey and the Cenotaph in Whitehall was unveiled. To me, and to many who had opposed the war, this seemed a desperately sad and even hypocritical affair, since its regal and military pomp was a boast of victory rather than mourning for the million of our countrymen whose death was symbolised by this one nameless body—a mourning in which we would have fervently joined. These feelings I expressed in a letter which was printed on the leader page of the *Daily Herald*.

The next day the *Morning Post*, the top daily paper of the propertied classes, honoured me with a long leading-article. It was headed: CONSCIENTIOUS CAD. Such a title conferred by the paper of the extreme Right delighted me then—indeed pleases me still. Today the word 'cad' has lost something of its flavour. Then, and especially to *Morning Post* readers, it meant 'not a gentleman', and nothing worse could be said of any man than that. The article concluded: 'The suitable treatment for a conscientious cad of the Francis Meynell type would not be shooting, or hanging, but kicking, or the hand of every honest man flat-heeled across the mouth'. There did not seem to be a single 'honest man' among the *Morning Post* readers: I was unmolested. What perhaps irked the writer specially was the fact that I bore a well-known 'county' name. And confusion of identity there was. My namesake of the aristocratic and rich branch of the family had a brick thrown through a window of his house, while I, mistaken for him, received a letter from the Unionist Party Headquarters reminding me that 'my' contribution to Tory Party funds last year had been 2,000 guineas and hoping for the same again.

At about this time I was asked by Arthur McManus, the chairman of the newly formed Communist Party in England, to redesign the title of its recently established weekly paper *The Communist*, which had made very little impact. I did this to his satisfaction, though not wholly to my own, and thereupon he invited me to become its editor for six months. I was drawn to accept by three things: my vague but fervent political convictions; my belief in myself as an unusual sort of journalist; and the chance for typographical innovation—there was not a weekly in the country that was not formal and dull in its appearance. So I agreed; and the ensuing months at the paper meant months also in the Party.

Arthur McManus was a Clydeside shop steward, a brisk, thoughtful and engaging little man, who didn't mind in the least that I knew no Communist dogma, had read no Marx or Engels and had never heard of dialectical materialism. The other members of his council did not share his tolerance and I had awkward summonses before them.

As I turn the pages of *The Communist* after some fifty years it seems to me that I did succeed, in my few months' editorship, in producing an unusual paper. It had two main characteristics: cartoons, sometimes six full pages of them in an eight-page issue, by a brilliant young Australian, Will Hope; and a number of serial 'supplements' such as historic revolutionary documents prepared by Raymond Postgate (my admirable assistant editor) and John Reed's *Ten Days that Shook the World*.

The new *Communist* was a circulation success. Sales grew from 8,500 copies a week at the beginning of January 1921, when I became editor, to 18,000 by the end of the month. Then suddenly orders from all wholesalers ceased. There was a police-inspired boycott. We went directly to the retailers, and by February 12 our circulation had increased to 40,000.

I doubt whether there could ever have been a political party organ that showed so little awareness of its party's ideology. Though now I was veering towards agnosticism, I was still a professed Christian and as a socialist I worshipped the revolutionary Christ of the Sermon on the Mount; so I caused Will Hope to do a series of cartoons showing a reverent drawing of Christ confronting our political enemies. These cartoons occupied five of the eight-page *Communist* of June 11 1921 and each was supported by a quotation from the New Testament. This was *not* in accordance with the Bolshevik ideology—it would have been more appropriate to the Salvation Army's *War-Cry*—and it contributed to the growing gap between me and the Communist leadership.

Indeed, *The Communist* was very little different in its temper and tone from the old weekly *Herald*. Like that forerunner, it was a paper by intention for working-class people but by its style addressed almost wholly to middle-class intellectuals. Even its front-page 'Notes of the Day' were allusively quizzical—for instance, whenever we quoted from *The Times* we referred to 'the bloody old *Times*, as Cobbett called it'. I cannot think that the out-of-work miner knew or cared who Cobbett was. The simple fact is that we wrote and cartooned for ourselves.

Will Hope became a little alarmed lest the growing furore caused by his excellent but ill-paid work for *The Communist* should deprive him of commercial commissions and even put him at risk for libel. I suggested seriously that he should change his signature to G. (for Guillaume) Espoir instead of Will Hope. It seems in retrospect an absurdly naive and give-away 'disguise', but he adopted it.

The Communist of April 23 1921 proved to be the most famous (or outrageous, as you please) and certainly the most expensive of its history. Early in the year, in the midst of a mounting trade depression, the Government had ended the war-time control of the mines and handed them back to the owners, who immediately announced a lock-out unless the miners accepted a reduction of

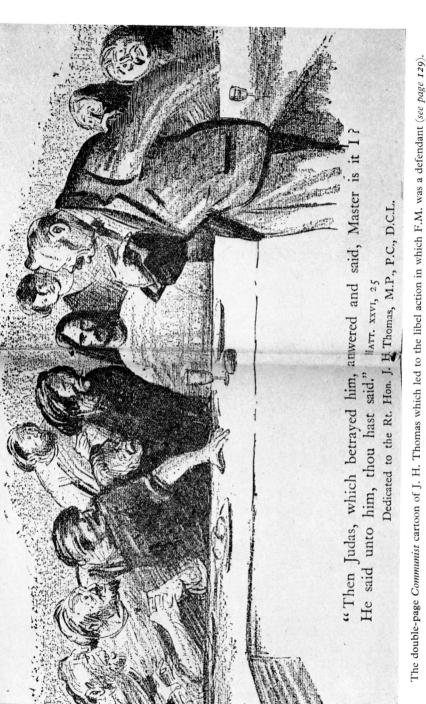

"Then Judas, which betrayed him, answered and said, Master is it I?
He said unto him, thou hast said." MATT. XXVI, 25

Dedicated to the Rt. Hon. J. H. Thomas, M.P., P.C., D.C.L.

The double-page *Communist* cartoon of J. H. Thomas which led to the libel action in which F.M. was a defendant (*see page 129*).

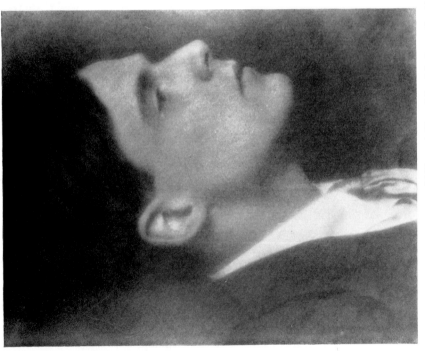

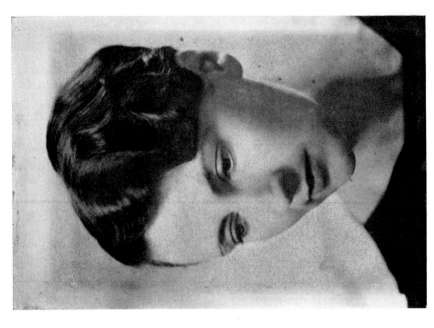

F.M. and Vera Mendel about the time of their marriage in 1923.

wages. The Transport Workers' Federation and the Railwaymen's Union pledged themselves to strike in support of the miners. This was the 'Triple Alliance', headed by Frank Hodges of the miners, Ernest Bevin and Robert Williams of the transport workers and J. H. Thomas of the railwaymen.

We had news of a secret meeting with Lloyd George, which was followed by the surrender of all the unions on the promise of a Governmental inquiry. The left wing of the Labour Party called this day—Friday, April 15—'Black Friday'.

The Communist published a full-page cartoon in which 'The Triple Alliance' became 'The Cripple Alliance'. It showed caricatures of Thomas with one leg, Ernie Bevin without any, and Frank Hodges with both his contorted, displaying themselves on a stage. The caption read 'Messrs Thomas, Bevin and Hodges play nightly to enthusiastic audiences of coal-owners'. Another full-page cartoon showed J. H. Thomas laying a wreath by the side of a dead miner, with the caption: 'I claim the right to lay the first wreath—I killed him'.

We weren't content with that. A middle-page cartoon showed a vivid drawing of the Last Supper with an unmistakable J. H. Thomas as Judas. In the original drawing one of his hands holds a bag with the thirty pieces of silver. Early in the run-off our printers, the National Labour Press, sent me a message to say that on legal advice the bag of money had been eliminated from the plate. That didn't save them. They, McManus and I were all served with writs for libel on behalf of J. H. Thomas.

Before the hearing of the action I had resigned my editorship. The libel action had alarmed me: I could not see how others were to be avoided if I continued to do an honest and unmuted job— and this would put my wife and child at financial risk. To myself I attempted to cover my main motive, which was plain cowardice, with two others. The first was the growth of unease between me and the council of the Party (other than McManus) because of my

failure in ideology. The second motive was our enforced change
of printers. The National Labour Press had refused to print us
any more, our new printers had abominable typefaces and typographical habits, and they made trouble about accepting those
special settings that I had so often designed and procured from
the Pelican Press. For me their attitude meant frustration in my
own cherished artifact. So it all mounted up, and early in May
1921 I wrote a formal letter of resignation and arranged to go back
to the Pelican Press at the end of June, when my six months contract with *The Communist* was to expire.

A few days after my letter of resignation, the police raided our
office, made arrests for 'sedition' and hinted that more were likely
to follow. Would I too be among these victims of the Defence of
the Realm Act (DORA, as it was called)? Ignominiously I asked my
father to make it plain to authority, in the person of Sir Basil
Thomson, that I had already resigned my post. To my father
Thomson replied affably that he had heard of my resignation, was
glad of this confirmation and hoped that I would 'have the good
sense to see through' my Communist friends. This abated my
fears, but I was (and still am) ashamed of what was something like
a secret supplication to an arch-enemy.

Some months after my return to the Pelican Press, I had to
face the J. H. Thomas libel action. It came before Mr Justice
Darling, who was notorious for his extreme Tory views and for
the severity of his sentences. There was never a question of settling
by apology. We had intended to denounce, which meant libel,
Thomas; and we thought the reporting of the case would further
expose him. McManus accepted my suggestion that we should
retain as our junior counsel my friend Maurice Healy, and his
uncle, Serjeant Sullivan (famed in Ireland for his power in cross-
examination), to lead for us. Douglas Hogg, K.C. (father of
Quintin Hogg), led for Thomas.

I went to the hearing with McManus, and we enjoyed ourselves.

Sullivan confused Thomas into admitting that he was not a socialist but that he meant every word of his socialist speeches; that he was party to a revolutionary movement which might result in the overthrow of the monarchy, but that he did not find this inconsistent with his oath as a Privy Councillor—and many other inconsistencies. At one moment of pause in his cross-examination, when there was some noise in court, Thomas pointed at McManus and said, 'I heard him call me Jimmy'. The Judge ordered McManus to stand up. No movement. 'Stand up, I say. Did you hear me? Stand up!' McManus was a very short man. He answered, 'I *am* standing up, my lord'. (Loud laughter in which neither His Lordship nor Thomas joined.)

Darling suggested to the jury that they should award what he said was sometimes called 'vindictive' damages; and after fifty minutes the jury assessed these at £2,000—a sensationally large sum in the values of the time. I was called upon to pay the £2,000, so I went bankrupt. Before a Master in Chambers I was quizzed by Thomas's counsel as to what I had done with the £75,000. My protest that this was utterly irrelevant was over-ruled. This nonsense made me all the readier to lie, and in any case I didn't want to involve the Russian Trade Delegation. I made a quick calculation. Would this sum, in £5 notes, go into a suitcase? The only measure that came to my mind was the Oxford Book of English Verse, with its 1,200 pages. Ah, pages of a book are numbered on both sides, so I must think of my standard as six hundred pages. I had to think of 15,000 £5 notes. Six hundred into 15,000, then, would give me 25 bundles the size of the Oxford Book. Easy for a suitcase. So I answered: 'Sir, I gave the notes in a suitcase to a masked man with a foreign accent, whom I had never seen before, one midnight on Hampstead Heath'. Thereupon the Master in Chambers adjourned the hearing.

The 'good ladies' (good indeed), Muriel De La Warr and Mary Dodge, have often appeared in my pages. Now they come in again. They had followed the account of my doings in the news-papers, and Lady De La Warr asked me to meet her not at her house but at her hairdressers, where she had the use of a private room and where no detective would follow her. There she told me that she and Miss Dodge feared that the probing of Thomas's counsel might reveal them as the donors of the funds which, years before, they had asked me to put into the *Herald* under cover of my name. Now, therefore, they would provide the money to pay Thomas off. This was done, my bankruptcy was discharged and I was freed from any more interrogations.

I ask myself why there is little about people in this chapter. The answer is that I remember more easily my public life in those years than my personal life. I had lost touch with my parents' world, and Eddie Marsh, for example, and almost all the people I had met through him, were so distant in politics that they became infrequent companions—though this does not mean that we ceased altogether to see each other. Most of my new and newly strengthened friendships had the *Herald* or other forms of the 'Movement' as background: Margaret and Douglas Cole, Raymond and Daisy Postgate, Walter Turner, Irene Clephane, Dick and Beatty Plummer and Joan and Clifford Allen.

My friendship with Margaret Cole began in my conscientious objector days, when she was still Margaret Postgate. When I met her she had lately resigned her post as a classics mistress at St Paul's Girls' School to take a dogsbody job at the Labour Research Department. She was heart and head in the 'Movement', a term that covered a multitude of sincerities: the Independent Labour Party, the British Socialist Party, the Herald League, the Shop Stewards movement. Her looks were handsome, even in-triguing, not beautiful in the full fashion of those days. Next to politics her passion, like mine, was poetry. It was a significant friendship for me. It would not, I thought, encroach on my marriage, which had become happily domesticated. In politics Hilda remained my ever staunch support, but she could not be (as Margaret was) a stimulant, since her political feelings were largely an echo of my own; and not in poetry was her heart, but in her music.

Margaret introduced me to the 'modern' poets of that time, and I enveloped her with my favourites, the seventeenth-century metaphysical poets. She herself wrote in the 'free verse' style, and I was so taken by her work that in 1918 I printed at the Pelican Press a small book of her poems. We went for country walks together, a political pamphlet in one pocket, a book of poems in another, sometimes the two of us, more often in a company of four or six. The language of sex is so evasive and frightened even today that it isn't easy to express oneself. Margaret and I never went so far as to have 'an affair', though *affairés* we were indeed in our kisses and contemplations. (Make what you can of that, Mrs Grundy.)

Many years later, in 1931, she wrote a poem which cast back to our war-time days together. With her permission I quote from it:

Come down into the valley, darling, darling.
The pool is dark with sunset, and your father
Will be asking what you've done with that girl you brought
                                                   from nowhere.

How can one write until the spell be broken,
How make clumsy lines for you to read them?
They would not sound like Marvell or like Herbert,
They would not be fine art, or quaint, or special,
Or nice to put inside a Nonesuch cover.

You are not a Lorelei; you are not heartless;
You have a heart, a heart romantic, silly,
A heart that wants to do the childish things,

The gallant things, the things in the story-books—
To climb the Jungfrau at dawn, to bring the water
To the pent city, to believe in something
Beside fine printing—to die on a barricade somewhere . . .

Oh Francis, Francis!
You do not break hearts, do you? You only put them
—Feeling a little dusty, a little tarnished—
With cool firm fingers, back on the shelf they came from.

Hilda and I, in the course of house hunting, stayed with Edgar
and Minnie Lansbury in Bow. We were there in January 1922
when Minnie died of pneumonia—the only time in my life that I
have been present at the very moment of death. Its cruelty to the
survivor rather than to the dying bit into me. Over the next
twenty years until his own death Edgar was near and dear. One
tends—or at any rate *pre*tends—to dislike 'compliments'. Edgar,
dying, paid me one which I hold still in his honour, not in mine.
Moyna Macgill, the actress, his beautiful and devoted second wife
and the mother of his famous children, came to tell me the news
of his fatal cancer, and asked me to come and say a last goodbye.
I stood for a few moments unseen beside his bed; then Edgar
opened his eyes and gripped my hand. 'Moyna told me', he said,
'that "someone" had come to see me. She didn't tell me it was
you. It's like having caviare when you expect sardines.' What a
phrase from a man who knew that he was within a few hours of
death!

IX

Mainly for Typophiles

I have already told of the odd fashion in which I came by financial support for the setting up of the Pelican Press in 1916. At Burns & Oates I had been something of a typographer, something of a printer at my minute Romney Street Press. At the Pelican I was to be printer, typographer, advertisement-writer, even occasionally publisher—occupations I was to develop in different ways and circumstances during the next decades.

The Pelican Press began in a dreary typographical epoch. World War I had shattered the few attempts to bring distinction to commercial printing. The function of 'typographer', now taken for granted by every publisher and advertiser, was non-existent; the printer's foreman compositor was left to do the designing. In commercial printing only Bernard Newdigate at the Arden Press, Gerard Meynell at the Westminster Press and Harold Curwen at the Curwen Press were offering 'style', with the revived Caslon Old Face predominant. In the mass of complicated Victorian dullness which enveloped the printing world one had to have a peering eye to discover their work.

Bruce Rogers, the great American typographer, was my hero. What he had done for book design in the United States I now tried to do in the design of 'jobbing' printing—catalogues, posters, press advertisements, political manifestos. A tall order indeed.

My first needs had been to find a suitable name and premises. I had in mind a sixteenth-century colophon device of a phoenix with a writing quill in its crest, and plumped for the 'Phoenix Press', but I found that there was already a press so named. Anxious still to keep the notion of rising from fire, I decided to lengthen the bill of the phoenix to make it a pelican, with that bird's symbolism added to that of the phoenix. It pleased me also that the new name preserved the alliteration. For premises I was lucky to find a house in Gough Square. It was large, it was cheap to rent, it was quiet; my office looked out on Dr Johnson's handsome house. It was to accommodate composing rooms only, since machining was to be done by its foster-parent, the Victoria House Printing and Publishing Company, which was integrated with the *Herald*. It was therefore important that our premises should be close to Victoria House. Fleet Street lay between it and Gough Square, but in those days it was not so crowded as to make the carrying over of type formes a difficulty. At Gough Square we made space also for a dining-room for the *Herald*'s small editorial staff—a symbol of the closeness of my concerns, for I worked almost as much for the *Herald* as for the Pelican Press.

I had no staff problem. The parent company gave me as foreman compositor A. H. Meaden. He was technically competent, he was willing to take the new view of commercial typography that I was determined to impose. We were easy colleagues, and later he became manager in everything except design and type equipment. I had no qualms about leaving the Press in his sole charge while I was away hunger-striking within a year of the Press's beginning.

The Press 'set itself from its beginning to do good printing for the daily, not the exceptional, purpose'. Settings for displays in the *Herald* and for its socialist pamphlets, were our early staples; but I wanted to work for ordinary commerce as well. That would help financially, but, more compelling, it satisfied my need as a typographic zealot and propagandist to influence typography generally.

Bruce Rogers had drawn inspiration for his bookwork from the sixteenth-century printers, particularly Tory and Estienne. I followed him into the past, but I was moved particularly by the Lyons school of Jean de Tournes, with his resplendent initials and the arabesque borders from which derived the fleurons or 'printers' flowers' of the seventeenth and eighteenth centuries. I have already told how Stanley Morison and I began to use printers' flowers at Burns & Oates; now, at the Pelican, I scattered them everywhere—to surround advertisements, for the borders of books, even to enclose political manifestos. In a Pelican Press puff I wrote: 'The eye first will be pleased; and then the mind's eye. For you will remember that these self-same patterns have gone to the making of fine printing with never a break (but for Victorianism) for four hundred years. Shakespeare's first editions, which served some Elizabethan hundreds, and the advertisements of London's Underground, which inform many millions—those are but brief bedding-places in the lives of these perennials.'

The printer's flower became the Pelican hallmark and when, rarely, I tried to use decorative rules our customers were apt to beg for the flowers they had expected. There has been some revival of printer's flowers in fairly recent years. Christian Barman revived them for the menus and announcements of British Transport Hotels in the 1950's,* where they are still in use. In 1960 the *Monotype Recorder* printed a special display of printer's flowers, both new and old.†

When I started the Pelican very few good type-faces for hand setting were available. I installed Caslon Old Face, Goudy's Kennerley and Forum, and Morris Benton's Cloister, the last three newly produced by the American Typefounders' Company. This narrow limit was no disadvantage: while our compositors were acquiring a new style, my style, they could not fall into the common error of a vast massing and messing of incongruous faces.

After a few months we were on our feet and able to buy a Monotype caster. We installed Plantin, Italian and Imprint, and persuaded Monotype to make in each of these faces a few special

---

* *Monotype Recorder*, Spring 1958.
† *Monotype Recorder*, Spring 1960.

'sorts' for us—ligatured ꜩ and ſt and italic *is as us in*, and a special lower case u̲ which carried half the capital Q's tail (in its standard form the Q had to swallow its own tail) and a lengthening of the descenders and ascenders of the Monotype Plantin. These characters (later called Nonesuch Plantin) are shown here before the normal ones:

g g j j p p q q y y *ff g g j j p p y y* b b d d f f h h k k l l Qu

Still later I searched abroad for well-designed types and could boast that the Pelican 'has always had in use some type held by no other English printer'. This was no doubt vanity in part, but it was also good commercial sense. In 1920 the Cochin faces were ordered from France, and then the Moreau-le-Jeune open letter and the Fournier decorated types. From Germany in 1922 came Walter Tiemann's Narcissus. We used such admirable living designers as Henry Ball, Frank Horrobin, Lovat Fraser, Doria Behr and Macdonald Gill to decorate the covers of some of our publications.

It was with real anxiety that in 1917 I sent Bruce Rogers some samples of Pelican printing. He had begun his notable work here at the Cambridge University Press. I presented myself to him at Cambridge. It was a lovely summer day, and I decided that there was one thing in the world at which I could be his instructor. I took him to a cricket match at Fenner's and explained—he was very patient—the techniques and formalities of the game. Soon I invited him and his wife to dine with Hilda and me at our house in Romney Street, telling him of our simplicities, and promising some piano-playing by Hilda. This was his answer:

"Dear Mr Meynell, I'm much relieved to find that you live in a slum, and don't dress—for I haven't had a dinner jacket for ten or twelve years. For the past five, we have lived from hand to mouth and knocked about from one lodging to another—dining mostly at cheap restaurants or making a stew over a gas-burner—so please tell Mrs Meynell we shall be frightfully disappointed if she gives us a regulation English dinner, and goes to a lot of trouble—don't let her, please.

I may add that we usually impress our own guests into service for the wash-up afterwards—but we of course don't insist upon this if there is a piano!"

It was a delightful occasion, and began one of my most treasured friendships, which did not end until B.R.'s death in 1957. I found his personality a complete confirmation of his work as a typographer. His line of talk was as firmly gentle as his drawing of a border or typeface. He was a propagandist but he was kind; he admired a great tradition and showed how one could adapt it to modern use; he treated the young aspirant as a fellow-worker.

By the spring of 1918 I was peppering him with samples of my work, including a vast quad crown showing of our type-faces. His answer was a blend of criticism and praise, both eagerly accepted:

"I have received your magnificent specimen-sheet of types—the poster and the smaller sheets. For the first, I have nothing but the heartiest praise (unless indeed I may be permitted the small wish that you had used rules throughout as division lines instead of section marks etc. It would have made a calmer page—and there is enough decorative variety in the types themselves). But this is a small carp—hardly more than a minnow, and it is on the whole the finest thing of its kind that has been done in modern days and I offer my sincere congratulations on mastering such a difficult subject. It *looks* simple enough, perhaps, to anyone but a printer, but I am well aware of the thought and work that went into it.

The poster too is most effective, though I don't think so successful as the broad-sheet of types."

D. B. Updike was another American typographical giant at his Merrymount Press in Boston. Once again with the vanity and courage of youth I sent him the Pelican type-sheet. His reaction too was great encouragement; in January 1921 he wrote to me that he had made our type-sheet 'one of the ornaments of my composing-room'.

One type was to remain a unique possession of the Press—a poster type that was elegant, condensed and bold, for which I commissioned a design from 'the finest printing craftsman of this day, and possibly of any day', as the Pelican pamphlet claimed. The reference was, of course, to Bruce Rogers. He was not easily persuaded to undertake the design. My intention or hope had been for lower case as well as capitals, for a feeling of the pen in the design and for narrower letter-forms than usual to get more matter into each line. Here is a letter he wrote me in December 1918:

"In regard to the type-design, your offer is a tempting one, just at present when income taxes are about due, though of course the problem of a lower-case is more vexing than of caps. alone. I enclose some sketches of both, but I am not at all confident that they are what you want. I fear I am not much good at this kind of letter as I'm not wholly in sympathy with the idea of making type look like drawn lettering, even in a mild degree.

Especially in lower-case when a single letter is repeated so frequently, the eye soon tires, I believe, of any marked eccentricity in its form. I have therefore made the lower-case even more regular than the caps—with the result that you will probably not like any of it. But you mustn't hesitate to say so, as I should hate to feel that the result did not meet your entire approval. It's really *your* type, you know—I'm just the draughtsman. So you will tell me frankly if you don't altogether like the sketches, and give someone else a trial. It would be comparatively easy to get more attractive letter-forms in this genre if it were not for the limitation in width. A narrow, and at the same time a heavy, letter is almost certain to be a somewhat gross one."

Then two months later:

"I've been working at your poster type design the last few days and I've got it pretty well 'roughed in'. But I have so many misgivings about the design that I'm sending it on to you in its present state to find out whether it is going to be what you want.

I fear it hasn't enough of the unusual in its make-up to satisfy your requirements and I don't want you to take it unless it does. I haven't been able to turn up any satisfactory (heavy) model for the caps (the lower-case doesn't exist I suppose) except the one Goudy used—and I musn't lay myself open to the charge of copying Goudy—even if I liked his type—which I don't. It looks well enough as he has shown it—just a line or two. But it would have become most tiresome and disagreeable in any quantity, I'm sure, and especially if enlarged.

I don't really like any of Goudy's types—except the Forum caps for very limited use. So I have fallen back on my own devices and started such a letter as I think I might like to use myself—but as I said in the beginning, I'm not at all sure it is what *you* want. You mustn't, however, take each letter as its final form, for they will doubtless all have to be modified more or less after they are all in ink (especially the A) but I can't do that at the present state of the drawing."

Indeed they did satisfy me, but the proofs were not pulled until four months later—June 1919—by which time I had left the Pelican for the *Herald*. (By what route I know not, the working-drawings for this type have come into the possession of the Victoria and Albert Museum.) The first stage in the making of the designs into poster type was to have them cut in wood. For some sad reason unknown to me the second stage, the casting in metal of the wood versions, was never reached, and the wooden types inevitably showed signs of wear by their use in perhaps a score of posters. They could still, I think, have been rescued in 1921, when I returned to the Pelican, but I found that my (by then) masters had little interest in the type and reckoned that no more money could be spent on it. I believe that the worn letters were later destroyed. The loss to typography has been lessened, I think, even annulled, by Berthold Wolpe's Albertus type, which admirably attains the ends and serves the purposes that I had in mind.

A large part of my pleasure in the Pelican was its and my close association with the *Herald*. I have already described how it gave me the opportunity to shape many of the *Herald*'s political proclamations, partly in their wording and wholly in their display. I also enjoyed enlarging the function of the Press by printing a few very small books. On these I set my heart as well as my types, for they were written by close and admired friends. Among them were Margaret Postgate's *Poems*, W. N. Ewer's *Five Souls*, Gerald Gould's *Monogamy* and Eleanor Farjeon's *Tomfooleries*. My own special preferences in poetry lay in the seventeenth century, and I made an anthology of Henry Vaughan and Andrew Marvell. Lines from a poem by Francis Thompson—

> Lo God's two worlds immense
> Of spirit and of sense
> Wed
> In this narrow bed—

gave an appropriate title and I called the book *The Best of Both Worlds: Poems of Spirit & Sense by Henry Vaughan and Andrew Marvell*. It was indeed a narrow bed—a crown octavo, diminished in its width to $4\frac{1}{2}$ inches, set in Plantin Monotype italics with the Pelican's special ligatures, printed on hand-made paper and sold for, I think, 3*s*. I added 'Notes' to my selection and I determined that the first sentence should run to exactly one hundred words. What silliness! I can only suppose that, generally and vaguely rebellious as I was, I needed to prove to myself that I still could be exact to an antic degree. My friend Martin Secker, one of the few publishers who had a real care for the style of his books, allowed his name to go on the title page along with the Pelican's device, and distributed the book for me.

A private printing for the Meynell family and friends was *Seven Unpublished Poems by Coventry Patmore to Alice Meynell*. This is pretty enough, but without any particular typographical interest. One of the poems specially pleased me because it testified to my mother's politics. It is titled 'To Alicia, seeking to make me a Radical'.

> Dear, either's creed one hope foretells.
>   Mine waits; yours, kindlier hastes—
> But what to us are principles
>   Who are one in Tory tastes?
>
> Bear in your hat what badge you may,
>   The Red Republic's even,
> So all your lovely ways obey
>   The Monarchy of Heaven.

We also printed two or three books for outside publishers, among them Raymond Postgate's admirable collection of revolutionary documents* and *Married Love* by Marie Stopes in 1918. (It was only many years later that she could use a more precise title for her pioneering books about the desirability and methods of birth control.) Our printing of *Married Love* brought an unexpected little problem. We were due to deliver 1,500 copies to the publisher, and since paper was scarce we printed precisely that number. The publishers complained that we had delivered only 1,415 copies. I made inquiries—and discovered that every

* *Revolution from 1789–1906* (Grant/Richards, 1920).

single employee of Pelican-cum-Victoria House, all eighty-five of them, had snitched a copy.

For its first three years I 'ran' the Pelican. At the end of 1918, when I went full-time to the *Herald* to help prepare its establishment as a daily, the Pelican moved to 2 Carmelite Street, a side-door extension of the printers of the *Herald*. It was my immense good fortune to find Stanley Morison free and ready to take my place at the Pelican as its typographer. Moving as I did only four rooms away from the Pelican office, I was able to keep in my own hands the designs for the *Herald*'s special displays. One of Morison's achievements at the Pelican was the design and production of Edmond Kapp's *Personalities*—those 24 superb and witty portraits of notables, published by the pioneering Martin Secker.

Both Morison and I, during our terms at the Pelican, developed a special kind of advertising for our work—special in the sense that it offered historical and aesthetic dissertations before the inevitable self-praise. Examples of this method of promotion are Stanley Morison's *The Craft of Printing* and my *A Printer's Miscellany* and *Typography*. I have kept some of these 'earlies', but the most ingenuous of them was absent even from my memory until I saw it in an otherwise unrepresentative Pelican packet at the Victoria and Albert Museum. It includes this innocent description of our costing policy and methods:

"Since the Pelican Press devotes itself to *good* printing, it demands for its fine product a fair price. We say 'a fair price'. It is not a fancy price. It is not an exorbitant price. It is based on the actual wages paid on the job with the addition of the appropriate percentage (arrived at by a scientific costing system) to cover the overhead costs of the department concerned, and then the percentage for profit. This percentage for profit ranges from 15% to 5% with a normal 10%, according to the class of work, the convenience of performance, and the risk it involves. It does not vary as between

THE PELICAN PRESS DEVICE

FIVE OF THE NONESUCH PRESS DEVICES

Stephen Gooden

Reynolds Stone

Tom Poulton

John Farleigh

McKnight Kauffer

The Lecturer

The President

The Designer

(*Above*) Fake Pelican Press and Nonesuch devices drawn by Edward Bawden for Double Crown menu, February 1928. (*Below*) Silhouettes from Double Crown menu, December 1933, showing F.M. the lecturer, Dr John Johnson of the Oxford University Press, the President, and Holbrook Jackson, the designer of the menu.

one customer and another; and our prices are *always* governed by this system, never by a plan of charging as much as we think the customer will stand without kicking. This holds not one whit the less when no estimate has been furnished."

Another of my early circulars was a dissertation on the phrase 'With 25 soldiers of lead I have conquered the world'. It was set in various sizes of the four Monotype faces the Pelican possessed, and the style of my prose was as mannered and florid as the style of the setting, a typical effusion of a young man now grown a stranger to me. The '25 soldiers' are the letters of the alphabet and the phrase is of antique French origin; our 26th letter, 'w', was added in the mid-seventeenth century. Here are my final two paragraphs:

With 25 soldiers of lead ... If it is not individually it is at least generally true. All the heights and depths and breadths of tangible and natural things—landscapes, sunsets, the scent of hay, the hum of bees, the beauty which belongs to eyelids (and is falsely ascribed to eyes); all the immeasurable emotions and motions of the human mind, to which there seems no bound; ugly and terrible and mysterious thoughts and things, as well as beautiful—all are compassed, restrained, ordered in a trifling jumble of letters. Twenty-six signs! The complete equipment of my child of six—and of Shakespeare. Two dozen scratches so chosen and so arranged as to make King Lear and the Sonnets! They are common to the greatest, and to us. They are the key to eternity. They are the stepping-stones to the stars. And we use them, one to split his infinitives, one to forge a cheque, one to write betting-slips.

Pause, gentle reader. Come back from the edge of this profound pool of sentiment and truth. Consider this in mitigation of the wonder. As literature is thus contained by a group

of symbols, so life is controlled by another and shorter series.
I make bold to declare that with eleven soldiers of lead—
eleven, no more—I could conquer the universe. You doubt it?
But first behold them:

$$9876543210£$$

Our combination of instruction, demonstration and promotion
was continued by Morison in a fashion as much learned as handsome when he joined the Monotype Corporation. There was a
happy interplay between Monotype and Pelican: Monotype produced its fine faces, Pelican showed how they should be used.

The Pelican Press was a successful commercial venture. We
offered settings for advertisements and by 1920 we were able to
list among our customers the Midland Bank, Rolls Royce, the
Architectural Association, the Everyman Theatre, Genatosan,
Heal's, MacFisheries, the Ministry of Labour and, among publishers, Basil Blackwell, Jonathan Cape, Chatto & Windus,
Longmans Green, Ernest Benn and Sidgwick & Jackson. Less
surprisingly, we worked also for the Labour Party. It was something of an achievement that such stalwarts of capitalism as Rolls
Royce should employ an off-shoot of the *Daily Herald*.

Looking today at the adventurous pieces of promotion we produced for the Pelican, I wonder if Morison and I did as well for
our customers as we did for the typographical revival and our own
enterprises. Once, however, it was the client company which
defeated itself. My friend Reginald McKenna was chairman of
what was then the London Joint City and Midland Bank. I persuaded him to agree that I should present to him and his Board an
illustrated argument for bank advertising, which didn't exist
then. I had the greatest fun with this project, which included
displays of the world-history of banking summarised (believe it or
not) in four advertisements and less than 400 words. One of these
was about Roman banking, set appropriately in Trajan capitals

within a fine border and with 'Senatus Populusque Romanus'
reduced to the customary SPQR. When I presented my series to
the secretary of the Bank's board these initials puzzled him. Then
suddenly light (or darkness) came to him. 'Ah yes, I see,' he said
'they stand for "Small Profits, Quick Returns".'

I had classified the public to be reached as (1) the bank's present
customers (few of whom knew of its executor and trustee services),
(2) other banks' customers, (3) first accounts, and (4) people with
'stockings'. The second category made it necessary for the Midland
to show the scheme to its rivals at one of their joint meetings.
Horror was expressed. If one bank started advertising, then they
would all have to... Furthermore, if many of the Midland's
customers were to take advantage of its 'special services' the bank
would have to abandon them. The plan, the most logical and eye-
catching I have ever made, was rejected, but I was entrusted with
the printing of some of their duller notices.

On my second return to the Pelican, in 1921, after resigning
from *The Communist*, I found a somewhat different Pelican. I was
no longer the boss. The limits of my narrowed function are
indicated by the colophon to *Typography* (1923). It reads: 'This
book was compiled and for the most part written by Francis
Meynell, the Typographer of the Pelican Press, of which J.
Atcheson Barrow is the General Manager and A. H. Meaden the
Manager'.

Into my minute office in Carmelite Street came Oliver Simon.
Our common interest was introduction enough. Fine 'jobbing'
printing was so rare then that we typophiles actually sent telegrams to each other when we came across outstanding examples.
Oliver was working for the Curwen Press, whose printing I much
admired; and he has written that I was 'the first young person'
who had printed in a manner that stirred his interest.* I wasn't so
young a person—I was nearing thirty, Oliver only twenty-six. We

* *Printer & Playground* (Faber, 1956).

started then an exchange of samples of our work that over the next twenty years must have amounted to a car-load.

Oliver was short, dark, handsome, a great enjoyer. In the thirty-four years I knew him he changed not one whit: the black hair, the untidy clothes, the easy giggle, the ambition. Our interests joined also in the cricket field and he was a constant and happily inefficient member of the cricket team, the 'Long Primers', which I set up in the early 'twenties. He was as ready to scorn as to admire, and he never really liked what I am sure he would have called my florid style: when at the Nonesuch Press I used Italian decorated end-papers in an edition of John Donne he said I had 'dressed the Dean in a tart's drawers'.

For Herbert, Oliver's younger brother, my friendship was much deeper. He had been to the U.S.A. to enter the flourishing cotton business of his uncle, was caught by type-fever and became a compositor in the famous firm of William Edwin Rudge. When he returned to England in 1921 he too came to see me in my Pelican cell, hoping that I could offer him a place alongside me there. This was not feasible: what I did offer him was a place in my cricket team.

Oliver started the Fleuron Society in 1922, the *Fleuron* magazine in 1923, the Double Crown Club in 1924 and *Signature* in 1935. The Fleuron Society died after two meetings which Oliver records were 'stormy'. Its only production was a sheet of note-paper bearing the names of the members: Holbrook Jackson (editor of *Today*), Francis Meynell (Pelican Press), Stanley Morison (Cloister Press), B. H. Newdigate (Shakespeare Head Press), Oliver Simon (Curwen Press). I don't think Oliver liked coming last even though that position was governed by alphabetical order. I gave the society its name, but did I contribute to the 'storms'? As I remember the meetings, a truer word would have been 'differences': Newdigate wanted to retain hand-setting and hand-made papers and specialise in narrowly limited editions;

Holbrook Jackson wanted no limits at all; Oliver was, I think, depressed by the number of strongly opinionated people who had come together (he could never adjust to a committee of more than one); I wanted to combine mechanical production with larger limits to editions.

At the Pelican I had already started on the setting of what was to become the first Nonesuch book, *The Book of Ruth*, but I was willing to subordinate my vague plans for a press of my own to Oliver Simon's wider scheme. When his scheme was aborted I still hoped for a renewed association with Morison, to whom I wrote:

"One thing which may sound trivial I beg of you: don't make too many book plans in which I have no share. I may need that interest and moral support very badly. And I am sure I have useful brains for it, so I don't ask it merely of your compassion."

Why this plaintive note? My personal life was at a distracted half-way point between the old and the new. I had left my old world of politics and special pleading; my return to printing was anxious and circumscribed. In short, I was sad about the past and anxious about the future. Morison and I didn't make books together, but we did collaborate happily in the production of the article on printer's flowers which opened the first number of *The Fleuron*.

Obviously it is not appropriate for me to attempt a judgement on the contribution the Pelican Press may have made to the development of English 'jobbing' as distinct from book printing. This has been generously done by others. Philip James, claiming in 1939 that the Pelican Press was 'only now to be seen in its true perspective', ended an article in *Signature* by saying that the Pelican 'not only gave delight in a starved and war-weary world, but was a powerful influence in the moulding of contemporary commercial typography'.

Today, looking back, I think that the historians of English printing have been over-generous in their judgment of the Pelican Press. The Westminster Press and the Arden Press, its forerunners, and the Curwen Press, its contemporary, did fine work more consistently.

To typographers other than book designers the style of Pelican printing must today seem old-hat indeed. But the odd necessity of its time was that the few forward-looking printers needed to look back to the high period of printing when type-faces had achieved simplicity and decoration was their servant. The age of the revived sans serif types and strange, un-useful margins was still far away. Each to his day!

X

Parting of the Ways

During my time at the Pelican and the *Herald*, Hilda was setting about re-establishing herself, after child-bearing, in the world of music. I had the pleasure of designing and printing her programmes and posters. I still have the the schedule of some of her concerts for 1918, and a neat little job it is. It reports seventeen recitals and concerts and much praise by the music critics. One concert at the Queen's Hall was in combination with Muriel Foster and Gervase Elwes as singers and Albert Sammons as violinist; another was with D'Alvarez, Gervase Elwes, Henry Wood and the Queen's Hall Orchestra. At one of the 'Proms' Hilda was the pianist. Her fee was three guineas. . .

Mary Dodge had given us a Whistler painting of Cremorne Gardens at dusk. It was a large canvas, dimmed by darkening of the paint as well as dark by subject. It had hung in our small drawing-room alongside a larger and lovelier landscape by A. D. Peppercorn, Hilda's father. We decided to sell the Whistler and accepted £550 for it from a Bond Street dealer—a moderate sum even for those days but sufficient for our plan to build ourselves a cottage at Greatham. We chose a site nearly half a mile from the paternal house: we wanted to combine independence with association. Macdonald Gill, brother of Eric Gill, was our architect, and a good job he made of it. We were helped with the cost by the £250 grant from public funds available for the building of any new house in the years just after World War I.

At Greatham our daughter, aged five, wanted to go to church, as her nearby cousins did. So to Mass she went, three times. Then, very bored, she asked: 'Don't they ever change the programme?'

By now Hilda and I had begun to break many of our ties of habit and habitat. Was there some unconscious portent or symbol in the fact that at a *Daily Herald* money-raising meeting at the Holborn Hall I prompted Hilda to put her wedding ring into the collection? And that I persuaded her that we would be wise to leave the house in Romney Street, where we had been very happy, for a small and comfortless flat?

After eight years of happy marriage I met and fell in love with Vera Mendel, and Hilda and I parted. To my lasting sense of shame I broke the news to Hilda by nothing more than a letter. Hilda never lost her full love for me nor I a deep feeling and sense of responsibility for her. We never ceased to see each other and quite soon after our divorce and my remarriage Hilda mercifully allowed me to bring Vera for an occasional weekend to the Greatham cottage. Twenty-five years later she wrote to me with a wonderful magnanimity:

"I wish you would believe that if our break was anyone's fault it was quite as much mine as yours. I have known it for a long time. And I wish, too, you would believe that, even apart from my having Cynthia, you have been responsible for most of the happiness of my happy life. I don't suppose it would occur to you, but I should have been much more of a dormouse if it hadn't been for you, more even than I am now, and it is much better, and more interesting, to be even a little bit awake. In fact, darling, instead of being a 'clod' you have given me all I ever had that I wanted. I hope you see that this is the truth. I wish I could say it better."

Vera was ten years younger than Hilda. She opened for me a new and exciting landscape of the mind. She had had a short, childless and unhappy marriage which had taken her to Greenwich Village in New York. There she was studiously interested in the psychological discoveries and questionings of Freud—of whom I had never heard. She was a 'Girton Girl'. She had near-perfect French and German; she even knew more poetry than I did. She was exact. She was unexpected. She once said, 'Why do people waste the night making love instead of talking?' When I was in a turmoil of doubt about leaving Hilda, Vera wrote to me: 'If in the end you decide that I cannot be your Wife, let me at any rate be your Man'. She believed that I was material still raw enough for her to mould. And, for a start, she was determined that I should have an operation on my left hand, injured two years earlier when a wine bottle from which I was drawing the cork collapsed in my hand. So when our 'affair' was still secret from everyone but Hilda, Vera conducted me to Berlin, where surgical skill was to be had with scarce-credible cheapness for anyone with English money. 'Here one is a millionaire on ten shillings or two dollars a day' I wrote to my mother.

When I woke from the anaesthetic the assertive pain was in my leg not in my hand. A ghastly doubt assailed me. Had the Herr Doktor misunderstood the operation he was due to perform? No, he had merely taken a slice of meat out of my leg to introduce it to my hand between the tendons and the bone.

In 1923 Vera and I abandoned the secrecy of our liaison. Hilda divorced me, and Vera and I were married at a register office with David Garnett as our witness. Our wedding-day celebration was to take four of my teenage nieces to 'No, No, Nanette'. Some months earlier my mother had died. My father said no word of rebuke about my divorce. I tried to persuade myself that he was able to shut out from his mind any knowledge of family actions which would cause him pain or shame. I was wrong. He wrote sadly to my old friend Maurice Healy, whose expected disapproval had kept me silent to him. 'That which hurt most', Maurice wrote to my father, 'was one letter which did not come'. Despite my silence Maurice remained my friend. Later he was able to write to me: 'I was talking to two young poet friends last week about friendship, and I told them not to make the mistake of thinking they had reached its greatest heights, for that only you and I had done'.

A few months before Vera and I were married, the child of our brain, the Nonesuch Press, was born.

XI

Nonesuch

How does one write about one's chief success—and it was a resounding one—without unseemly (and boring) boastfulness? I have attempted a half-solution of the dilemma by consigning to a separate page, and in small type, the opinions of some eminent judges and historians of printing.

It is easy, and false, for the bibliographer to think of Nonesuch as a knowing plan to change the manner and manners of publishing in general and to establish the typographer as a necessary character in a publisher's organisation. For me Nonesuch was a craft, a trade, a happy synthesis of my two fervours—poetry and print.

At the Pelican Press in its changed days and management I had already begun to hanker after more independence, personal and professional. Now I wanted to devote myself to books rather than to miscellaneous printing; so I made inquiries of several publishers. Would they allow me to print for them this, that and the other English classic which lacked any 'really nice' edition? My somewhat arch formula was to point out that if they chanced to be wrecked on the conventional desert island and made the conventional choice of the only two books to accompany them, the Bible and Shakespeare, they would not find a current edition of either fit for a tasteful shipwreck. The response was no more than a frown or a smile. So I myself set out to be a new kind of publisher-designer, an architect of books rather than a builder, seeking the realisation of my designs by marshalling the services—often mechanical services—of the best printing houses, papermakers, binders. We were lucky in our hour: we were the first to cater for a large, growing and unsatisfied interest in 'fine books' at less than

KIND WORDS ABOUT NONESUCH

By making conscientious, and not merely commercial, use of modern methods Mr Meynell has gone far towards proving to many of us that the future of fine printing lies in the hands of those who are prepared to follow his lead and to use modern machinery.—Stanley Morison: A Review of Recent Typography (*Fleuron, 1927*)

How often have I envied from a distance the triumphs in book design of such masters of the craft as Francis Meynell and Bruce Rogers.—St John Hornby: The Bibliography of the Ashendene Press (*1935*)

With the Nonesuch Press, appropriateness of design for each item is the main consideration ... seldom has there been such a well grounded knowledge of type combined with so nicely developed a visual sense.—Elmer Adler: The New York Times Book Review (*January 31, 1937*)

Most inventive of typographers, Francis Meynell keeps his admirers on their toes wondering what he will be up to next. He has, in fact, made book-production an entertainment as well as an adventure. We enjoy the Nonesuch books and feel certain that thier inventor enjoyed himself in their production.—Holbrook Jackson: The Printing of Books (*Cassell, 1938*)

In the early twenties there were still many people who thought that 'beautiful' printing could be done only by hand. It was Francis Meynell who most successfully proved this to be untrue, and made the logical step that linked the private press movement with general publishing ... The Nonesuch books were not specimens of abstract design like so many private press products, but were books that had a good reason for existing.—Ruari McLean: Modern Book Design (*Faber, 1958*)

In England the man who has most spectacularly bridged the gap from the hand tradition of the private press to intelligent control of the machine is Francis Meynell of the Nonesuch Press.—Joseph Blumenthal: Quarterly Journal of the Library of Congress (*April, 1965*)

the fine prices required by the great 'private presses' with their
limits of two to four hundred copies and their rigid retention of a
single style; whereas our limited editions went sometimes as high
as 1,500 and there was a vast variety in our types, bindings,
sizes.

At its small beginning in 1923 my new venture needed a very
little capital and modest premises. Vera Mendel supplied the first,
no less than £300. David ('Bunny') Garnett was the means of our
getting the second. I had met him when he spent a camping week-
end at Greatham, and I was astonished by the range of his apti-
tudes and intrigued by the expressive gaiety of his face and by his
habit of punctuating his conversation not by movement of the eyes
but by quick turnings of his head. He had just written *Lady into
Fox*, which was the beginning of his fame. Bunny and our acquaintances Francis Birrell and Ralph Wright ran a learned and enticing
antique bookshop, Birrell & Garnett, at 30 Gerrard Street, Soho.
Under it was a basement to let. What could be nicer than to site
our new little enterprise there?

To get the lease for us from under the nose of competitors,
Bunny assured the owner's agent that he was our partner and
signed the lease for us. We hastened to make a partner and an
honest man of him, particularly as his knowledge of the English
classics was greater than ours.

Somewhat sadly, I felt unable to approach Stanley Morison,
my close friend and collaborator in the past. I had left the Roman
Catholic Church, which had been a link between us and now became a division, and I had left my wife Hilda for Vera. He was
Hilda's friend as well as mine and would not have wanted to work
with Vera. Time and perhaps the fact that he later left his wife
(but not for another) abated the unease between us, and our friendship continued until his death in 1967, though with a lessened
intimacy.

An initial need was for a name and a device. Ralph Hodgson, to whom I confided our plan, waggishly suggested that I should call it the 'Pound Press'. He had lately seen and admired my father's seventeenth-century farmhouse at Greatham, which has in front of it a delightful yard or 'pound'. Every book, he urged, warming to his subject, should weigh a pound and cost a pound. . .

The name we chose was derived from the Tudor Nonesuch Palace. One of its tapestries surviving at the Victoria and Albert Museum held a pattern which seemed to me to have the makings of a good device. It showed a male and a female figure (which I secretly took as symbols of Vera and me) standing in front of the Palace. The name was chosen not in the sense of 'unequalled' but in the sense of 'unlike'. Moreover, 'Nonesuch' had its equivalent in 'nonpareil', the name of a very small size of type, only half as big as 'pica'. Thus in choosing our name we combined a possible boast with a streak of humility. Stephen Gooden, introduced to us by David Garnett, engraved the first form of the Nonesuch device, which we used on our notepaper and sometimes on our title-pages. There were to be many other versions, and for one of them E. McKnight Kauffer did in fact draw Vera and me from the life.

So there we were in 1923, Vera and I, in a cellar under Birrell & Garnett's bookshop in Gerrard Street, tackling the work of book production and distribution with David Garnett at call from the shop above us. It was an uncomfortable cellar, but a bottle of whisky and two decks of cards warmed some of its bleaker hours. Vera was twenty-seven years old, Bunny was thirty-one, and I, the entrepreneur, was thirty-two. For the first year I was still employed at the Pelican, and I did a good deal of Nonesuch work at my desk there, with early-morning and late-evening stints at Gerrard Street. Then Nonesuch became viable and I could afford to resign from the Pelican.

Nonesuch was small as a business. My two colleagues—Vera and Bunny—helped greatly but spasmodically. Vera looked after

the accounts and office management and also did some editing.
Bunny was a suggester of books and of editors. His chief love and
time-taker was always his own writing. My part was the final choice
of books, the design of every piece of printing that bore the Nonesuch name, writing our manifestos and negotiating with our
paper-makers, printers and binders. At the time of our highest
prosperity, in 1929, we employed only two office staff and our
trial-page compositor. He was Robert Willis, many years later to
achieve high distinction as secretary of the London Society of
Compositors and chairman of the Trade Union Congress.

For the first year Vera and I continued in the half light of our
limited premises, varying the task of book production with such
occasional diversions as 'invoice bees'—parties to which our friends
(among them Miles and Joan Malleson, Ralph Wright and Cyril
Joad) were bidden in order to help us, between drinks, with the
task of writing out invoices and such. This was a foretaste of our
long-continuing mixture of fun and work.

I myself 'travelled' the first books. I was received with varying
degrees of courtesy and support by the London booksellers. J. G.
Wilson of Bumpus's was pre-eminent among these. He was a
book-lover as well as a bookseller, and he inspired his staff with a
like attitude so that even junior assistants could give informed
answers to customers' vague inquiries. To him I went with a
mixture of hope and trepidation. He received me in that inner
office of his, where the shelves were crowded with the publishing
trade's newest offerings, of which he was able to give always the
impression that he had read the lot; indeed he had a reviewer's
talent for the quick mastery of the contents of a book.

He approved of what I showed him. Then, wagging a finger at
me, he said, 'Don't let me down. You must go on and on with
books like these. I've suffered from so many starters who had no
staying power'. He accepted my assurance that we had long-term
plans and promptly gave me orders of a size that astonished me.

After our first three books the demand was such that we had to ration booksellers' orders, and found it fun to be severe with those who had at the outset been discouraging, while to J. G. Wilson we supplied his orders in full.

We chose to publish the books that we ourselves wanted to have on our shelves, and from the beginning we declared our policy to be the making of books 'for those among collectors who also use books for reading'. (We used this teasing tone to our patrons through many years.)

In a charmingly self-effacing article on Nonesuch* David Garnett praises me for harmonising the form and subjects of the books I designed. 'Every book', he says, 'is like a caress and a compliment to its author.' But he also accuses me of having no genuine feeling that a text is sacred—'He would be capable of changing a word to suit the appearance of a paragraph.' There was some truth in this, but he and Vera and our many distinguished editors managed to keep me straight. The most charming as well as the most prolific of these was Geoffrey Keynes, a customer of the bookshop in Gerrard Street. There he was told of our enterprise and became my close friend and editorial collaborator.

He introduced us to John Sparrow, to whom, when he was eighteen and an undergraduate at Oxford, I entrusted the editing of one of our revivals of seventeenth-century poetry—Bishop Henry King's *Poems*. Even in his youth this future Warden of All Souls showed his independence of judgment. When in 1927 I sent him *The Temple*, which was bound in a cloth with the Nonesuch design worked into it (one of my favourite bindings), he wrote that he liked everything about it except the binding: 'I have to keep the parchment wrapper on for fear of mistaking the book for a cushion'.

Another of Geoffrey Keynes's introductions was to John Hayward, young, crippled, courageous, whose long career in

* 'The Nonesuch Press' in the *Penrose Annual*, 1936.

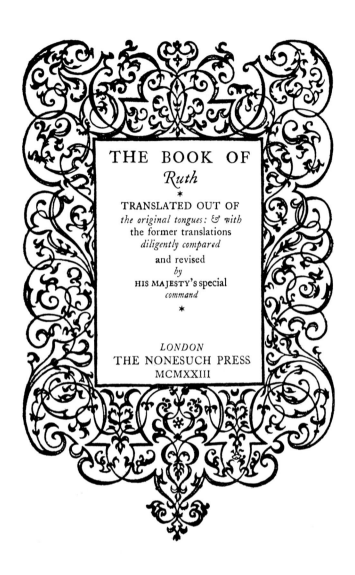

THE BOOK OF
Ruth
*
TRANSLATED OUT OF
the original tongues: & with
the former translations
diligently compared
and revised
by
HIS MAJESTY's special
command
*

LONDON
THE NONESUCH PRESS
MCMXXIII

The two examples of early Nonesuch pages here and overleaf show characteristic diversity of style. (*Above*) Title-page of *The Book of Ruth* 1923. Page size 9 × 5½ inches.

AND GOD SAID LET US MAKE MAN
IN OUR IMAGE AFTER OUR LIKE—
NESS AND LET THEM HAVE DOMI—
NION OVER THE FISH OF THE SEA
AND OVER THE FOWL OF THE AIR
AND OVER THE CATTLE AND OVER
ALL THE EARTH AND OVER EVERY
CREEPING THING THAT CREEPETH
UPON THE EARTH + SO GOD CRE—
ATED MAN IN HIS OWN IMAGE IN
THE IMAGE OF GOD CREATED HE
HIM MALE AND FEMALE CREATED
HE THEM + + AND GOD BLESSED
THEM AND GOD SAID UNTO THEM
BE FRUITFUL AND MULTIPLY AND
REPLENISH THE EARTH AND SUB—
DUE IT AND HAVE DOMINION
OVER THE FISH OF THE SEA AND
OVER THE FOWL OF THE AIR AND
OVER EVERY LIVING THING THAT

Text and illustration from the Nonesuch *Genesis* 1924. First English use of Koch's Neuland type facing woodcuts editing for me and others began with the Nonesuch Rochester in 1926. Years later T. S. Eliot gave him a home in his flat, a wisely generous and even self-sacrificing act, for John had by then little power of movement except in his hands; and years later still, in 1961, when I was given a book with inscriptions from many masters in the field of book production, John Hayward contributed to it with infinite care a picture to represent my helping hand. The colours soaked through to the other side of the paper and John, with a touch of sentimental humour that I found most moving, wrote above the soak-through:

Look, we have come through
Francis, thanks to you.

My method of Nonesuch was to use many styles and many different printers. I wanted variety for my own fun as well as because it would allow me to make the design of a book appropriate to its text. For our first 100 books I used 26 different type-faces and nineteen different printers. I gave our first three books to somewhat expensive specialists—the Kynoch Press, where Herbert (Bobby) Simon had just taken charge, the o.u.p. because I wanted their Fell type for Donne's *Love Poems*, and my own Pelican Press. For our fourth publication, *The Works of William Congreve*, I had to find a much cheaper printer to keep the price of the edition within reasonable bounds. Such a one presented himself: Mr William Brendon in person—head of the Plymouth printing firm of his name. He was clearly abashed by our cellar, but he persevered. He had seen, liked and bought our earlier three efforts; could he work for us? I explained the rigid conditions: he must obtain the Monotype type-face that I wanted to use and he must follow my lay-out, to which he agreed. After some poor interpretations of my intentions in the specimen pages which he submitted, on which I had no mercy, Brendon's did a fine job with our Congreve, and at a moderate cost. When I had to unload this four-volume edition from the printer's lorry we began to wonder whether the Press might not have to expand—indeed, one wall of our cellar did bulge alarmingly. Fortunately, part of this edition was delayed in Devon: the lorry carrying the books from the printers at Plymouth broke down before we did.

The Congreve was the first of our truly 'edited' editions. Our editor was Montague Summers, an odd character, an expelled but still dog-collared parson, stout, high-voiced. When I told him that we were to publish a Rochester for the series of Restoration writers that we had inaugurated with the Congreve, Summers beamed with pleasure and in a gay voice said, 'That is greatly to be regretted. Rochester is full of indecencies'. Then he became grave, almost sad, while he said, 'Happily his most horrid words appear in the early printings only as dashes or blanks'. Then, high-voiced and gay again, 'Most deplorably these words often come at the end of rhymed lines and so the rhyme will suggest the missing word'.

I made mistakes in plenty, and faithfully recorded them in the yearly issue of our 'Prospectus and Retrospectus'. The worst of these mistakes came in our first year, with our eleventh publication, a translation of the *Kisses* of Iohannes Secundus. I made public confession of the fact that its size of page was too big for the delicate contents, and the title-page too gaudy; and I asked subscribers to cancel their orders. About half of them did, and I enjoyed the destruction of the cancelled copies.

Paper was always an anxious problem because I ordered special makings to my own specifications in England, France, Holland and Italy; and twice they were failures and had to be destroyed. Vera and I made many journeys abroad to find hand-mades and (equally important) somewhat cheaper 'mould-made' papers using the pure rag of hand-made papers in a semi-mechanical process. One surprising discovery was a hand-made paper made in the Auvergne as a filter for beer-making. It served us well in a couple of books.

My experiments in type arrangements too cost us, and sometimes our printers, a great deal. David Garnett records that I made and scrapped twenty variants of the title-page for the Montaigne. And either William Maxwell of R. & R. Clark, or Walter Lewis, Cambridge University Printer (both have claimed authorship), said that he always lost money on the text of a Nonesuch book but made enough on the trial pages to see him right. . .

I tried to avoid solemnity in our Prospectuses and in one I made fun of Sir Archibald Bodkin, the Director of Public Prosecutions. He was eager to suppress any book or picture that disturbed the prurient (as we thought it) taste of the Establishment. Among his suppressions were *The Well of Loneliness* and, much more important, James Joyce's *Ulysses*, of which Bodkin himself wrote to the Birrell & Garnett bookshop: 'The book is grossly indecent and any person found dealing in it will be liable to criminal proceedings.'

There had lately been a great furore about an exhibition of pictures by D. H. Lawrence, which were seized by the police as being indecent. In the Warren Gallery at the same time were reproductions of Blake's pencil drawings which we had published two years before, and among these was his sketch for 'Glad Day', which shows a rhapsodically innocent naked youth. This too was seized by the police. What a chance for a leg pull! So I called our elegant 1929 Prospectus 'Bodkin Permitting'. It announced our Farquhar and our Kauffer-illustrated *Don Quixote*, and this was my foreword:

"In these days of literary censorship exercised by Sir Archibald Bodkin, no publisher can be positive in his announcement that he will issue such and such a book. Chaucer? Fie, his language is coarse. Plato? The less said about Socrates and his young friends, if you please, the better. Shakespeare?

He will perhaps pass unchallenged, for 'Lamb's Tales' doubtless exhausted the censor's interest in this prurient author.
Farquhar? Don Quixote even—? These too may corrupt the
corrupt, which is the current legal test of obscenity. With a
propitiatory bow to Sir Archibald we therefore give to this
list of announcements the precautionary title, *Bodkin Permitting*."

I took my anti-Bodkin tease into the realm of pure (impure)
invention. This was my 1930 Christmas card to a few close
friends:

> Archibald Bodkin, Britain's prude,
> Posted his Christmas platitude
> With a misprint that he'd ignored—
> Two words conjoined to make one word:
> THE PENIS MIGHTIER THAN THE SWORD.
>
> Bodkin! for once, our gratitude.

In 1924 Vera and I went for a walking tour in Italy. She, much
ahead of her time, was short-haired and knickerbockered, so we
thought we might both gain entry to an ancient monastery open to
male tourists only. We knocked at the door. After some delay it
was opened by a monk who, without raising his eyes from our
feet, intoned: 'Il signor, si, la signora, no.' A miracle of chaste
awareness? No; as we turned we saw the peep-hole from which
Vera's figure had been studied before the door was opened. This
holiday produced the one and only vast-selling Nonesuch publication, *The Week-End Book*, one of our unlimited editions. The idea
arose from the unwelcome weight of the books in our rucksacks,
so, as we walked, we imagined a single volume that might satisfy
our needs on such occasions. When we got home this made for
cheerful discussion with our friends who were experts in the
variety of subjects we wanted this book to cover.

I set to work on compiling the four poetry sections which

occupied more than half the book—Great, Hate, State and The Zoo, with an added 'List of Great Poems contained in many memories and most anthologies and therefore omitted from this book'. The next section, of Songs, was chosen by John Goss, himself a fine professional singer. He was full of gay and socially off-beat proposals (we shared the same political views) and he submitted his choices at audition-parties. This song section made so great an impact that Beaverbrook put John Goss in charge of a *Daily Express* sideshow—community singing at football matches. A section on games was written, drama-wise, by Eleanor Farjeon; Vera dealt with the Food and Drink portion; and Dr Maurice Newfield with the 'First Aid in Divers Crises' section, which included a neatly disguised aphrodisiac.

The launching of *The Week-End Book* was, for those days, unusual. We had a party—a Private View—to which the book-sellers were invited so that they might eat the food and drink the drinks described, listen to and join in the songs and play some of the games. They also had the unexpected pleasure of watching H. G. Wells engage in the new game of Tishy-Toshy*; and as the party went on and the drinks went down, orders which had been slender swelled handsomely. This was by far the biggest Nonesuch money-maker. With its several amplifications and redecorations, it sold more than half-a-million copies. Barry Neame, 'Mine Host' (as he called himself) of the Spread Eagle at Thame, home of many Wine and Food Society and other feasts, told me that at

---

* This game was first described in *The Week-End Book*. Two players stand at opposite ends of a table (the longer and broader the better) and throw a tennis ball to each other in turn, *always gently*. The server may roll, bounce, or full-pitch the ball, but it must not drop off the sides of the table, only off the end. The receiver must catch with one hand only and may not put his hand over the table or touch it with his hand. Cunning and 'length', not speed, win the point. If the receiver catches the ball lawfully neither scores. Game is five points.

one time he put a copy of *The Week-End Book* by the bedside in each room, but that one after another they were pinched.

Our friends were our editors and illustrators and our editors and illustrators became our friends. The *Anacreon* (1923) was a double first—the first Nonesuch illustrated book and Stephen Gooden's first appearance as an illustrator. He had served in the first war and there was still something military in his manner. He was ready to fight back, as I found when we opposed each other at hockey: an accidental hit on the shin was answered by a deliberate one. That was not his character in his work. Copperplate engraving, of all art forms, requires the greatest self-command and patience. I called upon that patience when he made a headpiece which I did not like for *The Latin Portrait* (1929). He made a new engraving and sent me a proof with the space below it filled with this verse exquisitely and minutely written to represent the type that the book would carry.

> Dear Francis: here displayed to view
> Behold now Venus, drawn anew.
> And though perhaps you think it rash
> For me to try to cut a dash
> To supplicate another muse
> And praise her as the Poets use,
> My chaste intent would never fly
> One hundredth part as rashly high.
> I merely fill the vacant space,
> Giving a body to the face.
> For who would not be rightly vex'd
> To have a Headpiece with no Text?
> With this excuse I take my leave.
> Your Humble Servant ever—Steve.

Later, Gooden (1892–1955) became, to my mild surprise but

very properly, the art-servant of the Establishment. The George Medal was based on his design; he executed the bookplates of the Queen, of the Royal Library at Windsor and of the British Council; and he worked also for the Bank of England. In all, he illustrated eight books for me.

At the end of 1924 Vera and I moved from a furnished flat to 16 Great James Street, taking Nonesuch with us. It was a graceful and prim panelled house which had been a coffee-house in the 18th century. Vera, with a little help from Nonesuch profits, was able to buy it. The upper two floors were our dwelling; the ground and first floors provided offices for Vera, Bunny and me, and the basement held my type-cases and hand-press as well as kitchen and pantry. From here we published all our books in the next twelve years.

The first book to carry this address was the folio *Apocrypha* (1924), with copperplate engravings by Stephen Gooden, followed during the next two years by the four volumes of the Bible proper in the Authorised Version, all decorated by Gooden, at 30s. a volume—our 'desert island' Bible. Stanley Morison called it 'a miracle of cheapness' and credited me with the successful redesigning of a number of letters in the type-face used for it.* I sent it to Bruce Rogers and I was delighted—he was still my typographical god—with his reaction: 'I send you my heartiest (and most envious) congratulations... I envy you the faculty of being able to tackle such really important subjects in such quantities and with such qualities.'

The closest of our illustrator friends was Edward McKnight Kauffer, the American who won fame in England but is still strangely unacknowledged in his own country. My first acquaintance with him was in 1919, when I bought as a poster for the then new *Daily Herald* a lovely design of his—a flight of birds that

* 'A Review of Recent Typography', by Stanley Morison: *The Fleuron*, 1927.

might almost be a flight of aeroplanes; a symbol, in those days of vain hope, of the unity of useful invention and natural things. Winston Churchill, keen-eyed, was intrigued by it, called Kauffer to a meeting and invited him to design a new flag for the Royal Flying Corps. This was not Kauffer's line and nothing came of it. Frank Pick of London Transport had better luck. He commissioned a series of posters which justified many an otherwise ugly London hoarding and indeed made a new movement in what had become a declining and despised art. Kauffer was an example of the abandoned truth that art is indivisible: that a man with the root of the matter in him can paint or design rugs (as he did for Arnold Bennett) or make posters or illustrate books or decorate a room or parti-colour a motor-car (as he did for me) or scheme an advertisement.

In those days, and indeed to the end of his life, Kauffer's appearance and manner gave no inkling of his hard beginnings. He told me that, working as a handy-boy in a San Francisco bookshop, he read many more books than he helped to sell. His knowledge impressed a customer, who sent him to art-school. From there he joined a travelling theatre company as scene-painter and shifter, and even as shoulder to an important member of the company who drank too much for steadiness. When he came to England he was already an 'exquisite,' delicate in face, figure and manners.

Ted Kauffer used to enlarge his conversation, often witty and sometimes with a sly undertone, by generous quotations from his favourite books, among them Burton's *Anatomy of Melancholy*. He had not yet illustrated any book and I suggested that he should tackle the *Anatomy* for us. It appeared in 1925 with scores of his line drawings. Years later he told me that while he was at work on this I bombarded him with forty letters, nagging, beseeching, criticising or praising the drawings as he delivered them singly or in batches, with long gaps, over many months. He had the generosity to conclude 'What thrilling moments we had!' Kauffer's illustrations were a breakaway from the strictly representational which was the habit of the time, and they shocked Sir Edmund Gosse, who called them 'infantile scrawlings'. (Abuse from him was as pleasing to me as other people's praise.)

For a year or two Ted used as his studio a room next to my office at Great James Street. I found his pronouncements on aesthetics distracting when there was work to do, so I nailed up a list of 'red-herring' words ('functional', 'the Artist' and so forth) which he was not to use during office hours on pain of a fine of sixpence a time. Admired though he was, his was not so lucrative a success as to make it easy for him always to pay us his quarter's rent, but the total of his sixpences made a substantial contribution.

There was no such sixpenny escape from George Moore. While *Ulick and Soracha* (1926) was at the printers he came almost daily, hung up his square bowler hat and settled down to read aloud to us the revisions he had made in his last batch of proofs. Each time it was an entirely new text. The first version was almost illiterate. The second grammatical but undistinguished. The third a transfiguration. It was fascinating to see the process of his composition at close quarters and our feelings were undisturbed by anxieties about the printer's bill, for he had proposed at the outset that he should pay for his own corrections. They exceeded the original cost of the setting. I used on the title-page a somewhat mannered type, Civilité, which I felt had something appropriately Gaelic about it. George Moore disliked it: 'I think that title-pages should be formal as gravestones. The fancy printing in *Ulick and Soracha* looks like Persian... I would have liked to omit all criticism but he who admires all things admires nothing.'

I have already mentioned that Geoffrey Keynes was the most fecund of all Nonesuch editors. Professionally he was a distinguished surgeon. Is there perhaps some relation between the mending of the nerves and bones and muscles of the human body and the correction of manifold errors in an important but un-established text? Geoffrey Keynes is a past-master of both these skills. I cannot guess which of his two arts has meant most to him—but it is obvious that many more thousands have come under the influence of his pen than of his knife. Between 1925 and 1957 he edited or compiled no fewer than sixteen Nonesuch books.

Geoffrey is one of the most eager and generous men I have known, a patron as well as a performer in the arts. He is the only close male friend of mine who has not been a games player. Instead he builds brick walls at an age which in anyone else would be considered old. While he was at work on our three-volume Blake (1925) Geoffrey came almost daily to Great James Street in his open car—little did he care about bad weather—on his way to surgery at St Bartholomew's Hospital. When our discussions could not be finished without delaying an operation I sometimes continued as a passenger in his car, struck almost dumb (doubtless to his relief) by the icy blast. His contribution to Nonesuch scholar-ship was of the highest and his well-wishing has been of extra-ordinary value to us. He lives now neighbourly to us in the country, and the old times and the new are scarcely distinguishable from each other.

Has any man written learnedly, and often gaily, on so many subjects as James Laver? In 1927 he read to me his delightfully mannered narrative poem, 'A Stitch in Time: or Pride prevents a Fall', with its final couplet:

> I am no priest, be vicious as you please,
> But not, Belinda, in a darned chemise.

I begged to be allowed to publish it, and he confessed that this indeed was his plan. My design was a folio in the eighteenth-century formal style, to accord with the poem itself. Various fussifications, such as the marble-paper covers, forced the published price up to 3*s.* 9*d.*, no less. The 1,525 copies were over-subscribed before publication and copies reached three times the published price in the bookshops.

I had lately met Arnold Bennett for the first time. I found myself talking at him instead of listening to the great man as I had hoped to do. Why? Because when he spoke he revealed two rows of upper teeth, one behind the other—a fact embarrassing to him I felt, and so to me. Our next meeting was in print, for he reviewed 'A Stitch in Time' and queried the propriety of our use of the word 'Press' in our publishing enterprise. I answered him in our 1928 Prospectus. I wrote that Mr Arnold Bennett's view 'is not a serious misapprehension, but such as it is it needs correction', and I explained that we maintained at Great James Street a small typographic plant (with a one-page sufficiency of many different types mainly given by the Monotype Corporation) on which we produced experimental pages 'whereby the style can be established for books too various in their format to be dealt with by any one printer', and where occasionally we composed small books in the Jansen seventeenth-century types which the Nonesuch Press alone possessed. I concluded: 'This Prospectus is likewise homework. A copy has been sent to Mr Bennett'.

'The Farjeons' (they were so often thought of as a family) meant much to me. Herbert (Bertie) I had met before World War I when he visited my sisters at Greatham. Joan, his wife, was one of the beauties of her day, and her nature is like her looks. Eleanor, his sister, had been 'Tom Fool' in the *Daily Herald*, to which she contributed day after day her topical verses in which she managed to combine politics, wit and sentiment.

Bertie was the writer and producer of the 'Little Revues' which made his fame in the late '30s and '40s. World War II was not an easy time for the theatre. Farjeon's contracts with artists and investors contained a suspension clause 'if the theatre is bombed or the country invaded'. The Little Theatre was in fact blown to pieces in 1942. It may interest the theatrical moguls of today that the total capital he needed for a show was £1,700. In several of these shows I invested the usually profitable sum of £50.

Farjeon had the air of an easy collaborator, but he had his own determinations. I had met Hedli Anderson and much admired her singing, and I urged him to engage her in one of his 'Little Revues'. Bertie wouldn't have her; she was, he said, 'too good to be disciplined in what is after all *my* revue'. But he joyfully engaged Joyce Grenfell for her first performance on the stage. I had a minor part with Stephen and Mary Potter in plotting this. They arranged a party at which the young amateur would perform, and I undertook to bring Farjeon to it. It clicked. Joyce Grenfell was a delight of his various revues from 1936 to 1942.

Revues, however witty, are ephemeral, but Farjeon's reputation in another field will last, for he prepared with infinite patience and scholarly exactitude the text of the Nonesuch Shakespeare. It came to be regarded as the finest Shakespeare text. The seven volumes took five years to produce and all 1,600 sets were sold before publication.

The page presented a typographic problem. There were to be marginal notes, and I decided to use the Fournier type for its combination of elegance and legibility even in its very small sizes. The difficulty was that this type has its capital letters a little larger than usual in relation to the 'small' letters. Since Shakespeare used a capital for innumerable nouns, the first trial pages delivered a series of optical bangs, and I had to have all the capital letters redesigned to be a little smaller instead of a little larger than normal.

Gordon Craig, actor, producer and thundering theorist, whom Vera and I had met and then dodged in Venice, asked for this Shakespeare with a pleasing (and unnecessary) cautionary phrase—'unless it be Bowdlerized for the Exemplary'. T. E. Lawrence, as Aircraftman Shaw, used extreme terms of admiration of the

Shakespeare in a letter to David Garnett: 'It satisfies. It is final, like the Kelmscott Chaucer or the Ashendene Virgil. Every word which Shakespeare uses stands out flowing. A really great edition ... altogether a triumph', and more in the same vein. I sought his permission to quote him. Garnett was our ambassador. Lawrence appealed to the group of friends with whom he chanced to be: 'I don't want my letter to be reprinted, I hate the advertising of my name and opinions', he protested. To his chagrin his friends supported his view. 'After all,' they said, 'you are not a Shakespeare scholar.' This decided Lawrence—an instance of this great man's sad dichotomy. 'It is my duty to give permission', he said. And so his letter appeared in our 1929 Prospectus.

It is not public performances and successes that make a close friendship and mine with Herbert Farjeon came from common political and sociological views (he too had been a conscientious objector) and from a great liking for the slightly lesser things of life, like punning, leg-pulling and most of all cricket, of which more in another chapter.

Stephen Potter, though he edited three Nonesuch Books, was much more of a friend than an editor. Games, physical and verbal, were our tie from our first meeting in 1925. He was several inches taller than my six feet, better at tennis, equal at ping-pong, worse at cricket, supreme at tricks of the tongue. He and Mary Attenborough ('Att') were on their way to their marriage two years later. Already she showed her great talent as a painter and she too had the skills and enthusiasm of a games player.

It was between sets of tennis that Stephen and I discussed the possibility of his editing a 'compendious' Coleridge, which indeed came happily to pass in 1934. In 1935, when Nonesuch was at a very low financial ebb, we published a swank book of Coleridge's selected poems, chosen by Stephen. Among my few records of the time I find one which reports his payment for this as £5.

In its relations with other publishers Nonesuch avoided

antagonisms, even avoided competition. When I found that Peter Davies and the Nonesuch were both planning to re-issue Cobbett's *Rural Rides* we met and tossed for it. He won, and our editorial work was made over to him. Osbert Sitwell suggested that we should publish a satire on Noel Coward; Coward that we should publish his satire on the Sitwells. To both we said no. How pleasant it would have been to issue them together in one book!

Herbert (Bobby) Simon did much printing for Nonesuch, first at the Kynoch Press and then at the Curwen Press. Until his retirement in 1970 he was still in business, important business, as a printer. His simplicity of manner hides an expert knowledge of many things: the history as well as the practice of typography, the economics of survival through times of changing techniques, and (his hobbies) the history of textile mills and of railways. He is a demonstrative democrat: he has never yet travelled first-class and when he entertained for the Curwen Press he chose a teashop rather than the Savoy.

In this high time of one of its revivals, printing produced admirations which sometimes grew to friendship or even devotion. Thus I first met Beatrice Warde in her editorial writings for the *Monotype Recorder*. Her pen-name (and soon for me her pet-name) was Paul Beaujon. We had much to do with each other professionally: Nonesuch required and was given many special services by Monotype. By 1929, when I commissioned her to design the headpieces for our 'compendious' edition of John Donne, we had become 'Dearest Meynell' and 'Dearest Beaujon'. In 1933 she commissioned Eric Gill to make a portrait of me for the *Monotype Recorder*. Gill had long been a friend of my family. Twenty years earlier he had appealed to my father to find him religious reassurance: 'I find my unbelief very present'.

My father had been the decisive influence in getting him the commission to carve the Stations of the Cross in Westminster Cathedral, and my brother Everard had been the chief promoter of the sale of his wood-engravings. For me Gill had cut the book-plate which I still use, and I had bought his beautiful low-relief of a girl in Capal-y-Finn stone. Now, in my new infidel and his new dogmatic days, we had no longer any association. He did not make the sitting for my portrait a pleasant one. Clad in his usual imitation monk's habit, with biretta on head, he gave me no word of welcome, was silent through the sitting and at its end merely nodded me away. After the drawing had been reproduced in the *Monotype Recorder* Beatrice gave it to me, and in an engraved version it was used in the *Nonesuch Century*.

In 1956 I chaired a lecture given by Beatrice Warde to the English Speaking Union. I had spoken a poem of hers in a BBC broadcast of war poetry at the time of the blitz on London: I needed it now, could not find the text and asked her for it. Sending it she wrote: 'It recited itself to me complete one morning in London 1941'. Here it is:

When will you understand?
   Mark what I say:
Whatever you hold in your hand
   Will be blown away.

Must you learn for yourself?
   Listen: take warning;
Whatever you put on the shelf
   Will be gone by morning.

Soon you must play your part.
   What are you learning?
Get it by heart! By heart!
   I have seen books burning.

Many years later I edited an anthology of poetry, called it *By Heart* and printed the last verse of her poem in my foreword. These were my concluding words to the reader: 'May the need for that warning never recur. May peace be in the world and poetry in your heart'. That is my one persistent and frightened prayer.

Only once in our deep friendship was I at odds with Beaujon. When my son Benedict was seven, she was shocked to realise that he had not been given Christian baptism or instruction. It was Christmas-time and with scorn she asked if he didn't celebrate even the birth of Christ. I told her, with inappropriate levity, that he was about to celebrate Father Solstice. She denied me my kiss, and in a calmer mood brought Benedict into a booklet with the allusive title *The Shelter in Bedlem*, which she printed for her friends at Christmas 1937. It is a clever polemic against unbelievers and the likes of me. My copy was inscribed 'F.M. from Beaujon', and with it this note:

> "Dearest Meynell: Nobody else will spot the veiled reference at one point in this pamphlet to a relative of yours.
>
> And this inscription to you is in fact the Dedication of the book. I don't care for printed dedications. Devotedly yours."

This was the reference, in the epilogue to her pamphlet:

> "I'd spent the first of the Two Minutes simply enjoying the sensation of being able to hear myself think. I remember that what I did hear myself think was: '*What's to become of that little son of F's who got his presents from Father Solstice?*'"

At the 200th dinner of the Double Crown Club in June 1969 I sat opposite Beatrice Warde. She seemed still her younger self, and made a concise and witty impromptu speech. A few weeks later she died.

Nonesuch could not make friends with so amorphous and large a body of people as its customers, but we took them into our confidence in our Prospectuses and once or twice we consulted them.

With *Bodkin Permitting* we sent a ballot card asking for their choices in the outer-wrappings of books. Here is a record of the voting in which nearly 500 of our regular subscribers took part: for plain slip-in case, 164; for fancy slip-in case, 48; for plain glacine, 212; for printed jacket, 35; for fancy paper jacket, 20. This showed that the general view confirmed my own growing opinion that money should not be deflected from the book itself. At an exhibition of Nonesuch books in 1933 we showed for the opinion of visitors several trial pages for our newly announced *Herodotus*. This was a gesture more than an inquiry, for I had meanwhile made my choice.

The sales of Nonesuch in the United States did much to establish our reputation as well as our financial success, and they too brought me many friends. Random House, New York, became our sole distributor. It came about in this manner. Into my office one day in 1927 walked a complete stranger—a brisk young man swinging a silver-headed cane which caught my envious eye. With a mixture of humour and assertiveness he said, 'My name is Bennett Cerf. I have come to inform you that henceforth Random House is to be your sole selling agency in the United States'. In the same mood I thanked him for his courtesy in telling me about it anyway. We grinned together and confirmed our alliance in the next few days with a mass of legal documents—safeguards, protocols, guarantees and such like, to which neither of the High Contracting Parties was ever to refer.

In 1929 Bennett and his partner Donald Klopfer invited me to be their guests in New York. They paid my passage, hired me a handsome apartment, taught me how to throw playing-cards into a hat as an office diversion from the work of publishing and introduced me for the first time to the gamble of the stock market. About this Donald is quoted in the *New Yorker* (May 16, 1959):

"Bennett and I were active in the stock market. We did some of our trading through Saint Phalle & Co., which was conveniently located on a floor below us. On our way to lunch, we took Francis down there, and guaranteeing him against loss, had him buy two hundred shares of Stone & Webster. In a few hours he sold out at a profit of two thousand dollars. 'Can one do this during the lunch hour every day?' he asked."

Bennett and Donald took me to a party about which I boasted to my musical niece Alice:

"On my first night in New York I was one of a party of eight which included DICK RODGERS. Truly, Dick Rodgers, young, handsome, witty, gay and very sympathetic; Dick Rodgers, who wrote the music of 'My Heart Stood Still', and is a half-millionaire out of it. And after dinner, theatre and nightclub, we went to his apartment and he played for us the numbers out of his new show, to be produced in a few weeks—'Spring is Here'. They are *lovely*.

I had to write to tell you this, so that you may know what a very fine (as well as lucky!) fellow you have for an uncle. *He knows Dick Rodgers*."

I also became friends with Elmer Adler, the designer and third partner in Random House. He introduced me to Rockwell Kent, who gave me one of the twenty-five copies of a comic little booklet which he printed about Adler in April 1929. Gaiety seems to be a mark—a printer's mark—of the great American book-artificers. Elmer Adler manœuvred an honorific occasion for W. A. Dwiggins, that versatile home-grown type-designer and emblem-maker, and for me, the foreigner, at the American Institute of Graphic Arts. This was preluded by a pretty little parody pamphlet of which twenty-eight copies only were printed. It was signed jointly by Roland A. Wood and John S. Fass. It was titled *Eulogy in a City Club House*.

Full many a flower is born to blush unseen
But now have come two posies, passing fair,
To blush and show a proud (though modest) mien
Nor waste their sweetness on the desert air.

No mute, inglorious Caslons have we here,
But these, who by the magic of their hands
Have won acclaim in places far and near.
And scattered printing o'er two smiling lands.

Far from the madding crowd we gather round
Twin lights, to fortune and to fame well known.
To Meynell and to Dwiggins praises sound;
Thus ends our Eulogy. Our muse is flown.

In the event, the original 'elegy' would have been a better
theme than the eulogy. I had not realised that I was expected to be
the main speaker, and in any case I was not accustomed to the
hard drinks that flowed early in the meeting. So confusion was my
main contribution.

A year later I printed on my hand-press and sent to members of
the Institute what I hoped would be taken as an apology. Like
theirs, it was a very small booklet. It was a selection of my mother's
writings in a cover of Chinese silvered paper. It was not well
received. I am not sure that it was even acknowledged. Doubtless
they would have welcomed words on typography, not poetry.

With the growth of business, Vera's interest in Nonesuch
began to lessen. She had done quite a deal of editing and book-
choosing in the early years, but her chief employment was as
company secretary, and as early as 1927 she had begun to be bored
with this. So she accepted a surprising invitation to go on trial for
six months as editor of the London edition of *Vogue*. This was not
a success: indeed, Vera did not really expect it to be. Her views,
her attitude, were different from those of the American proprietors

and the English management. Even her vocabulary was different. The social correspondent submitted a report of a big dance which began with these words: 'On Friday the second of Lord Camrose's balls came off.' Vera circulated this to the sub-editors with a large query mark. Nobody confessed to seeing that these words were capable of a far-from-intended interpretation.

In due course the American editor-in-chief of all editions of *Vogue* visited London and, with Harry Yoxall, the London manager, politely told Vera that her six-months engagement would not be renewed. At their parting Harry Yoxall said: 'Please, Vera, don't look at us as if you despised us and the whole set-up'. 'Dear me, Harry,' said Vera, 'and I thought I had a poker-face.'

Nonesuch limited editions sold to the full of their hundreds, but we published also a series of 'compendious' volumes in un-limited editions which sold in their many thousands—they still do through the Bodley Head under their post-war name, The None-such Library. Among these was a William Morris.* I sent copies to George Lansbury, Ramsay MacDonald, Clifford Allen and Stanley Baldwin. Their replies make almost a résumé of their political characters. G.L. saw in the social essays a conscience-pricking reproach about things left undone. MacDonald, then Prime Minister, defending his own runaway politics wrote: 'It is a matter of profound regret to me that the so-called Socialist Movement has fallen into the ruts of Poplarism'.† Clifford Allen, who had supported the un-socialist MacDonald Government, warmed my heart and restored a precious friendship in his reply:

"How generous of you. Nothing that has happened to me during these three bitter years has touched me so deeply as

* *William Morris: Selected Writings*. Edited by G. D. H. Cole, 1934. It had 696 inviting pages bound in buckram with end-pages of Morris wallpaper and was then priced at 8s. 6d.

† Meaning 'Lansburyism'.

your gift and your letter. Bless you above all for writing of this book as common ground; indeed it is. Nothing will ever change that for me. But that you should care to say so makes me realise how these past few years have been more lonely than the war itself. Do grant me the compassion of which Morris writes in the last paragraph of your book, even if you cannot understand."

Stanley Baldwin did not answer for eighteen months: the book had been mislaid. But when he did answer (he was now Prime Minister) he covered two 10 Downing Street pages with his close handwriting, to apologise and explain. The Perfect Gentleman. His postscript meant even more to me than the kindly letter. I had appealed to him to allow the entry of Berthold Wolpe, the brilliant German typographer who, with Rudolf Koch, had designed ornaments for the Nonesuch *Iliad* and *Odyssey*. Because he was a Jew the Hitler régime had declared him unfit to practise his art in Germany. Baldwin's postscript said simply: 'Wolpe is coming into England in September'.

In 1936 we published the *Nonesuch Century*, in which we celebrated our first hundred books. There A. J. A. Symons, of 'Baron Corvo' fame, who ran his own First Edition Club, wrote the 'Appraisal' and Desmond Flower, already a skilled and devoted typophile, compiled the bibliography with that studiousness and independence of judgement which already marked him then (he was still in his twenties) as it does today. For me, I wrote notes in the bibliography on most of the hundred books and described our first years in 'The Personal Element'. The *Century* was given the startling honour of a leading article in *The Times*. I guessed at Stanley Morison's hand in it. It gave even more pleasure to my father than to me. He wrote: 'One mention in a *Times* leader is fame; your multiple mentions are immortality'. In a spate of honorific articles those by Elmer Adler in the *New York Times* and by Holbrook Jackson in the *Listener* gave me special pleasure.

St John Hornby, whose published approval I have put among the kind words on page 156, now wrote to me a laudatory letter about the *Nonesuch Century*. I quote a sentence which demonstrates the professional precision of his eye:

"I only detected one printer's error in the book, if 'error' it can be called—on page 16 between lines 14 and 15 there seems to be a two point instead of a three point lead."

A. J. A. Symons was a strange man, or mixture of men. He had an extraordinary ambition about fairly ordinary things, and in the forty years of his life he created a legend about himself as a dandy, a wine-bibber, a gambler with infallible systems, a littérateur, a collector, a wirepuller, a promoter of clubs, and more than all as a man of great affluence with no visible means of support. He dressed elaborately and he had what I called a 'double-breasted waistcoat' accent, and he disciplined his handwriting into an elegant formality well before the italic-hand revival had made its mark. His affectations in dress and manner, his snobbery and odd ambitions, were a cover. He had been apprenticed to a furrier when he was fourteen, so lacked a 'normal' education; and Julian Symons, his brother, reveals in words true and tender that A. J. had something else he wanted to hide—he had a psychopathic shame that his father was a Russian-Jewish immigrant and that the English name was an adopted one.

A. J.'s conscious ploy was to suggest a mystery, with just a hint of grandiose, even royal, origin. It became a private game among his friends to invent ancestors for him. He was very tall, but one surprising guess—he boasted of his knowledge of horses and racing —was that his father had been a jockey. Vera's comment on this was: 'Then his mother must have been a giantess in a peep-show'.

A. J. founded the First Edition Club, which lost money for all its backers but did good work with its book exhibitions and published a number of worthwhile books, chief among them Ambrose

Heal's *The English Writing Masters*. The Saintsbury Club, with its twice-a-year meetings at Vintners' Hall to honour wine and literature, and the Wine and Food Society were also A. J.'s inventions. He had a true literary flair which rediscovered, almost invented, Frederick William Rolfe, 'Baron Corvo'. As I became familiar with him, in that world of books and comfortable affectations which we inhabited together, and later on as a near neighbour in the country, I liked and admired him more and more, so that I was proud to have his learned side express itself in his contribution to the *Nonesuch Century*.

The war of 1939 brought on A. J. three devastations. The woman he loved left him; his investments, gambles in antiques, collapsed; and he became gravely ill. Debts overwhelmed him and I set myself to collect a substantial sum of money towards his expenses. Many of the people who subscribed had suffered loss through him before, but they were ready again to open their purses because they had never been able to close their hearts to him. I have never known a man so heroic in disaster. His courage was remarkable and so was his new-found simplicity. I regarded him now as a hero and something of a saint. My last memory of him is at our house in the country. For an after-lunch rest he lay on our lawn in the bright sunshine. His eyes were shut and on each eyelid he had put a penny. 'They will put them there when I am dead,' he said. 'They serve a more comfortable purpose now.'

Paradoxically all the praise and celebration over the publication of the *Nonesuch Century* came at a time when Nonesuch was in financial difficulties. I have no precise figures to quote because virtually all the pre-war records of Nonesuch were destroyed early in the war by Sir Robert Leighton, the representative in England of George Macy, the then proprietor, who was in the U.S.A. Neither George nor I was aware of Leighton's action. Leighton took the odd view that it was better to destroy our records than to risk fire from possible bombing. A small number of miscellaneous letters

and one costing-sheet for the books of a single year happened to
be in my own hands, and these survive. I have, therefore, to rely
on my own estimates based on the fact that one-third of the price
of our books was for their manufacture, one-third for the bookseller's discount and one-third for overheads and profit. So I calculate that in our first year we made a gross profit of £1,600 and in
1929 (our top year) something over £11,000; at that time our overheads were still very small. Then decline, as we were hit by the
slump (or as an Indian friend of mine called it, 'this mundial bad-
time'); so that by 1933 we were down to a gross profit of £800.
Two years earlier our declining income had sent me in search of
other work which would still leave me free to preside over Nonesuch. Vera's interest had virtually ceased since the birth of our son
in 1930, and there was growing disharmony between her and me
which made another reason for my own change of occupation.

Financially, Nonesuch had always lived from book to book.
Our suppliers had from the outset shown a gratifying confidence;
now they shared our own anxiety as the bottom dropped out of the
collectors' market. Nonesuch had to find more capital. New capital
and new brains were supplied by Cecil Harmsworth and his sons
Desmond (now Lord Harmsworth, the painter) and Eric. They
were nephews of the 'Press barons', Northcliffe and Rother-
mere, but their interest was in literature and art. They were
hopeful, gentle and pleasant partners. David Garnett, who had
just finished his history-novel *Pocahontas*, stayed on the Board out
of kindliness, certainly not for pelf—his total remuneration was
£5 a monthly meeting. (In the early years of Nonesuch he had
five per cent of our profits.)

Desmond and Eric Harmsworth shared in the production of the
Nonesuch programmes of 1934 and 1935; but the slump was too
much for us, their investment was exhausted, and in August 1935
we welcomed proposals for a complete take-over from George
Macy, founder-owner of the Limited Editions Club of New York,

a man who combined a skilful devotion to the arts of the book with a necessary business sense, a hardness sometimes of words with an invariable generosity of actions. Beatrice Warde had a perceptive view: 'Artists and designers generally say that George Macy is a good man to work for. Printers, blockmakers, and others may use different-sounding words, but we must remember that in their language of craftsmanship "holy terror" is a term of tribute that nearly means what it says'.

Macy and I were not strangers, for he had presented himself to me almost as if on a pilgrimage when he visited London in 1931. Our negotiations took nearly two years, were harsh when they were written, easy and even gay when they were spoken. He wanted me to stay on the new Nonesuch board of directors, but since the strategy as well as the money was to be all his I felt bound to refuse. At length we came to an understanding. For his part he would settle all our trade debts (which he did by the issue of debentures to our printers and binders) and would include in his programme the books I had planned for 1937 and 1938; and I for my part would continue as designer of all Nonesuch books.

Not unnaturally, George wanted to emphasise his new manage- ment by a move to more spacious premises in Russell Square and by a greater publication than Nonesuch had ever before attempted. This was a complete Dickens in sets of 24 volumes, plus a uniform book-shaped box to contain one of the original illustration-plates, all of which he had bought from Chapman & Hall, the original Dickens publisher. I think this Dickens must have been originally a project for his Limited Editions Club, since the elaborate editorial scheme was so instantly available. I doubted whether the anxious England of 1938 was easy-minded and easy-moneyed enough to absorb a set of books costing 48 guineas and I disliked the dispersal of the plates. Alice, my niece-secretary, shared my feelings; whereat George told me, 'Alice is not loyal'. In a fashion both we the doubters and he the believer were proved right. The sale was alarmingly slow at first, to George's shocked surprise. But in the end how right he was: after the war the plate in each set proved a powerful selling aid, the edition was eagerly sought after, and now it fetches many times its original price—a set has recently been sold for £980.

I was given, indeed at George's insistence I even claimed, more of the credit for the handsome style of this edition than I deserved. This should have gone to Harry Carter, since my Nonesuch work was usually confined to an hour or two at the end of the normal working day. Harry Carter, now Archivist of the Oxford University Press, was my Nonesuch understudy; sometimes indeed my overstudy. It was he, and not I, who chose the typeface for the Dickens and persuaded the Monotype Corporation to produce it. He found the brilliant illustrator, Mildred Farrer, for the *Comus*, and made the topographical researches, and then the map, for White's *Selborne*, two of the seven books planned and on the way before Macy took over.

The war of 1939 was not a setting for limited editions. George Macy needed all his powers of adaptability to proceed with a series of *Ten Great French Romances*, in translations and with fine illustrations. For most of these he used a combined Nonesuch and American imprint. Because war-stricken England could not afford to produce or to import the rag paper this series needed, the typesetting only was done in England and the paper-buying and the printing had to be done abroad from English plates, first in France, before she was overrun, and then in the United States. I designed the books and Ernest Ingham and his Fanfare Press were the ingenious type-setters. For the volume *Dangerous Acquaintances* we used type-like figurines to identify, above each letter, the writers whose correspondence makes the novel. I commissioned Berthold Wolpe to design these figurines. More than the illustrations of Chas Laborde these added to the sight and sense of the book.

After the war, with the general shortage of consumer goods in England, Macy's Nonesuch became profitable and he was able to redeem all the debentures. Then, with wonderful magnanimity, he returned to me the use of 'Nonesuch' as my mark. I became a publisher once more, but as a hobby, not as an absorption, for I was by then in an utterly different and challenging job as Director-General of the Cement and Concrete Association.

XII

Fun and Games

From the beginning of our joint enterprise Vera and I limited our books to an average of eight a year because we reckoned that any more would distort our social and personal life. Work for None-such was seldom allowed to interfere with other pleasures—with travels abroad and parties and dancing and games and good eating at home. Why should it? The planning and pondering over a text and editor and artist and printer and type need not be done only in office hours. One's happiest thoughts may come on the dance floor or in the bath.

We entertained a great deal in our years at 16 Great James Street. We had a wide circle of very diverse friends: 'intellectuals' like Bertrand Russell, Cyril Joad, Harold Laski, Geoffrey and Margaret Keynes, Kingsley Martin and David Garnett; a bevy of editors, illustrators and printers; my old friends from the *Daily Herald* days, chiefly Dick and Beatrice Plummer and Irene Clephane; humane politicals like the Coles and the Postgates, the Ewers and the John Stracheys; theatre people like Charles Laughton and Elsa Lanchester, the Farjeons, Collette O'Neill and Miles Malleson; *and* my games-playing friends.

In our little world we were, wrote Margaret Cole, 'the glass of fashion and the mould of form'.* We liked to think of ourselves as at any rate siblings of 'the Bloomsbury set', and true Blooms-buryites like Maynard Keynes and his dancer wife, Lydia Lopokova, and pre-eminently Lytton Strachey, were admired party-comers though not close friends. When Ray Garnett (Bunny's first wife) came in her own face to a party she was silent and apart; but if it was a fancy-dress affair she wore a mask, and

* *Growing Up Into Revolution* (Longmans, 1949).

was then the gayest, the most approachable and approaching of women. A guest so constant that he assumed something of the role of host was Garrow Tomlin, son of the judge, Lord Tomlin, and brother of Stephen, the sculptor. He was better than I was at the little arts of life (where I could admire and even copy him), but a failure at its larger business, which enabled me to keep up my self-confidence. His attentions to Vera tempered my own lessening sense of duty to her. He had gaiety, even when he failed for the second time at the reputedly easy Bar Finals. He enjoyed exaggeration: like one of my grand-daughters two generations later, he declared his wish to have a dozen children each by a different spouse. He was my willing teacher, I a failing pupil at distance-swimming in the south of France and ski-ing in Switzerland. I even imitated him in his desire to learn to fly, but I went no further than my first lesson; my instructor had difficulty in landing the plane, so rigid was my frightened hold on the joystick. Garrow persevered. Yes, he persevered until he crashed his plane and was killed in 1931.

Virginia Woolf was only once a party guest. Undistracted by the clamour, she gazed fixedly into my eyes and with a firm grip of my hand said: 'The Hogarth Press may not make any money— but at least [the grip tightened] at least we did not publish *The Week-End Book*'. She was surprised when she heard me guffaw this to the rest of the company. I had other ways of putting my party foot in it—as when, to their complete embarrassment, I introduced to each other two of my most admired friends, Bertrand Russell and Ottoline Morrell. I did not know that they had decided years before that they would never see each other again.

Great characters can have odd relapses into pettiness. It was so with Bertrand Russell, always a hero of mine as well as a friend. In 1930 he asked me to be trustee for a fund he had established for his two children. When he and Dora were divorced I became involved in a dispute between them as to who should pay for their children's clothes. I did my best to make a reasonable accord between the parents. Dora was an equal friend, but I now saw more of her than of Bertie, and favoured her stance in this and other pathetically trivial developments of their quarrel. In May 1935 Bertie wrote grudgingly to me that he had accepted my decision about the payments for the children's outfits. But his conclusion was definitely against me:

"During the divorce proceedings, at a time when I had all the cards in my hand, you intervened and *forced* me to negotiate with Dora... As you compelled me to enter into the concordat, it is clearly up to you to see that it is carried out."

Dora was not, in my view, the trouble-maker, and I had clearly lost my influence over Bertie. So no accord was established.

Yes, a great man can have his littlenesses. This, thank goodness, was not my last touch with Bertie. In the 'sixties we were together on the platform of a C.N.D. (Campaign for Nuclear Disarmament) meeting. He grasped my hand, saying, 'I suppose we shall be doing this kind of thing to the end of our lives'. He did. I hope I shall.

Occasionally we had the pleasure of welcoming Paul Robeson at our Great James Street parties. Once when I was dispensing from a bottle of Martell brandy it happened to be so angled that Robeson saw only the first four letters on the label and assumed that they were to develop into Martini. He said, 'Please give me a long glass of that.' A little surprised, I complied. He took a big swallow; there was a spitting splutter. With the clearing of the misunderstanding and of his voice he was able to entrance us with his singing. Occasionally he demonstrated some typical American football attitudes and moves—he had been a master footballer in his youth—and I had fears for the furniture.

Miles Malleson was compère at a home-made cabaret for one of our parties. I printed a programme for its 'Twelve o'Clock Trollops'. Bertie Farjeon appeared in it with the name of

'Farty Burgeon'. Elsa Lanchester was 'Our Elsa', assisted by 'Childe Harold' (Scott). Mlle Rambert, the one performer given her own name, danced—or perhaps it would be fairer to say revolved fast and elegantly on her belly on the floor. Garrow Tomlin came as Adam, dressed only in a fig leaf. In another party we included the whole female chorus of 'Blackbirds', a very successful London show with a coloured cast. One of these girls soon disappeared, to our inquisitive alarm. We reassured ourselves by a private roll-call of the males of the party: none was missing. As the party broke up and I saw our guests to the door I found her, safe and fast asleep, curled up under the pile of coats in the hall.

Cyril Joad was a public 'character' of the time and a friend very dear to me. With me he reversed his usual high-hat posture into one of almost embarrassing diffidence. Having written a novel—a surprising departure from his clever popularisations of philosophy—he gave me the proofs to read. I never allow friendship to modify judgement, so I told him that his book was hopeless, a parody of a novel. He said, 'What a good idea! I shall write a short preface explaining that parody was always my intention.'

Cyril had a series of love-affairs. When I met the girls I found to my surprise that every one of them was called Maureen. Cyril explained: 'I tell each of them that it is my favourite name and that it specially suits her. But of course my real motive is that it avoids the embarrassment that I might utter another girl's name in my sleep'.

As a young man Cyril was an unsuccessful civil servant in the Ministry of Labour. In those days everyone wore hats and Cyril had a special technique with two of his. One he kept permanently on a peg in his office so that it would be thought that he was about the building somewhere; the other was on his head as he left the Ministry for his studies and frolics around town.

He went once to his Chief of Establishment and asked if he

could have special leave to go to India. 'Certainly not', was the reply. 'But why do you want to go?' 'To give some lectures', said Cyril, 'and perhaps to accept a professorship at a university.' 'That', said his Establishment officer, 'is a *very* different matter. You are welcome to special leave on the understanding that you do not return.' The visit did not take place.

Later Cyril became the most famous broadcaster of his time in the 'Brains Trust' programmes. He was the super-Muggeridge of his day: and he refrained from sneering at the holders of opinions he himself once cherished and later abandoned. Like Mr Muggeridge, Cyril Joad in his later life rediscovered God. About this, Professor Dickinson of Leeds said to me, 'I think Cyril pronounces God with the G soft and the O long'. Cyril was my tutor at tennis, I was his at cricket. As partners we once reached the semi-finals in a county tennis tournament, but batting in my cricket teams Cyril seldom survived a single over.

The 'twenties was the great age of jazz—the foxtrot, the Charleston and finally the 'black bottom'. We invited friends to professional dancing lessons at Great James Street. We made up parties or went in couples to dine and dance at David Tennant's Gargoyle Club, playground of the 'intellectuals', where in summer one danced on the roof. And we went often to Elsa Lanchester's 'Cave of Harmony' in Soho, where she performed with Harold Scott and Charles Laughton.

Quite as important to me as dancing and parties were games of all kinds, but especially cricket. I have been a games-player all my life. I first handled a toy cricket bat when I was five, in the long basement passage of our house, my brother Everard being the bowler with a tennis ball. My last cricket match was in my sixties at Greatham in August 1958, when I retired with an honourable split finger after holding a hard catch. Between these extremes I won my cap at preparatory and public school for cricket, hockey and soccer, created my own cricket team to play against village sides, took an occasional place in Jack Squire's 'Invalids XI', captained the local village team when we had a house in Essex, and played for Sudbury when we moved to Suffolk. And nearly fifty years ago I started the annual match of Meynells and their friends against neighbouring Sussex villages—an event which still flourishes in the care of my nephew Jake Dallyn.

I can and do boast that I once played against W. G. Grace. Before I reached my 'teens I went to watch the Winchmore Hill team play London County, a side invented for the great W. G. to captain when he had retired from county cricket. At that time my convention was to dress myself in flannels and cricket boots whenever I watched solemn-class cricket. Now by a marvellous chance one Winchmore Hill player failed to appear and I (the only spectator in white) was invited to take the vacant place. I made no runs and fortunately had no catches to drop. I was shocked to find that Grace took no more interest in the match after his own innings, but played bowls within our sight while his side fielded.

The 'Long Primers', the cricket team I established and captained in the 'twenties, were a diverse lot, ranging from Miles Malleson (actor and playwright), John Strachey (expressive left-wing politician), Harold Monro (of the Poetry Bookshop), Herbert Simon (printer), Edgar Lansbury (who once with a sound like a pistol-shot broke an achilles tendon when he ran to save a boundary), George Hamilton (poet and civil servant) and William Mellor (then still at the *Daily Herald*), all good at the game, to Cyril Joad and Kenneth Walker (surgeon and story-writer) who were novices. Between these extremes were Herbert Farjeon, who boasted that he was the slowest bowler in the world, Geoffrey Boumphrey (propagandist for the duties of the eye and the pleasures of the tongue), John Langdon Davies (already a multiple man, with achievements in life and letters as many as the runs he made) and Stephen Potter. Too rarely the 'Long Primers' included

Alec Waugh, Clifford and Arnold Bax, and Desmond Flower, so adding literature, music and bibliography to our after-cricket festive boards.

Oliver Simon was our accident-prone wicket-keeper and his successor was my teenage nephew Wilfrid, exact and vigorous, whose deep-throated appeals sometimes startled an umpire into an unexpected acquiescence. We usually won our matches, but only by a discreet margin. Clad in my pads I sometimes waited for an innings that proved unnecessary: we had won already. No matter, the wait had its usual pre-innings purgative effect.

Herbert Simon has given me this cricket reminiscence, characteristically omitting any mention of his innings of 88 against Arundel or his capture of all ten wickets against Fittleworth in (I think) 1924:

"The 'Long Primers' played on some beautiful village greens, most often at Aston Clinton in Buckinghamshire, where we hired the village cricket ground every other weekend and there was a very good inn called the Bell. In our days the proprietor was Mr Gladding, who had quit a Stock Exchange post for the more congenial task of hotel-keeping. It was very simple, comfortable and the food was good plain English stuff. Strawberries were strawberries, not deep-frozen wool, and the salmon deserved its hollandaise. After-cricket evenings at the Bell were memorable. Very often we had John Goss to sing his haunting sea-shanties and there was the talkative and argumentative Cyril Joad.

Among our players was R. D. Best, who was what I may call a natural number-eleven batsman. On one occasion there was a photo-finish. Our opponents had made 212: we in reply were 212 when our ninth wicket fell and there was just Bob Best to go in. A small whisky, and he was propelled out of the pavilion towards the wicket. The first ball he received nearly bowled him; the second struck him a painful blow on the bottom. As the ball skidded off his body towards long-leg we all bellowed 'Run, run'. After an agony of suspense he did run, and won for the Long Primers its most famous victory— by a bum-bye."

When I played for Jack Squire's 'Invalids' I sometimes found myself promoted from my accustomed place at number five or six in the batting order. Jack was not a good organiser. Too often when play was due to start several members of his team were still absent, and he had therefore to be accorded first innings even when he lost the toss. Then he would say to me, 'Go in first and keep an end up until the 3.30 train comes in'.

Watching cricket at the Oval and Lords took many of my summer hours. I was for a short time a member of the Surrey Club and for a longer period of the Middlesex. When the Australians were in England, Herbert Farjeon and I often went together to the Test Matches. We had an elaborate but economical betting system. The toss of a coin decided which of us backed England and which Australia. Payment had to be made at different rates for no-balls, wides, maiden overs and byes. Once when I was *for* Australia, I had a special piece of luck. The English wicket-keeper retired hurt and Woolley, the great Kent batsman, took an unaccustomed place behind the stumps. Inevitably he let through dozens of byes—at sixpence apiece for me.

In 1938 I took James Thurber, that great comic writer (greatness means humane wisdom as well as wit), to Lords. He had never before seen any cricket, and this was a thrilling Test Match. I begged him to look upon the game as a ballet as well as a battle; he welcomed that phrase, told me that he would use it in his own report, and delighted me by asking me to take him to Lords again the next day.

All cricket lovers enjoy chatting about the game, as Neville Cardus and John Arlott have proved to me and sundry. Myself, I so enjoy John Arlott's and Brian Johnston's radio commentaries that nowadays, watching cricket from my armchair, I turn off the television sound and put on the radio.

I had one chance, only one, of being myself a cricket reporter. After I left *The Communist* George Lansbury failed to make me *Daily Herald* correspondent in Rome, a passport having been refused me; as a sop and solace he gave me the reporting of the Australian Test Match of 1921 at Leeds. I took the job on with enthusiasm and filled many columns with my description of the match. In one respect at least I showed myself to be a novice. At regular short intervals in the afternoon, messengers came to the Press-box for dispatches to be telegraphed to the newspapers. I did not notice that on the Saturday of the match only the Sunday-paper reporters used the messengers: reports for Monday's papers could be sent by train. I went on giving my report, paragraph by paragraph, to be telegraphed. At the end of the day's play the *Morning Post* man teasingly asked me if the *Daily Herald* was about to produce a Sunday issue.

Tennis I played eagerly and even fairly well after professional coaching, some of it at Queen's Club, where I was a member for a short time. Sometimes my ball-boy was the youthful Dan Maskell, now famous as a tennis commentator. I partnered Stanley Unwin in matches of Publishers against W. H. Smith—gay affairs these. Once I made a September pilgrimage with Gerald Gould in my somewhat inadequate car to tennis courts in the south of France: bad weather overwhelmed us. In the 'thirties, regular summer visits to Talloires on the Lake of Annecy were made robust by tennis at nearby courts with Alix (Bay) Kilroy and her skilled sister Angela (Toto), Evelyn Sharp (now the Baroness) and the Potters. Stephen and I indulged in 'gamesman-ship' long before he made the word famous.

Squash rackets was a convenient game for a busy Londoner—at my level it was short and a quick sweat-inducer. One had to go some distance for a tennis court, but as a Savile Club member I was allowed access to the squash rackets court of the 'In-and-Out' Club in Piccadilly, and there I often played against Stephen Potter. I had also many eager and equal games with Ambrose Heal (developer of the great store in Tottenham Court Road) on his own court. Once and once only I played against Winnington Ingram, Bishop of London, patron of my friend Eileen Walker. The Bishop had his chaplain as the 'marker' and every time I won a point the marker called 'let'. The Bishop, or rather his marker, won.

I once led a foursome against the table-tennis team of an Indian Students Union. We lost every game except one—when I had lured a totally unsuspecting Mohammedan into drinking a double whisky before I played him. At the end of the match the opposing captain intoned a polite excuse for the failure of our middle-aged team: 'Of course it is not possible to play table-tennis after you are twenty-five years old'. (I have here used the current name for what I still call ping-pong, as it was known when William Orpen gave me my first lessons on the dining-room table at Palace Court.) Having won the ping-pong tournament on my sea-voyages to and from the United States in 1949, I added to my *Who's Who* list of recreations 'Trans-Oceanic Ping-Pong'. Would that suit *Who's Who*? By no means. It was edited to 'Oceanic Table Tennis'. At seventy-nine I still play on the same dining-room table which belonged to my parents, warning my opponents that if they beat me they will never be invited to the house again.

Vera was a lovely dancer, but she held games in contempt. Her fun was with phrases. When we looked for domestic staff she composed an advertisement for the *Church Times*, whose readers, practising Protestants, would be likely in her view, or pretended view, to be specially conscientious and loyal. A man-and-wife would not do, because only one of them would be likely to work, yet the couple must be happy together. So her advertisement read like this: 'Wanted, cook and housemaid, Church of England and Lesbian'. It produced an exact and very satisfactory response.

As a music-addict Vera made much use of our large-trumpet gramophone. When a favourite Mozart record became too scratchy she told me that she longed to be rich, really rich. This was by no means in accordance with her or my social attitude. She explained: 'So that I could have my own private trio'. The nearest we came to this was to organise through Nonesuch a series of six concerts at the Wigmore Hall in 1926. Music for me was bound up with my feeling for Hilda, and I hoped that these concerts might be the means of persuading her to start her musical life again. Our friend Hubert Foss, head of the Music Division of the Oxford University Press, planned these 'Period Concerts . . . illustrations of the history of music from 1580 to the present day'. It was an odd adventure for Nonesuch. I commissioned from the Cambridge University Press a Prospectus of the concerts, on hand-made paper, and circulated it with the Nonesuch 1926 Prospectus and Retrospectus. The concerts were crowded and Hilda's piano playing in two of them won personal and press admiration; but my hope that she might be tempted back to a public career came to nothing. She devoted herself to our young daughter and to piano teaching.

Vera and I had regular French holidays. Our plan on one of these was to bathe in a different river every day. I was well advanced in a trial growing of a beard, which was rough and red and horrific. When we came to the Rhone Vera decided that the current was too fast for safety. I did a show-off dive and was carried helpless for a hundred yards till I managed to get to the bank and scramble out. Here was a lovely young girl, a shepherdess guarding a few sheep. She saw me climbing naked from the water (that was my habit), screamed, crossed herself, cried, 'Mon Dieu, le diable, le diable!' and fled towards the nearby village. I am sure she had a breathless story to tell to the parish priest and the villagers of her miraculous escape from the fiend.

We conformed to the week-ending custom. We had made close friends during the early 'twenties with Oswald (Tom) Mosley and his wife Cynthia (Cimmie) and occasionally we were their guests at Denham. On one of these weekends Cyril Joad was a fellow guest. The evening wore away with Cyril (short and rotund) monologuing on politics to Oswald (tall and thin), who dutifully pretended to listen. Vera rose to go to bed. 'I am tired,' said she, 'of watching a serpent being fascinated by a rabbit.'

Our friendship with the Mosleys was a divided one, Tom's for Vera, mine for Cimmie. She was the daughter of Lord Curzon and she had his qualities of gentleness, self-depreciation and wit. Tom was then a fellow Labourite, but to me he was always sardonic or withdrawn. He played painful practical jokes and I was one of his victims when at a cocktail party he offered tit-bits which looked enticing but proved to be slices of soap spread with shredded tobacco. I saw him watching me when I put this to my mouth and determined to deprive him of his pleasure at my pain; so I controlled my expression and consumed the tit-bit. Then I had to rush out of doors and be sick.

In 1931 Mosley founded what he called the New Party to be a 'ginger group' of the Left. A grand idea we thought, a quicker way to true socialism, and Vera and I joined the group, as did John Strachey and Cyril Joad and many of our friends. Then horror. One day John Strachey came straight to us from a critical meeting of the New Party committee: 'Tom has gone fascist. I have had fears for some weeks, and now there is no doubt about it'. That was the end of the Mosleys for us—of both political association and friendship.

Others of our weekends were spent at Garsington, which had become the country home of those charming characters Ruth and Tommy Lowinsky: Tommy a richly talented romantic painter, Ruth the perfect hostess, simple and inquiring in talk and highly sophisticated in such things as the planning of meals. At a small luncheon party at their London house in Kensington Square I made a double first-acquaintance—with the wrist-befrilled Max Beerbohm and with Ruth's own invention of a delicious camembert ice.

It occurred to me that the talents of Ruth and Tommy might well be combined in a Nonesuch cookery book, and they cheerfully agreed. Tommy made the stipulation that there must be some copies on hand-made paper, for which he would pay, besides the ordinary edition. When the drawings had been made and the recipes proofed for *Lovely Food*,* the Lowinskys came to dine with us, Ruth bringing with her the manuscript of her introduction. I said that I would read the introduction when we had dined. During dinner Ruth showed a mounting uneasiness and afterwards begged for the return of the introduction, in which, she said, she wanted to make some changes. I persisted in reading it aloud. It included a passage on how to choose your cook from among the applicants for the post. 'Never correspond with a cook—see her and then ask her for her idea of a good menu for a dinner-party. If she suggests as an inspiration that it should start with grape-fruit and go on to *Consommé à la Royal*, a nice sole and a bird, you can stop her before she proceeds to the inevitable meringues and sardines on toast. Give her up as hopeless.' A mounting un-easiness? That, except for the sardines on toast, was the identical dinner, course by course, that we had provided.

Vera had longed to bear a child, but after five years of dis-appointment believed herself to be sterile. She decided that a weekend house of our own in the country would make a helpful distraction. So in 1928 she bought, adventurously, a tumbledown, double-gabled house called Bradfield in the Essex village of Toppesfield. It was built as a manor house in 1430 and enlarged in 1681. We jointly spent on making it habitable many times the few hundred pounds its freehold cost Vera. Our first 'camp-in'

* *Lovely Food: A Cookery Notebook* (Nonesuch, 1931).

there was made jocularly formal: we wore evening dress and Garrow Tomlin made a ceremony of lighting the first candle.

As blatant non-believers Vera and I were not on terms with Canon Lampen, the rector of Toppesfield, but we were on his conscience. He wrote to us to say that he understood that we were 'about to take into your employment a maiden of this village who, although her parents are Wesleyans, is a very earnest Christian'. It had come to his notice, he continued, that both Vera and I had been divorced and he would warn the girl against coming to us. We set up a competition among our weekend guests to provide us with an answer that would best exploit the Canon's 'although' phrase. I don't remember the winner, but later I had my own retort of a different kind. I had entered the 'over-forties' race at the local fête. The rector was among the entrants. I allowed him to lie first until a few yards from the finish, then I let myself go and won by a paunch.

While a bathroom was being built at Bradfield, Jane and H. G. Wells welcomed us each weekend to a bath and, weather permitting, to a game of tennis at their house in Little Dunmow. One feature of H.G.'s game was comically wrong: to receive service he stood on the service line; he could return only the shortest of short services, but the comedy of his stance won for him many double-faults. H.G. had put my mind ajar by his writings when I was still at school. Now he really opened it with his logical talk, the more pleasing to me because it was against habit and authority. He commented on the threatening aspects of the day with an extra up-turn of his high voice at the end of a sentence, as if he were asking a question and even wanted one's answer to it. If any-one did attempt an answer he was tremolo-routed. Nevertheless I have one contrary memory. Some twenty years later I dared to argue with him at the Savile Club when he declared that there was no hope of a true community of nations after the war. I said that we must still strive for it. He gave me an emphatic 'You have always talked nonsense' and turned away. Two days later, again at the Savile, he sought me out and said: 'I want to apologise to you for what I said the other day. I was testy and rude. You were right'. I cherish these generous words, spoken though they were in his tentative old age. Was it, I wonder, the only apology of his life?

Jane Wells died in October 1927. H.G. asked me to print the speech he wrote for her funeral but hadn't the heart to read. I hoped that this might be my little gift to her memory, but H.G. didn't agree: 'The care you are giving it is your tribute'.

H.G. celebrated his seventieth birthday at his flat in London with a small dinner-party. Vera and I were his only non-family guests. Marjorie, his daughter-in-law, had planned the meal to consist of one dish only, H.G.'s favourite. It was smoked salmon. This was a shock to me: I had always refused what I had thought of as raw fish. What could I do but attempt what I assumed would be a difficult swallow? I have been a smoked-salmon enthusiast ever since.

Near to Toppesfield is the larger village of Great Yeldham. In the early 'thirties I captained its cricket team. I provided all the side with large-peaked cricket caps. This sartorial extravagance was not due to vanity, but to tactics. In every village team there are one or two fielders worse than the rest. Opposing batsmen quickly get to recognise the good and the bad fielders and take or refuse their runs accordingly. Our caps were face-obscuring and so valuable run-savers.

I planned to make a grand occasion of the opening of the new Great Yeldham cricket pavilion. Flying was a newish private pastime then and David Garnett had just learned to pilot his own aircraft. I thought it would be gay and exciting to have him fly over and drop the cricket ball from the air for our opening match. Then, knowing nothing of ballistics, I had a sudden fear that the ball would gather such speed in falling that it would have a cannon-ball effect and might go through the roof of the new pavilion. I made anxious inquiry of Desmond ('Sage') Bernal, one of my few scientific friends, and was reassured; but I had not realised how difficult it would be to aim from an aeroplane, even at so large a target as a cricket field. We saw Bunny fly over, but we never found the ball.

By accident or by friendly imitation this patch of Essex countryside was to become almost a duplication of our London environment. A. J. A. Symons came to nearby Finchingfield and to our village or immediate neighbourhood came Att and Stephen Potter, Dick and Beattie Plummer, and Harold Hobson. Our house is now owned by Michael and Elizabeth Ayrton, Beattie (now the Baroness) Plummer has moved to what was the Potters' farm dwelling, Alan and Babette Sainsbury (he too has now properly been be-Lorded) now possess the Plummers' house: an admirable continuum.

Games and life can come close together. I had played cricket more than once at Mickleham and I returned years later in search of the cricket ground and its memories. There were many changes in the village and its approaches, and I found the wrong field. I wrote these verses.

MIRAGE AT MICKLEHAM

This country was not strange to me
Nor quite familiar grown.
I knew it not by stack and tree,
Only by wood and down.

Dazzled by dappled land and light
And scarce-transparent shadow
I thought I saw that quickening sight—
The field close-set, the men in white—
Cricketers in the meadow.

And yet no batsman takes his guard
No ball is bowled, no hit is heard.

The haze is blown, the yew-tree stirs.
For sign of life I search the sward.
Only white stones, these cricketers—
Only white stones in the churchyard.

XIII

Farewell and Hail

Late in 1929 I went to a dinner party given by Kenneth Walker and his first wife, 'Tim'. (Kenneth was a charming failure in my cricket team.) Among the guests was a school friend of Tim's, Alix (Bay) Kilroy, who was to become the most important person in all my life. (She will be Bay, her family pet-name, in all my proud and happy references to her.) We found that we had another mutual friend in Garrow Tomlin, but we had never met through him; he kept his admirations, which included Vera and Bay, in separate compartments. Bay told me that in 1924 when she was at Somerville she had been taken (very shy and fish-out-of-water) to the rooms of a notorious aesthete where the cynosure of conversation and eyes was the Nonesuch *Genesis*. Bay, eleven years my junior, had been one of the three first women to achieve (in 1925) the administrative grade of the Civil Service, where she was the winner of her own subsequent renown. To me then she was simply the ideal dancing partner when the Walkers took us, after dinner, to a tennis-club dance at Grosvenor House. In the first two years after our meeting we saw little of each other. We both had other serious involvements.

In February 1930, after gynaecological treatment, Vera achieved her greatest desire with the birth of our son, Benedict. We reported him to our Nonesuch friends as a 'strictly limited edition'. His naming proved a difficulty. His maternal grand-mother urged that his first name should be William after her dead husband, and that he should be baptised in the family christening robe with water brought from the Jordan. We wanted neither the name nor the christening, and we suspected that it was the social rather than the religious aspect of baptism that appealed to Vera's mother. In this we were proved right, for a double bargain was happily concluded: 'William' as his second name and (my proposal this), instead of christening, entry on the waiting list for membership of the top-gentlemanly cricket club, the M.C.C. . . .

For Ben's birth we had moved from Great James Street to a house in Gordon Square, which had ample accommodation for child and nurse. Kingsley Martin and Edgar Lansbury and his second wife, Moyna Macgill, became tenants of the flats we made above the Nonesuch office at Great James Street. This removal from an intimate house, a house I loved, had also its effects on my association with Vera, just as the move from Romney Street had, I think, contributed to the break of my first marriage.

Not that the new home was an unpleasing house. It was spacious and well sited. Its previous occupants had been Clive and Vanessa Bell, and Clive Bell had painted a great mural in the drawing-room. Audaciously, I added gold wallpaper columns to each side of it to 'collect and contain' what seemed to me disorderly elements. Near to us lived Maynard Keynes, Charles Laughton and Arthur Waley, famous for his translations of Chinese poems. I saw Waley one evening mounting his bicycle with some difficulty because he was in full Court dress, silk breeches and stockings and sword and all. I asked him where he was going in that guise. He said, 'To a dinner at 10 Downing Street in honour of an oriental prince'. Next day I saw him again, this time in normal clothes. 'How did things go last night?' I asked. 'Oh, I was a great success,' he said. 'I was the only one dressed like that.'

To Benedict, Vera transferred both the grandeur and the minu-tiae of loving attention that she had given to me in the first years of our marriage. She made it clear too that she and only she was to be Ben's effective parent. This enlarged the growing gap between us. In the fashion of our time and neighbourhood and friends, we enjoyed plentifully what is now called the 'permissive' attitude towards extra-marital affairs. We believed that the only prurient thing about sex is the mystery and pretence with which convention surrounds a natural function and delight. However, we failed to have the needed emotional tolerance and after eight years of our marriage, with its shared ecstasies and happy commonplaces and achievements, and its horrible jealousies and angers, we became painfully estranged. We were too deeply involved for this to become a mere neutrality. We became hostile towards each other. I still respected and admired Vera—but more easily from a distance, both in space and time.

Benedict was brought up on principles which would now be attributed to Doctor Spock. Discipline was minimal and he was encouraged to choose for himself. The results were not quite what Vera expected. I remember one pointed incident. The small Ben is being pressed to say what pudding he would like for his lunch and after listening to a number of suggestions he stamps his foot and, almost in tears, cries, 'Can't the *cook* choose?'

Vera had been psychoanalysed in New York, where she had lived during her former marriage, and she insisted that it was proper for Benedict also to be analysed, when he was seven. I saw no abnormality or unhappiness in him that needed treatment, and I came to the view that his sessions with the analyst were disturbing rather than reassuring him. Vera promptly bade me go and talk to the analyst. I went. The analyst said, 'I suppose you know that your son is a homicidal maniac?' If he had said that the boy suffered from a little bit of this or that I might have taken it seriously. As it was, I said: 'Yes, indeed, I am aware of that, but how did you find out?' He said: 'Ben carries a toy pistol. I have watched him as he comes up the stairs to my consulting-room. At each landing he pauses and shoots imaginary enemies.' That was enough even for Vera. She agreed with me that the analysis should be ended.

Nonesuch being no longer profitable enough to support us, I

was now also three-quarter time at work in the film industry. There I had some success, which Vera explained to me: 'You have a second-rate mind, but you only have to compete with people who have third-rate ones'. There was too much truth in this assessment and too little kindness for my liking.

I found solace in other attachments, some fleet and fleeting, one deeper and so more of a mixture of pleasure and pain. From one of these girls when she was ill came these lines:

> Since you so tastefully elect to stay
> Close-fitted in a built-in functional life
> With architectural niches set for play
> And work and delicately spaced 'twixt wife and wife,
> Why disarrange some neat time-tailored frill
> To telephone me here—when I am ill?
>
> My dear, however vibrant warm your tone,
> We cannot copulate by telephone.

There was one figure in the long landscape of my approaches and alienations on whom I began to gaze with love and even hope, who gave me cool appraisals as well as warm comfort in my despondencies, who had much of my first wife's single-mindedness and largeness of heart and of my second wife's trained exactitude of mind, who was young and beautiful. This was Bay Kilroy. She has filled full and fulfilled my life during every one of the forty years that have passed since we discovered each other.

In 1932 she and I went to Paris together and in the following summer we and her sister and cousin had an idyllic holiday at Talloires on the Lake of Annecy. From that time on our love grew and we became one another's best. For Christmas 1933 I wrote lines to her, and set and printed them myself, with this colophon: 'This edition is limited to one copy, for Bay'.

AUTUMN

The pear-tree in my orchard now
    Is over-laden so with fruit
That the once taut and sterile bough
    Is bent right back upon the root.

How is it with our ripening love?
    With our surprising harvest, how?
Quick, with our baskets to the grove,
    Lest fall the fruit or break the bough.

We must not go anhungered now.

Bay had interesting parents. Her mother, Hester Dowson, one of a well-to-do Midlands Unitarian family of ten, had insisted on having a career, which was then most unusual for a girl in her circumstances, and had become a trained nurse. She was a natural rebel. She did not accept hospital discipline and wrote to *The Times* from University College Hospital about the cries of animals suffering under vivisection there. For this she was sacked. She wore her hair short, considering it hygienically proper for nurses, and once she cut off the pigtails of fellow nurses in their dormitory while they slept—she was sacked again. She was one of the brave few who volunteered to go to India at the time of the terrible outbreak of the plague in Bombay in 1897. The young nurse with whom she shared a bungalow died of the plague.

In India Bay's mother met a British naval doctor who became her husband. Her bringing up of Bay, her three sisters and her brother, had a character of its own: the little girls were dressed in home-made 'shorts' (none could be bought for girls in those days) and if the children seemed to their mother to be 'too good', she established a 'mobbing day' when they were to be as naughty as they liked. When Bay and her elder sister went to their first boarding-school it was with precise instructions that they were to hold a midnight feast at the end of term. Under this training her children became, if not rebellious, independent-minded.

Lancelot Kilroy, Bay's father, was a very different kind of person. He came from an Army background and was himself a Surgeon-Commander in the Navy. Where Bay's mother was a Liberal and an innovator, he was a Conservative and a conformist. He was a devotedly conscientious man with an impelling sense of duty and great integrity, but everything for him was either black or white; there were no greys. After he retired from the Navy, he made a one-man business of inventing and tying salmon-flies, which he sold through shops in London. When I asked him if he would be my guest for a game of bridge at the Savile Club he refused. Why? Not because I was a still-married man paying court to his daughter, as I had half expected from a father of conventional views. No. He said: 'My fly-tying has made me a tradesman. As such I could not enter a gentlemen's club.'

Bay's family was almost as clannish as mine, and she and her sisters and brother were especially close both to each other and to their mother. When I first knew Bay it was quite usual for all four sisters to go dancing with their partners to 'Chez Henri' or the 'Gargoyle' together. I called them the 'Kilrush'. Of her sisters I knew best Angela (Toto), who married Jack Rendle. She and I were frequent tennis partners.

My happy and stimulating life with Bay was full of business-hour lunches, evenings of dancing and occasional weekend visits to Toppesfield (when Vera was not there) and to Greatham (whether or not the ever-tolerant Hilda was there). We took a regular summer holiday at Talloires, always with friends. Consistently among those friends at weekends and on holidays was Evelyn Sharp, beautiful, brilliant and didactic. She had been at Somerville with Bay, was now like her a civil servant, and had become my friend no less than Bay's. Evelyn would never miss a jaunt if it was adventurous, like a bicycling tour in France in the depths of winter with snow and ice on the roads.

One bicycling party brought Bay and me to the château country. I thought it would be fun to call on Charles and Fern Bedaux at their Château de Candé. Vera and I had stayed with them in the early 'thirties. They had a *grand tenu* dining-room with a French *capitaine* and Italian waiters, a French *maître de cuisine* with a *chef saucier*, a *chef potagier* and a *chef patissier*. Guests could opt out of a formal meal by going to the always-open cold food bar, manned by Englishmen. The head gardener was English too; a Scotsman was in charge of the eighteen-hole golf course; a German presided over the library. One was called by house-telephone every morning to ask what one wished to eat during the day.

All the money had come from the 'Bedaux Unit', the first labour-measuring 'productivity' system, sold to many vast American corporations. With all his opulence Bedaux was a sadly disappointed man in one major thing: he had no child. He wanted desperately to perpetuate his name, and set out vainly on many expeditions to little explored lands in the hope of finding an unnamed river or mountain that he could cause to be called after him. He had a cure for all business ills: he sent me detailed proposals for 'saving' the Nonesuch Press in 1935 and a year later he claimed that he alone knew how to revitalise the British film industry. His end was desperate. He was arrested after the war as a collaborator and died in prison.

But now we are back in 1937, on our bicycles. We presented ourselves at the lodge gates of the Château and asked to see Monsieur Bedaux. The Château was obviously in occupation, but we had a cold, almost hostile, reception from the porters, who even refused to telephone our request to the Château. We wondered whether this was due to our bedraggled appearance. We learned in the nearby village that the Duke of Windsor and Mrs Simpson were honeymooning in the Château. Clearly we had been judged to be enterprising English journalists.

Bay willing, Vera and I kept something of a public face together, which we all thought desirable for Ben's sake. I continued
to live at the smaller, cheaper, house in Woburn Square to which
Vera and I had moved from Gordon Square in 1935. Bay and I
rarely took holidays or spent weekends alone together. Nevertheless at Easter 1938 we did go by ourselves, very discreetly, for a
trip to northern France in Bay's old Citroen. Our progress was
slow and from garage to garage because of car troubles. We spent
a joyous evening at the Lion d'Or in Bonnétable, then owned and
operated by the Lucard family. Before dinner we came upon the
daughter of the house polishing the already shining panels of the
bedroom doors, and from our window we watched Monsieur
Lucard sorting out hillocks of spinach with infinite care in the
courtyard. At the exchange rate of 173 francs to the pound our
delicious seven-course dinner cost just over 2s. a head and our
bottle of Mouton Rothschild 1928 set us back another 4s. 3d. . . .
Madame Lucard came at the meal's end to inquire whether all had
been as we wished. We offered her our praise and our thanks.
With arms demurely folded, she bowed and said: 'On est content
de son métier'. Then she passed serenely on to the next table.

On est content de son métier! With scarce an exception our
varied jobs have justified Bay and me in echoing to each other this
gentle boast of contentment.

The hotel, alas, was destroyed in World War II.

XIV

Other People's Wares

I go back to 1930 when I needed some supplement to my dwindling Nonesuch income. Could I find a profitable use for my typographic know-how? In the design of advertisements? In general this was still clumsy and uninviting, even though the more progressive advertising agencies occasionally commissioned designs from such dedicated printers as Bernard Newdigate, Harold Curwen, Gerard Meynell, Bobby Simon and Stanley Morison, and my own Pelican Press. Surely, I thought, one could have more influence, as well as more money, from a position within one of these agencies.

In 1929 I had written *The Typography of Newspaper Advertisements*.* Though priced at the then enormous sum of two guineas, it was a quick success. After a somewhat pompous thesis, I showed a large variety of good but little-used display types and a gallery of well-designed English and American advertisements, printed on newsprint, as were the originals. Most of my English specimens were the work of no more than three advertising agencies: W. S. Crawford, the London Press Exchange and Charles W. Hobson. The Crawford advertisements were usually signed with a minute 'Ashley'. They were the work of Ashley Havinden, Crawford's designer-in-chief. Would there, I wondered, be a place for me beside, or indeed cheerfully below, this master of his art? No, there was none.

It was at this moment of disappointment that I was pressed by Charles Hobson to join his advertising agency. He was a retired master-mariner turned printer and advertising agent. He had been a client of mine at the Pelican Press before he started his own

* Ernest Benn, London.

short-lived Cloister Press, where Stanley Morison and Walter Lewis (later Printer to Cambridge University) worked together. Hobson was a subscriber to all Nonesuch editions and a member of the Double Crown Club. I joined him early in 1931. My job was to be a three-quarter-time one, the other quarter remaining Nonesuch's.

The agency was established in a beautiful eighteenth-century mansion in Park Place, St James's, and I was given a noble room next to Hobson's own. This I furnished with Arnold Bennett's rug, desk, sofa, stools and chair, which I had bought after his death. I was now in my first job under a virtual stranger. I was very shy—so shy that for my first fortnight I could not bring myself to ask where the lavatory was. Instead I took myself to the nearby Ritz Hotel. Vera took no interest in my new job. We were already far apart. It was Bay who knew of my trepidation and often telephoned me to ask how I was faring.

Hobson's chief copywriter was Marchant Smith. In manner he affected grandeur. Once when he was processionally descending the grand staircase, his pretty young secretary had begun to mount it. I saw her turn to make way for him, trip and fall. Passing her prostrate body Marchant Smith said 'A curtsey would have sufficed, Miss X'.

Hobson had struck a new note in the advertising style of the day with his personal, conversational copy for Buoyant Chairs: 'Get up out of that chair, Kenneth, and let your father sit down'. His type arrangements were direct, unconfused; he had learnt a lot from Stanley Morison. Even so, there was still plenty of room for reform.

At our staff conferences, when a client's problem was to be solved, it was risky to pull Hobson's leg, which made the effort more tempting, because he might take as serious what was merely satire. We had to plan a campaign for a firm marketing a tinned fish somewhat misleadingly called salmon; sales resistance was

caused by its most unsalmonly colour. I suggested that the advertisement line should be 'guaranteed not to turn pink in the tin'.
It was only after half an hour of discussion that Hobson decided
not to put this proposition to his client. At another staff conference
we discussed the problem of the makers of Brasso, a metal polish.
Brass was decreasing in popularity and with it the sales of this
polish. I asked how many holes there were in the sprinkler top of
the tin. 'Five,' I was told. 'Make it seven of the same size,' said I.
'You will find its sales increase by about two-fifths without any
advertising.' This time Hobson was merely, though briefly,
annoyed.

My gag approach could be of use. We did the advertising for
the Central Electricity Authority, which had occasional serious
power cuts in the course of establishing the national grid. I was
irked that gas had as its advertising slogan 'Gas never lets London
down'. Then it chanced that there was a big gas explosion in the
road at Holborn. I told the gas advertising agents that if they did
not abandon their slogan, ours would be 'Electricity never blows
London up'. It worked; they dropped their phrase.

Already prominent in the electricity industry in the 1930s was
Harold Hobson (no relation of my employer). He was, and is, a
close friend of mine. I had known him since the days when he
visited Greatham with David Garnett in 1915. Harold is tall and
powerfully handsome; his is the more commanding profile in a
drawing, in which I too appear, of the Gracchi, made by Tom
Poulton for the Nonesuch Plutarch. When the electricity industry
was nationalised after the war, Harold was too determined an
individualist and too much the conservative—our politics are
pylons apart—to allow his name to go forward for high office. He
liked, still likes, to coin the carefully distorted and thus striking
phrase: about this appointment he said it offered 'no room for
scope'. Harold arranged that I should be invited to the 'World
Power' (i.e. electricity) conference in Stockholm in 1933. It was a

pleasant and even useful visit. The conference habit had not then grown to its present extravagant (in all senses of the word) proportions.

'Creative' work in an advertising agency can be, usually is, dull and exacting. I had plenty of it at Hobson's but I now remember only a few of my involvements. One was an account for the first zip fasteners to be used in clothing. Bobby Simon continued to sound his admirable new tune to Imperial Chemical Industries at its Kynoch Press and got agreement to the transfer of their 'Lightning Fasteners' advertisement account to my care at Hobson's. He had faith in my typographical capacity and (I suspect) was moved also by his realisation that a new account credited to me would strengthen my position at Hobson's. Pleasant encouragement for what I designed came from Noel Carrington, the handsomest of Bloomsburyites, a powerful preacher of 'fitness for purpose' and a London representative of the Kynoch Press. I have always had the habit of using the products I advertised. How was the zip to be used by a man? Only one use seemed possible—as a substitute for fly-buttons. I pressed my tailor to make the daring experiment on a pair of my trousers. He warned me: 'Be very careful, sir, or—how shall I put it, sir?—or there may be a painful entanglement'.

A significant meeting for me at Park Place was with Ernest Ingham. He was the manager of the Fanfare Press, which was commercially associated with Hobson's through the London Press Exchange, to which both companies were affiliated. Ingham was an imaginative and flexible young printer, equally eager to instruct and to learn. Here was a happy chance to combine my continuing Nonesuch and my new Hobson responsibilities. In 1931 I gave Ingham the first* of the eight Nonesuch books that he printed for me. His sense of style was shown in the intelligent variety of his equipment and in the choice of his staff. I learned from him as

* *Lovely Food*, by Ruth Lowinsky.

much as I taught. It is an unfair oddity that his work has not been fully recognised by the typographic historians.

After four years of hard work I decided to claim a place on the Board of Directors of Hobson's parent company, the London Press Exchange, which had become very intrusive in the affairs of its subsidiary. Without that promotion I would leave. I was invited to a formal interview followed by a chatty lunch. I did not pass this double scrutiny. So out I went or, more accurately, out I was pushed.

Some anxious months followed, with nothing but little-remunerative work for Nonesuch, until in January 1935 I became a columnist on the *News Chronicle*, the now defunct Liberal daily, then edited by Aylmer Vallance. Three times a week I had to fill a half-page with jaunty paragraphs. My feature was called 'Between the Headlines'. I chose for my pseudonym the name 'Brevier' (eight-point type), so continuing my type-size naming habit.

Filling my space acceptably was no easy task. Name-dropping was the heart of the matter—not 'society' names but those of the intellectuals. I reported the doings of my friends in the arts and also in the eats. (I was a member of the Saintsbury Club and of the Wine and Food Society.) There had to be anecdotes aplenty, some real and some fanciful—like that of the British diplomat in Russia who, served with caviare on bliny, remarked to his host, 'Excellency, the pancake is good, but the jam on it tastes a bit fishy'. Under my anonymity I was even able to write about Alix Kilroy on her birthday and about our friend Evelyn Sharp. Family? Yes, I puffed the first novel of my niece Barbara Lucas and anecdoted about my father. And little bits of my politics could be smuggled in, such as hostile references to Hitler and Mussolini, then on the way to the disastrous height of their power.

I was a constant party-goer and every party had to produce its paragraph. Sometimes a name dropped with a clang: Charles Laughton was cross with me about my description of the small gymnasium designed for him by Wells Coates, where, said I, he strove to reduce his girth. I lacked tact, but malice I kept only for unlikeable public figures.

Meanwhile my work for Nonesuch was still heavy but un-remunerative; and since its debts were mounting I was pressing forward with the plans for the introduction of new money and skills from George Macy.

Now came a surprising new offer. My journalism caught the eye of George Archibald,* secretary of the British division of United Artists, one of the biggest distributors of American films. Our mutual friend Dick Plummer arranged a comfortable meeting. George Archibald then introduced me to Murray Silverstone, the managing director of United Artists. In those days everything about the advertising of films, by far the largest public entertain-ment, was blatant and bad; every new picture was 'super-colossal' and the greatest that had ever been made. Type and illustration, commanded from the parent companies in the United States, were loud and unlikeable. Murray Silverstone and George Archibald believed that this could be corrected and thought that I could be the corrector. I was offered the job at £1,500 a year (against the £900 I earned from the *News Chronicle*); and I saw too as large an opportunity to better the standard practice as in any work I had done before.

'Show business', dominated by films, was a strange new world for me. It had a behind-the-scenes attraction, but in the forefront was the formality of a large organisation with its super-command in remote Hollywood. My entrepreneur, George Archibald, was easy and generous and a buffer when I needed one between me and my new boss, Murray Silverstone, a cheerful American.

Silverstone planned a cocktail party at the Savoy to introduce me to the film critics and technical journalists. I persuaded him to

* Now Lord Archibald, for many years Chairman of the Federation of British Film Makers.

make it a farewell party to my predecessor with me as no more than a side-show. This bashful policy was successful. *Today's Cinema* reported: 'Meynell made a direct hit with the gang'.

My office was at one end of a long passage in the United Artists building in Wardour Street; at the other end were the offices of Murray Silverstone and George Archibald. 'You got the better end', said Silverstone. 'At our end we got all the pigeons, their noise and mess.' On my first day in the office I asked Silverstone why it was my duty and not the sales manager's to send out a weekly news-letter to provincial cinemas. Silverstone explained: 'You haven't met Teddy Carr yet, huh? He's the finest salesman in England, maybe in the world, he can speak more lies to the minute than any man I know, but he can't write letters'.

Silverstone had principles. 'See here, Francis,' he said, 'you've got to be honourable in business. Isn't that so? Well, we encourage a guy to build a theatre somewhere and promise him our pictures and then Teddy doesn't give them to him. So that isn't honourable, is it? So to hell with Teddy, and that guy shall have them. It isn't as if the opposition house was making good offers for our pictures.'

It had been decided that I should be put under instruction for a few weeks by Sam Cohen, publicity manager for United Artists in New York. His first two letters to me tickled me by the delicacy of his approach to familiarity. They arrived in one envelope. The first began 'Dear Francis Meynell' and closed 'cordially yours, Sam Cohen'; the second began 'Dear Francis' and ended simply 'Sam'. When a few weeks later he joined me in my office he was shocked to find that my staff consisted of one assistant and a secretary. 'In your job', he said, 'there ought to be three high-ups: one to decide on the work, one to do it, and one to tell Hollywood that it has been done.'

My functions were several: to see to the design of the advertising for West End premières of the films we were distributing; to cajole film theatres to use our displays and not their own in their foyers; to feed the critics and gossip-writers with news and to be their host at first nights; and to publicise and entertain the American film stars when they visited London.

Once a fortnight a new film had to be sold to the success-determining London public, and the problem was that it always arrived from Hollywood with its advertising already made, but made for a public different from ours. For example, one film arrived with the instruction that it should be described as one of the most 'pretentious' films ever made; and the information sheet for 'Les Misérables' included an instruction on how the difficult word was to be pronounced: 'Mizayrobb' was the American phonetic.

In place of photographs of stars I commissioned drawings by artists, among them Leonard Beaumont and Doria Behr and Ted Kauffer, and later Mariette Lydis. For 'Modern Times', which had its première in February 1936, I used signed drawings of Charlie Chaplin by eight different artists. My policy for copy was to get away from the shouting 'super-colossal' technique and to substitute information given in little more than a whisper. 'You look after the nouns', I advised in a talk to the Regent Advertising Club, 'and let the critics look after the adjectives.'

I had scarcely warmed the seat of the chair in my new quarters when Walt Disney, whose films we distributed, made his first visit to London. His Mickey Mouse series had made his name famous, but he himself was something of a mystery in this country. 'Make his poyssanality known' was Silverstone's order to me. Disney struck me as an amiable backwoodsman who had seen little, heard little and read nothing at all; which meant that his genius—not too large a word—was all his own. My favourite among his cartoons was 'Peculiar Penguins'. With a bevy of press photographers I took him to the new Penguin Pool at the Zoo. I squeezed my son, aged six, into the picture and he appeared with Disney and penguins in a score of newspapers.

Walt Disney's 'Band Concert', with Donald Duck the comically rebellious member of the orchestra, was about to be shown. Toscanini, the great conductor, happened to be in London. I dared to invite him to a small first-night party. He came; I enjoyed his enjoyment even more than the film. At the end he said with a deep chuckle to the reporters, 'I too have my Donald Ducks'.

My most successful ploy about Disney, judged by the number of press lines it produced, was a lecture I gave to the English-Speaking Union. David Low, the cartoonist, took the chair and described Mickey Mouse as 'the only public figure in the world today who is universally beloved'. I spoke somewhat drearily about the Disney techniques, but I showed a veritable anthology of his cartoons, perhaps their best showing ever.

Among the film celebrities that it fell to me to entertain was, I am glad to say, Fredric March. He came to London in September 1935 for the opening of 'The Dark Angel'. Vera and I gave a dinner party at Grosvenor House to celebrate its first night. The forty guests included Fredric March and Merle Oberon, the stars of the film, the Laughtons, Raymond Massey, the two Douglas Fairbanks, Noel Coward, Alexander Korda and the top film critics. No, I did not have to pay for this party, but in Clan Meynell fashion I managed to include in it my daughter Cynthia and my niece Alice.

My meeting with Fredric March was a delightful experience. It was his first visit to England and he wanted to see things other than St Paul's and Buckingham Palace. I took him to the 'Prospect of Whitby', then a charming and unspoilt pub on the Thames in the remote East End. And to a cricket match at Lord's. We had our lunch at a neighbouring pub and March told me what a new pleasure it was for him to be in a public place and not to be recognised. At that moment a man came up to him and asked for his autograph. His displeasure—how shall I put it?—was not extreme. He wrote his name in the proffered book. Its owner gasped with disappointment. 'Gorblimey, guvnor,' he said, 'I thought you was 'Erbert Sutcliffe.' (Sutcliffe was the leading all-England batsman, handsome indeed in very much the same way as Freddie March.)

Among the many film acquaintances I made, Fredric March and his wife, Florence Eldridge, became and remain our close friends. We visit them and they visit us. To a post-war party in our country house came an elderly and somewhat dour woman. The next day she confided to me that she thought she had made quite a hit with the famous Freddie. Alas, I knew better. He had told me that his mother had taught him always to seek out the least attractive girl at a party and be specially nice to her.

Douglas Fairbanks Sr. was an engaging character; he was person to person (and that included me), never the great man to his stooge. He noticed the early signs of baldness on my head. 'Why, that's happening to me too. Don't you do something about it?' I told him yes, that I had tried going to a woman who coaxed raw egg into my scalp. Fairbanks was eager for her address. 'It didn't do me any good at all', I told him. 'Perhaps you didn't believe?' he said.

Alexander Korda was a looming figure in the film world. I was introduced to him by H. G. Wells, whose 'Things to Come' Korda was filming. On one of our visits together to the studio we watched the 'rushes' of part of the film, which was directed by Korda's younger brother, recently arrived from Hungary with little knowledge of the English language. One critical sentence of seven words was recorded seven times with the emphasis on a different word each time because the director had no understanding of the intention of the sentence. H.G.'s derision was decisive. On our journey back to town he said: 'I think I must have a Guardian Bungle'.

Arthur Bliss composed music for this film. It included a double fugue to represent the first appearance of the vast and

ceaselessly moving space-machine. 'He ought to have remembered', said H.G., 'that machines of the future will be soundless.'
I ventured to suggest that a composer would find it difficult to
indicate soundlessness by his music.

Everyone at United Artists was in awe of Sam Goldwyn, producer of many films we rejoiced to sell. Of his celebrated tricks of
the tongue I remember: 'A verbal contract isn't worth the paper
it's written on'; 'Include me out'; and his saying 'Bon voyage'
to each of us in the office as his goodbye when he was about to
leave for Hollywood.

Necessarily I had several sessions with the British Board of
Film Censors, then headed by Brooke Wilkinson. From Twentieth
Century Fox I received this typically wordy cable:

WE HAVE IT IN MIND TO MAKE A FILM DEPICTING
THE LIFE OF MARY THE MOTHER OF JESUS WITH
MADELEINE CARROLL IN THE NAME PART STOP
PLEASE ASCERTAIN THE REACTION OF THE BRITISH
BOARD OF FILM CENSORS TO THIS PROJECT STOP

I put the proposition to Brooke Wilkinson. He preferred to
deal in generalities. His answer was: 'If this is to be a religious
play the following rules must be observed: the Divine figure may
appear as a light or a shadow, but otherwise only as an arm—and
not beyond the elbow; there must be no smoking in the cinema;
music must be religious; advertising must be in gothic type.' The
last condition amused me particularly, but I was never to challenge it because the film was not made.

Miriam Hopkins came to England in 1936 on a European
holiday though ostensibly for the première of 'These Three', one
of the best films of that era. I found her a charming as well as a
lovely companion. In life she repudiated the 'hard woman'
character she was often given to act in films. Her tongue could
twist against herself. One night at the Gargoyle I was down to the

last silver coins in my pocket with just enough for the taxi to take first her and then me home. As we went to fetch our coats she noticed the fruit machine. She asked what it was and I told her that it was a quick and silly way of losing money. 'Oh, let me try', she said, and I had to produce a precious half-crown. She pulled the handle and out came three. 'This *is* fun', she said, and put in another. Out came five, and at the next pull three again. Then she had a run of bad luck—two insertions without a win. I tried to persuade her to stop. 'Just one more', she said and out tumbled the jackpot—97 half-crowns. The attendant offered to change the coins into notes. 'Oh no,' said Miriam, 'I want every one of them. When I get to my room at the Savoy I will arrange them on the mantelpiece and in the morning Mary, my maid, will see them and say, "Oh, Miss Hopkins, you *were* busy last night".'

When Bay and I took Miriam out to dinner and then on to dance at the Dorchester we were made to feel like celebrities ourselves because we were followed by boys on bicycles eager for her autograph.

Do I give the impression of little in my film life but parties? That would be very false. The new style of advertising was proving a success, but that did not lessen the effort. A success with one film set a standard for those to come. The English trade papers made much of the new style. One carried an article by me headed 'What film advertising has done to me', balanced by an article headed 'What Francis Meynell has done to film advertising'. This latter was the more generous because it was by Pat Dixon, a man of talent, then engaged in rival film publicity. But what impressed my masters most was the surprising applause of American trade papers. I was, for example, described in *Motion Picture Herald* as the 'poet, publisher and publicist extraordinary' who has 'revolutionized British film publicity'.

In short I was riding high, but it was nevertheless a surprise when Mark Ostrer asked me if I would transfer to his company

Above) F.M.'s cricket team at Greatham *circa* 1925. Standing third from left: William Mellor, hen F.M., Edgar Lansbury, Miles Malleson, A. N. Other, Herbert Simon. Sitting second rom left: Oliver Simon, A. N. Other, my niece Mary Saleeby (now Dr Fisher), John Dallyn Viola's husband). (*Below*) 'Bradfield' at Toppesfield, F.M.'s and Vera's weekend home, photographed for *Homes and Gardens*, February 1934.

*Crown Cement is a name and
a brand justly famous for
over one hundred years—a name
and a brand too proud in
service to suffer itself to
be mischieved or fribbled away.*

THE RUGBY PORTLAND CEMENT CO. LTD.
CROWN HOUSE, RUGBY

(*Left*) Walt Disney, 1935. His 'Peculiar Penguins' had just been released and F.M. took him to the new Penguin House at the Zoo.

as publicity director of the many-sided Gaumont-British
Picture Corporation. I allowed a fatter salary and the prospect of
more power and less work to win me over. I bade farewell to
Murray Silverstone and George Archibald after only thirteen
months with United Artists. Beachcomber in the *Daily Express*
commented 'per ardua ad Ostrer'.

My new employers were the largest film producers in the country
and also the largest cinema owners. The object of my work was the
same as at United Artists, getting the public in, but at different
stages in the chain between producer and public.

My new office was in Cork Street, Piccadilly, where Gaumont-
British put at my disposal a small elegant house. I immediately
set about a considerable reorganisation of the many publicity
activities I was now to be responsible for. G.-B. employed altogether
16,000 people and had a capital of nearly £16,000,000. They had
three film-making studios, many London and provincial cinemas,
their central distribution organisation and also Bush Radio and
Baird Television. Most of these had their own publicity organisa-
tions when I arrived. It was my duty to co-ordinate and supervise
them. A problem was to do it without the hurting of feelings.

In August I announced my new set-up with quite a fanfare of
trumpets in the film press. I would work on newspaper lines: the
separate publicity sections for G.-B.'s many different activities
would be our news-gatherers, our reporters as it were. For the
're-write' sub-editorial function at Cork Street I tempted John
Ware away from the entertainment page of the *Daily Express* and
Rodney Hobson from Siviter's Advertising Agency. I was the
remote approver.

Film production for Gaumont-British was under the care of
Michael Balcon. He was welcoming to me and I went often to see
him at the studios at Shepherds Bush. I was by no means embarrassed by the fact that the only room that could be found for
me there was Jessie Matthews' dressing-room.

Once a week there was a somewhat pompous lunch meeting at the Gaumont-British head office with Isidore Ostrer in titular and Arthur Jarratt (in charge of the cinema side) in vocal command. Isidore Ostrer was head of his family and so head of the business. He was revered by his younger and very efficient brothers. He wrote poetry, which made a private bond between us. Mark Ostrer was an easy companion, but Jarratt I found too much of a know-all. Mark Ostrer had open ears, Jarratt only an open mouth.

A frequent embarrassment was the duty to attend the private first showing of a picture in our own small theatre. The twenty or so people it accommodated usually included some of the film's stars: the time was always after a well-wined lunch and I had difficulty in keeping awake. Fortunately the nodding of my head was apt to wake me; but would not its movement, I wondered, be noticed by those about me? There was one way to safety. When I met my fellow-viewers again I tried to make it clear by jerking movements of my head that this was my usual wide-awake mannerism.

Embarrassment could come from too much as well as too little zeal. Arthur Jarratt arranged a visit to England of Dutch cinema proprietors and I was bidden to welcome them. How better to do this than in Dutch? I submitted my remarks to Gustav Renier (author of *The English: Are They Human?*) and he made a translation for me with phonetic spelling. I learned it by heart and had my pronunciation corrected by him daily on the telephone. As part of my practice I even rang Bay at the Board of Trade, where she was engaged in foreign trade negotiations, to see if my Dutch was good enough to deceive her. She asked me, in slow and careful tones, to hold on until she called an interpreter. My speech to the Dutch film-men caused surprise and pleasure: they did not expect the lazy English to know their tongue. When the formalities were over they thronged about me, talking to me in Dutch. Not a word could I understand or reply.

My new duties included a share in the organisation of some charity first-nights which Queen Mary attended. I was interested to see that as she passed down the row of us welcomers in the foyer under a battery of press cameras, she moved her lips as if she were speaking, but in fact uttered no word. Some of these so-called charity affairs seemed to me rather fraudulent. I composed for myself but for no-one else this undeliverable speech of welcome:

"Your Majesty, my lords, ladies and gentlemen. Those of you who have been dunned into buying expensive tickets for this somewhat drab film which you are about to see will be glad to know that a small proportion of what you have spent will in the end actually go to the charity. This does not often happen, and perhaps the observation is irrelevant on this occasion because most of those to whom I am speaking have not paid for their tickets.

The Gaumont-British Corporation, which has generously given the film, has not got as much publicity out of it as it would like, but at least it can be said that Mr Maurice Ostrer has his photograph in the programme and that Mr Arthur Jarratt regards this, his third presentation on like occasions to H.M. Queen Mary, as yet another step upward in the social scale."

Arthur Jarratt made it. He was knighted in 1946.

Among my responsibilities was publicity for Bush Radio and Baird Television and in my office in Cork Street stood the earliest of television sets designed by Baird. The only receivable picture that I remember was of tennis at Wimbledon. On January 4 1937 we held at the Dominion Theatre the first public exhibition of television on a cinema screen. I wrote to George Bernard Shaw asking him if he would preside and be televised from the back of the hall on this significant occasion. His refusal was decisive. On my letter, which he returned, he scrawled: 'No: damn it: I'm too old. The spectacle would be too revolting. G.B.S.'

My Cork Street organisation did not last many months. There were financial quakes in Gaumont-British and approaches from John Maxwell, the owner of the rival Associated British Picture Corporation. In the autumn of 1936 Maxwell beat Gaumont-British to the post by announcing an agreement between the two film empires which had not in fact yet been finalised. My masters bade me summon the Press to hear a joint and revised statement. It proved to be the most embarrassing press conference of my career. For more than an hour I had to soothe the reporters while Ostrer and Maxwell continued to fight it out off-stage. When at last they appeared they had no more to say than that Maxwell had joined the Board of Gaumont-British. The terms of any further agreement remained—and I am told still remain—unknown. The resulting decline in British film production and the increasing influx of American producers caused Micky Balcon to transfer to Metro-Goldwyn-Mayer. At his farewell lunch I said of him, praisefully and truthfully, that he could think of three things at once and talk of four.

A minor consequence of the new Gaumont-British policy was that six months later an economy programme moved me and my section out of Cork Street into the Gaumont-British main office in Wardour Street. Now in the ramifications of big business I had lost my influence and almost my identity. I was a number on a door and on a telephone extension. I had to tell somebody to tell somebody to do a job: often I could not even see the result of these tellings. In this mood I received a letter from Francis Ogilvy, a stranger to me, asking if I would like to join Mather & Crowther, the advertising agency of which he was managing director. I sought information from Dick Plummer, then advertising manager of the *Evening Standard*. He gave me a hopeful report. It appeared that this old family firm was being rejuvenated, with two policies in amiable conflict. Francis Ogilvy, supported by the chairman, Laurie Mather, was set on improving the style of its advertising, with eyes wide open to the new techniques of market and media research; whereas Gordon Boggon, the vice-chairman, was a master of the old and profitable slap-on-the-back-and-have-another-drink technique.

To Francis Ogilvy's question I gave a cautious answer. An appointment was made. I arrived at the due time and was told that he was 'too busy' to see me. That took me down a bit, but I disguised my annoyance. Francis confessed to me later that this was planned as a test of my equanimity. In his place he had designated his younger brother, David Ogilvy, to show me round the agency. David was twenty-six years old, I was forty-six. Though not yet an *éminence grise*, he was certainly a *curé gris* in the agency—of no authority but great influence. It was he, I learned, who had inspired the original approach to me.

Some months passed before I heard from Mather's after this double inspection. In that interval I was promised by Sir William Crawford, who was then Adviser on Public Relations to the General Post Office, that I could get the Post Office account—quite important financially and very important in prestige—whenever and wherever I wanted it. He had kept me in mind since he had failed to find me a place in his own agency. I mentioned this, naturally enough, when Francis Ogilvy next wrote to me. There followed a quick interview with the chairman and vice-chairman. News of the decision to appoint me to their Board came to me in a romantic telegram:

"The time of the singing of birds is come and the voice of the turtle is heard in our land. David Ogilvy."

My turtle voice was to give me at any rate much pleasure, for I was to share in as well as supervise the copywriting and layout of advertisements. Financially I was at ease: a salary of more than £2,000 plus sundry expenses. Soon I brought into the agency those three men of talent who had already worked with me: Leonard Beaumont, to head a design unit; Marchant Smith, to lead the copy writing section; and Pat Dixon, whose talents—that rare combination of imagination and exactitude—served Mather's well in film and radio advertising until the outbreak of World War II, when he joined the BBC and devised such famous programmes as the Goon Show.

With me came also my Gaumont-British secretary, Kathleen Selby, who became Mather's librarian, and, more predictably, my niece Alice, who had long worked with me at Nonesuch. I was to get as good as I gave. Here in 1939 I first met Pamela Hayman (Zander). She became my secretary at Mather's in 1940 and has been my helpmeet for thirty years—first at Mather's during the war, thereafter at the Cement and Concrete Association, then at Mather's again. In all these years she has been some cells of my brain, almost all my memory, and always the fingers of my hand in the planning of the twenty-three Nonesuch books that have appeared since Nonesuch restarted in 1953.

Characteristically and properly Mather's did not allow me to jump over T. D. Morison, the Media Director, who had been given to understand that he would have the next vacancy on the Board: so I became Tom Morison's junior by some minutes—and this I happily remained for twenty-four years. Tom Morison is the most Scottish Scot I have chanced to know: rich in voice and elegant even in laughter, with an exact, an engineering, mind. When I came to know him well he disclosed to me his secret vice: he wrote poetry. I dissuaded him: his verse was not as good as his tidy prose.

'Greetings telegrams' were a new Post Office adventure and it was my job to make them known. For ninepence you got a festive form, to be hand-delivered in a golden envelope. Even with my 'creative' reinforcements I thought it well to employ a number of eminent designers from outside the agency. I provided the copy, and the early striking layouts were made by Oliver Simon, J. H. Mason, James Shand, McKnight Kauffer, Ashley Havinden and, indeed, Francis Meynell. I printed the designer's name at the foot of each display. For the first time in advertising the 'little art' of pure typography was thus honoured.

An early adventure at Mather's was a summons to a meeting by one of the firm's old clients, J. Sainsbury. Tom Morison and I, the new brooms on the Board, were entrusted with the mission. We presented ourselves confidently to Alan Sainsbury, who with his brother Robert was keeping his admirable enterprise in the forefront of an ever-changing market. Our reception was cool, very cool, and we were elated when after much discussion we came away with instructions to develop a new campaign on the lines I had suggested. Alan told me later that his intention in calling that meeting was to give Mather's the sack. The Sainsburys and I became and remain close personal friends. In business too; for in July 1967 I took part in a Sainsbury–Mather lunch to celebrate forty years of their association.

In composing an advertisement my hope was to use the unusual phrase and display, to attract attention by novelty, by a play on words—a new manner then, though a commonplace of advertising today.

Thus 'Snowfire' cream would serve young women 'for ever and a date'; B.S.A., mysteriously represented by the drawing of a slide-rule, was 'not a mystery but a mastery'. On a bus side we shouted: 'Choose a Kiaora-or-a-Kiaora-or-a-Kiaora.' Two services of the Rugby Portland Cement Company I headlined as a *syzygy*—an eye-catching word doubtless known to you but not to the ordinary.*

David Ogilvy's roving commission took him to the United States for a study of American advertising. He returned with very different views from mine. With some generosity, and even condescension, I arranged that this bright young spark (my junior by twenty years) should meet me in formal debate before the whole

* The O.E.D. definition is 'yoke, pair, copulation, conjunction'.

staff. He overwhelmed me. He had the findings of research, I had only opinions. Part of his thesis was that advertisements were proved by research to be more effective if they were set in crowded small type. He had counted the number of words in a hundred inches of advertisements by our most successful competitor and in a hundred inches of ours: they used 1,500 words, we used 900. As to the methods of approach, the best headline words were 'How to', 'New', 'Price reduced', 'At last', while the best subjects for pictures were, in this order, Sex, Babies, Animals. I did not want to produce 'formula' advertisements. I wanted Mather's to have a face and features of its own... And yet?

David Ogilvy later achieved, and worthily achieved, unequalled personal power and success in advertising the whole world over. When he established his own agency in the United States did he suffer a conversion? Certainly he tailored his formulae to fit particular selling situations; he used them as foundations, not as buildings, and he left himself free to exploit the values of the unexpected. One of the most famous of all advertisements—it was his—is surely that for Rolls-Royce: 'At sixty miles an hour the loudest noise in this new Rolls-Royce comes from the electric clock'. No formula promoted that. In 1963 he wrote his brilliant *Confessions of an Advertising Man*. ('Confessions': surely that should belong to his list of proved magic words?) In the copy he gave me he wrote: 'The older I get, the more I admire you'. I say the same to him.

Mather's in my time abounded in 'characters'. Laurie Mather, the admirable chairman, treated all the staff at any level as his co-workers. The thing I most cherish in my memory of his conduct of the firm was his unvarying probity. The question was always 'Is this true as well as profitable?' An instance: we were offered the rich advertising of a nerve-soothing miracle pill; we had the pill analysed and it was found to be nothing but dressed-up salt; 'No, thank you' was the answer to the makers. Again it was our habit to temper the claims of our clients by making to them the discreet argument that an under-statement was in the end more believable than an over-statement.

Francis Ogilvy had a cosy sense of humour. He seemed always a little embarrassed by his own eloquence. Standing on one leg, with the other wrapped round it, he declaimed lines new to me though already famous in the trade:

> If your client moans and cries
> Try a name-block twice the size.
> If he still should prove refractory
> Insert a picture of his factory.
> Only in the gravest case
> Should you print your client's face.

Today the 'gravest case' seems to occur often, particularly in financial advertisements. Francis Ogilvy's purposive absences from a set occasion with client or staff made his attendances all the more significant. One thing never varied: his devotion to the living English tongue. The Fowler brothers could not have faulted him. When he 'dictated' a letter he was in fact reading from a word-by-word draft hopefully hidden from his secretary. Pamela Zander tells me that when on occasion she had to 'take' his letters his easy eloquence outpaced her meagre shorthand. All was well, for as soon as he left his office she recovered his draft from his waste-paper basket. What is happiest in my memory of Francis? Not his brilliance, not his skill, not his success, but the fact that he was always both immensely vital and intimately kind. Flat words these: and they stand for a man who was something of a mountain.

An utter opposite to Francis was hail-fellow-well-met Gordon Boggon. His stout body and smiling visage and open look (open too was his cocktail cabinet) made me and a host of others feel an easy companionship. He was essentially a generous man: he gave as freely out of his own pocket as he did out of the firm's—and as richly when he was short of money as when he was flush. He had lost a leg in World War I and his tin leg became a part of his personality. He could even take it off with effect. In 1931, when Ramsay MacDonald was campaigning for a National Government, Gordon took the chair at some of the rowdier meetings. He devised a quietening technique. Without his tin leg and supported by crutches he hobbled on to the platform. He knew that no one in the audience would throw things at a one-legged man.

Of my friendships within the agency, a significant one developed slowly but very surely with Stanhope Shelton. He came to Mather's in 1939, just before the war, with a humble account. He himself was not humble; he made it clear to all that he had views of his own about creative work. Francis Ogilvy, quicker than I was to see his potentials, instructed me to give him his head. Of all Ogilvy's decisions this proved to be the most fruitful.

Among our clients Halford Reddish became my kind and continuous friend. Sidney Bernstein, who had gallantly supported in his cinemas my stylistic efforts at Gaumont-British, brought us together. Reddish wanted to safeguard his company name, 'Crown' Cement, for there were rumours of impending regulations which might restrict the use of the word 'Crown'. This gave me the chance to do what I most liked: to use few and odd words set in elegant type within delicate borders. A half-page in the *Financial Times* had this as all its text:

"Crown Cement is a name and a brand justly famous for over one hundred years—a name and a brand too proud in service to suffer itself to be mischieved or fribbled away."

With Alan Sainsbury my friendship was based on a multi-likemindedness: we were both of us socialists. With Halford Reddish it was an attraction of opposites, for he was the complete

Tory. He taught me to be brief in correspondence. Advertising often condones the use of three words where one would do; in the letters that pass between Halford and me we use one word where three would be justified. For him this is a symbol of the elimination of waste, one of his master-creeds; for me it is a much-needed discipline. After the war Halford Reddish was to introduce me to another of my lives.

XV

Clubman

My clubs. That possessive 'my' indicates what clubs were, and (in diminished numbers) doubtless still are, to their members. Of mine the most political was the short-lived '1917', the most affable was the Savile, the most gaitered and gartered was the Athenaeum. There were also the dining assemblies, called clubs but not so in the full sense of the term: the Double Crown, which specialised in typographic matters; the Lucretian, membership of which was limited to 23, all of whom (with one exception who shall be nameless) were and are dignitaries of the arts and sciences; the Half-Hundred, now demised; and the Saintsbury, which still flourishes to indulge in wine and food.

The first of my clubs, the '1917', was a humble open-for-lunch-only meeting-place in Gerrard Street. It was founded by people who today would be called 'Labour Left', and its name was a tribute to the first (Menshevik) Russian Revolution. Most of its members were anti-war, but, that apart, they were almost Irish in their divisions of opinion. After the Bolshevik revolution a pro-Communist group monopolised the 'long table' and made almost a club within a club, a conscious huddle within the muddle. Alfred Bacharach was its leader and Miles Malleson his lieutenant.

Ramsay MacDonald, a founder member and the club's best-known politician, was not welcome at 'the table'. Interesting characters were Henry Nevinson, Charles Laughton, H. N. Brailsford, Raymond Postgate. Bay joined the '1917' before I knew her and when I was no longer a member—a lost chance of an early meeting. The club, tiny and rather unkempt, died before the last war. Its premises now house strip-teasers.

With the Savile Club I had a filial connection; in the early years of the century my father was a member when the club was housed in Piccadilly. In 1947 I took him to its new location in Brook Street. Frank, the old-time head waiter, greeted him with a bow of recognition though he had not seen him for more than thirty years. When he served us with coffee it was with manifest embarrassment that Frank confessed that he could not remember if my father took sugar.

I was proposed for the Savile in 1935. To my surprise I was elected despite my 'disreputable' political past. I indulge now in some name-dropping because a list of my supporters shows the variety of the club's composition. It includes Alan Kingham (civil servant, then honorary secretary for elections), Jack Squire (poet and editor), G. P. Wells (scientist son of H.G.), Alan Barlow (civil servant), A. D. Peters (literary agent), Richard Church (author), A. J. A. Symons (man-of-all-letters), Alec Waugh (author), W. R. Darwin (stockbroker), T. Balston (collector and bibliographer), G. Wren Howard (publisher), J. C. Pritchard (administrator) and R. D. Best (manufacturer).

The Savile is an unpretentious and happy club which lives up to its motto, 'Sodalitas Convivium'. It is characteristic that standard jokes reported to new members are always 'against' the club. One involves Frank again. Long ago he found a £5 note dropped by Rudyard Kipling. Restoring it to Kipling, Frank said 'Lucky for you, sir, that it was not found by a member'. Again: when Savilians were guests of the sartorially smarter Guards Club, one of their members was heard to say of ours: 'It's rather amusin' meetin' these middle-class chaps, but why do so many of 'em make their own trousers?'

Chief of my Savile Club friends was Alan Barlow.* He was ten years my senior and immeasurably wiser in all the fairways and fashions of life. He was for me a synthesis of all Savilian qualities:

* Sir Alan Barlow, Bart., G.C.B. (1881–1968), leading Treasury civil servant and collector of oriental ceramics.

man of the world, of the dining and card tables, of conversation or of appropriate silences, of a knowledge of poetry, and of high distinction as a civil servant.

Of all my friends, in and out of the Savile, Stephen Potter is the most difficult to write about because of the quick changes of mood which gave him a multiple personality. He was demonstratively grateful for the editorial work I gave him at Nonesuch and at times indignant that I didn't give him more. He could be happy about the admiration which I showed for Att, his lovely first wife, and for her paintings, and suddenly angry that she, not he, was the object of my homage.

Only in one particular—an important one to him and to me—was he always equal, gay, easy. That was in our games together over nearly fifty years: tennis, squash, Savile snooker, ping-pong, bridge, 'tishy-toshy'. Here he was indeed my leader as well as my mate. There was our partnership in 'gamesmanship' as well. To an ardent chess-player he boasted once that he and I played mental chess together on our walks. 'Who usually won?' 'Oh, it was very equal', he said. So it was. What we did was to toss for white. Whoever got black immediately resigned.

Sir Thomas Barlow, Alan's elder brother, was a Savile stalwart. Richer than many members, he was in all other respects the ideal Savilian: a fine talker, an unassuming man of public as well as private enterprise, a moderately competent bridge player. To me he was something of a hero, a man of the widest culture and yet with a brilliant business head. He had the best private collection of Dürer prints in Europe and the best collection of Hocks in England. He showed his sense of humour when he rescued me from perplexity. My son Ben was about to go to his first boarding-school and his grandmother expected me to have a guiding talk with him. He already knew the 'facts of life'. What more could I tell him? Tommy Barlow supplied me with just the thing. At his own first party, he said, he was standing alone and very shy, fingering his white tie, when an obvious man-of-the-world came up to him. 'Your first party, I presume?' 'Yes, sir.' 'Then I will give you a piece of advice which will stand you in good stead for the whole of your life. If they serve wine-jelly, and they probably will, help yourself to the knobs. They always make the damn things upside down, and all the wine runs into the knobs.'

Ben was pleased with the story and told it to his headmaster —whose wife, when Vera and I went together to the school, folded her arms at me: 'That was a very selfish story that you told your son', she said. She was not a woman of perspicacity. She insisted that Ben was happy because she had heard him whistling on the stairs—she had apparently never heard of anyone whistling to keep his courage up. We found Ben so miserable that he spent the time of our visit in tears. The remainder of the term was made bearable for him by our kindly friends Norman and Monica Ewer who lived nearby and took him in as a lodger so that he could finish the term as a day-boy. Ben's next school—Beltane—was informal and co-educational and he was completely happy there.

Another Savile character was Alison Russell,* who went faster round the billiards table than anyone except 'Billy Nick'.† Russell's sudden death was a sadness which I committed to verse. This gives, I think, something of a Savile as well as a personal picture, so I print it here.

CLUB EPITAPH

'One diamond', said my partner, and the man on my left,
The onlooker, said in my ear, '*Sad about Russell*'.
'What about Russell?' said I, and to my partner
'One no trumps'. '*He died yesterday. It's on the board.*'
'Two no trumps' from my partner. And I: 'No, no, no.'

* Sir Alison Russell (1875–1948), chairman of many legal committees under the Colonial Office.
† Sir William Nicholson, the painter.

'*Heart failure, boarding the train.*' No, no, no. Not Russell.
The debonaire. The petulant young-old Tory. Who would not
    be compelled by the people
But had imperatively his noblesse oblige. Who disdained
    his Prince
Because he had not shaved to receive the Zulu chiefs.
Who had never lost his youth or found his heart's desire.
Who walked faster than any man but never broke a queue—
(Hearts, yes!) Who went the round of the billiard table
As if it would whisk away in fifteen minutes. Who waltzed
Strauss waltzes most uncomically. Who partitioned Palestine
Against all prejudice, his own the utmost, because that
    was cricket.
Judge, athlete and aesthete, passionate painter, legal
    draftsman in love
(Boasting that he loved it) with the comma and, more,
    with the colon
That promissory *in aeternum*; anathematising the full stop.
Dandy painted by Orpen and able to look at himself
In the portrait, in the mirror, in the mirror, in the portrait
Morning by morning for fifty years with a candid recognition.
My most unlikely friend.

'But partner, the heart on the table! Can't you count?
    The heart was good!'
So it was. I am sorry. So it was—till the last violent flurry.

When this appeared in the *Sunday Times* it brought me many
letters of praise. No, not of my poem but of Russell himself. And
one correction: the portrait was not by Orpen—though he was a
Savilian—but by an artist whose name I cannot now remember.

Alan Barlow proposed me for the Athenaeum. I was gratified,
as I reported to my father, by my election early in World War II.

PEACE ON EARTH AND MERCY MILD TWO FOR A WOMAN & ONE FOR A CHILD

New Year card 1937 designed by Leonard Beaumont for Vera Meynell and F.M. *à propos* Franco's bombings in the Spanish Civil War.

(*Above*) Reading the news at Talloires of Franco's insurrection in 1936. Photograph taken by Stephen Potter shows, left to right: Bay Kilroy, Evelyn Sharp (Baroness Sharp), Bay's sister Angela (Mrs Rendle), F.M., Mary (Att) Potter. (*Below*) Cobbold's Mill, our home from 1945 to 1967.

I made journeys there on my bicycle. It was, however, a little too highbrow and ecclesiastical for my complete liking though its steak-and-kidney pie was the best in London.

Björn Prytz, the Swedish Minister in London during the war, was one of our closest friends and he too belonged to both the Savile and the Athenaeum. It was our habit when we had dined out together to go to the Athenaeum for the midnight war news. When it was closed for the staff holiday we could use the 'Senior', immediately opposite. There on a critical night in the war we went, eager for news. The 'Senior's' hall porter looked us up and down with a grave condescension: 'From the Athenaeum, gentlemen, I presume? There is a member of *yours* prostrate upon *our* stairs'. There was. We knew him well and we carried him to a taxi and saw him to his home.

Barnett Freedman, the admirable and charming artist and illustrator, a Jew and a cockney, was newly returned from a war-artist job as a Major in the Marines when he was elected to the Athenaeum. He told me of his first visit. 'I thought I'd be out of me depths there, and so did me taxi-driver. When I said "Athenaeum, please, mate" he looked at me unbelieving-like and said, "What, *you*?"'

The Double Crown Club, born in 1924, is a fraternity of experts in the several crafts of printing. It was Oliver Simon's brain-child and the *accoucheurs* were Hubert Foss and my cousin Gerard Meynell. We meet at dinner four times a year. We are professionals meeting as amateurs, and the exhaustion of many subjects for discussion has not robbed our fellowship of charm and dignity, of learning and even love. Though tradesman and artist meet artist and tradesman at club dinners—publishers, printers, binders, typographers, illustrators, papermakers—it has always been anathema that private business should be sought or even talked.

There is the same fixed but easy formality at each of the dinners: a president who comments on the appearance of the menu (designed and often printed at his own expense by a member), a reading of the names of the guests, and then a learned address and consequent argument.

Holbrook Jackson was the first president of the club, and fulfilled a much more important function as its dinner secretary until his death in 1948. A pioneer and patron the stylistic revival of commercial printing (he gave orders to and boostings of the Pelican Press), he became a most learned and readable writer, in some two dozen volumes about authors, printers and illustrators of books.* He had the presence of a prosperous business man, full stature, confident posture (despite his asthma), correct-for-the-occasion attire. I was fond as well as admiring of him, and I looked forward to singing his praises to his face at a Double Crown lunch in honour of his seventy-fourth birthday. Alas, that day proved to be his death-day, and my speech became an obituary.

I doubt whether any other member talked as much as I did in the early years of the club—occasionally as president or chairman or address-giver, but chiefly as argufier. In 1926 I was asked to speak at the eighth annual dinner when Eric Gill was to open the discussion on the artist's function in book production. I refused: 'The letter I deserved and expected from *you* was: "I am directed to ask you whether you will refrain from speaking . . ."'

A collection of Double Crown menus and invitations would make a notable anthology of graceful yet sprightly 'occasional' printing over nearly five decades. In 1930 the great type-designer Rudolf Koch was guest speaker and my friend Elmer Adler, the American typographer, was also a guest. The very elaborate menu which I designed and printed was, I think, my best-looking

* In *The Printing of Books* (Cassell, 1938) he found a place for me among my peers, devoting a whole chapter to my work as a typographer. It was not all praise: he scolded me, justly, for my omission of the original footnotes in my Kauffer-illustrated edition of Burton's *Anatomy of Melancholy*.

Double Crown contribution, but I had reason to break the habit of naming the designer; a tipped-in notice confesses that 'the incompetent and careless designer' had made a mistake in recording (happily not in announcing) the date of the dinner. Koch himself had one anxiety: he told me that he possessed no dinner jacket. I assured him that in special deference to him we too (who in fact never 'dressed') would wear day clothes. Everything went well: the speech, the food and wine, the questions and commentary.

When it was my turn to be lecturer or president I did not find it easy to be both recondite and bright, as the listeners—learned, vocal and wine-inspired—expected; but since few of them survive to correct me I will assert that I was always a success. Certainly I look now with unmixed pleasure at the relevant menus. Edward Bawden greeted my presidency in 1928 with leg-pulling versions of the devices of the Pelican Press and the Nonesuch Press. In 1933 I was asked to speak about my work at Nonesuch. The menu, designed by Holbrook Jackson, showed silhouette portraits, by Ernest Potuczek and Edwin Hunter, of the president (John Johnson, Printer of the Oxford University Press), of the designer and of me. Ernest Ingham put them in their delicate flowered surrounds. For my paper on 'Art Jargon', twenty years later, Barnett Freedman illustrated the menu with comic 'Portraits' of some real and some imaginary art critics.

Double Crown dinners have almost always been held at Kettners, where the club has been admirably served. Prices? Without wine, dinners have cost members 10s. 6d. in early years, 16s. in the 'fifties, thereafter proceeding to 20s., 23s., 30s., and 40s. (December 1969) for a shorter meal—a progression which shows with what care the committee counts the coins of its members. For its continued combination of orderliness and gaiety the Double Crown owes much to Desmond Flower. Besides his virtues as occasional president and lecturer, he has acted as dinner secretary for more than twenty years. Of the club's original members there survive only four: Christian Barman, Geoffrey Keynes, Herbert Simon and myself; but the intent of its founders flourishes still in its seventy members.

The Saintsbury Club meets twice a year on the birthdays of Shakespeare and of George Saintsbury, writer and wine-bibber. The rendezvous is Vintners Hall; there is good food and superlative wine (mostly the gift of members) and a formal literary address. Some thirty-five years ago the address was given by the portly Hilaire Belloc. He arrived pent-up in a much too small dinner-jacket borrowed at the last minute from A. D. Peters, his literary agent: he hadn't realised that Saintsbury dinners were black-tie affairs. Duff Cooper, proposing Belloc's health, stumbled through the first half-dozen lines of his *Heroic Ode in Praise of Wine*. Belloc prompted him and then challenged him to complete the poem. Whereupon Duff Cooper recited, indeed declaimed, the whole poem—all of its 250 lines. He splashed and poured its richness about us. I have since wondered whether the early hesitation was deliberate to make the later flow more impressive.

Belloc's speech was for him unusually and frankly anecdotal. Its climax was such that I remember every word of it: 'And when at last I am called to the Kingdom of my Heavenly Father, Sir, I shall say, I have forgotten the name of the village, I have forgotten the name of the girl, but [and his voice became resonant] the wine was Chambertin'.

One other memory I have of Hilaire Belloc and wine. I had the excited pleasure of lunching with him when I was still in my 'teens. Talk was, inevitably, about wine. I had lately saved up to buy a single cheap bottle of claret, my first wine investment, and I waited my chance to make a casual-seeming reference to this. Belloc said, rattling the French r's that he cherished: 'A *bottle*? A single bottle, did you say? My boy, always buy yourr wine by the barrrell'.

Once only have I been in the chair at a Saintsbury Club dinner and once only have I given the address. Any Saintsbury member was allowed a single guest; the address-giver was allowed two. Mine for this occasion were Alan Barlow and Ernest Pooley; Björn Prytz had brought with him Prince Bertil of Sweden; M. Cartier, the Belgian Ambassador, had as his guest M. Spaak. But it was towards Percy Fender, the Surrey and England cricketer, whom I had so often admired at a distance, that I anxiously looked to see if now *he* was watching *me*.

André Simon was the honorary cellarer of the Saintsbury Club and an expert in the wine trade. To him I appealed when I was invited by Bay to a New Year party at her flat in the early 'thirties. I knew that she would be unlikely to provide much in the way of alcohol—it was only recently that she had progressed from tea to beer at her parties—and I wanted to impress. I decided to take with me not a mere bottle, not even a magnum, but an imperial (eight bottles in one) of champagne. Even André Simon said it was doubtful if he could find an imperial at short notice. Find one he did, and he warned me to be very careful how I carried it since the glass was no stronger than the glass of an ordinary bottle and the explosive power of the champagne very much greater.

In the taxi I wrapped it in my coat and held it between my feet, turning my head away at every bump in the road. At midnight the party assembled with expectant glasses. I begged people to stand clear, then dewired the cork and expected an immediate up-thrust, a euphonic explosion, of the wine. Nothing happened. I shook the bottle. Nothing happened. I banged it on the floor. Nothing happened. Finally we had to knock its head off with a hammer... Nevertheless the champagne was full of fizz and worthy of Simon's recommendation.

It was in André Simon's *Wine and Food Quarterly* that I read an article on 'The Pleasures of Dining Alone'. My own view, and his, is that shared pleasures are far the best, but how pleasing if not persuasive I found the sentence: 'When one dines alone it is

[245]

surprising how often the bottle comes round'. André Simon invited me to an august wine-tasting at the Jardin des Gourmets in 1935. There were eight of us, supposedly claret-connoisseurs all. Our object was to determine whether 1924 was likely to prove a great year for claret. The consensus was that it had a fine future as well as a beguiling present. Two by two, eight significant clarets were put before us. I was relieved to find that my own preference for the Château Brane-Cantenac was shared by André Simon. Ordinarily one doesn't drink a red wine with fish. To make this possible a noble dish was devised: salmon with a red (Chambertin) sauce.

I wrote a foreword to André Simon's book *The Art of Good Living*,* in which he was practical in terms of food and drink and I more word-conscious. It gave me my chance of putting into print the campaign I had already waged at many restaurants where I had returned to the kitchen fish described on the menu as 'sole' but which proved to be lemon sole, dab sole, ditchfish sole or some qualification of sole. I object even to the adjectival 'Dover' sole. A sole is a sole is a sole. Leave any adjective, say I, to the soft and flabby substitutes. This misnaming of sole never happened at the Ivy under Monsieur Abel. It was my favourite restaurant, but it was years before I could get recognition (which meant a well-placed table) there. I took to wearing queer ties and to stuttering. Still I was not remembered. Then one day I said: 'I shall sign the bill, not pay it. You can open an account for me'. There were consultations and scrutinies. From then on I was recognised. Victor Gollancz had a more masterful way with him. At the end of a meal he hurried out, saying to the waiter, 'Sign the bill for me'.

In 1937 Jack and Molly Pritchard founded the 'Half-Hundred', which they nicknamed the Poor Man's Wine and Food Society. It had some pleasant rules. Wives were not allowed to propose their husbands for membership nor husbands their wives, though both

* Michael Joseph, 1951.

could be elected if separately proposed. There was an impoliteness
fine of 2s. if a member failed to give notice of his absence from one
of the monthly meals. A member must plan, and if he please may
cook, at least one dinner; and its cost must not exceed 5s. a head
for food with another 5s. for wine.

The members were word-wise as well as food-wise—among them
Philip Harben, Wells Coates, Julian Huxley, the Dick Russells
and Raymond Postgate, who with his *Good Food Guide* has
done so much to raise the standard of hotel cooking in England
—an odd achievement for a classical scholar, historian and novelist. He has invented for himself the name by which he does *not*
want to be remembered: 'the English Stomach'. No, he prefers to
be thought of as translator of the *Agamemnon* of Aeschylus.

Philip Harben, broadcaster and writer about food, had a mis-
print in one of his books* that actually emphasised his meaning:
'Once the cake is in the oven it begins to rise. This is a critical
time . . . until that crisis is past the cake should be left undisturbed
in the oven. Don't keep peeing in to see how it's getting on.' Was
it an 'r' or a 'p' that was missing?

In another of his books† Harben did me the honour of a quotation: 'That great epicure Francis Meynell once told me of his
cooking method, "I throw in everything in sight". It is courage
of this sort that produces some of the world's finest dishes.' Well!

Alan Barlow, my patron in so many ways, got me accepted as a
member of the Lucretian Club. Its limit of twenty-three members
was characteristic of both its science and its whimsicality, for this
number was established by the gloriously irrelevant fact that 23
is the atomic weight of sodium.

In my time there were four dinners a year, and at each a learned
—a really learned—address was given. Here indeed I was out of
my depth, but the waters were made amiably smooth by the

---

* *The Way to Cook* (The Bodley Head, 1945).
† *Cooking Quickly* (The Bodley Head, 1946).

kindness of such fellow-members as Alan and Thomas Barlow, Cecil Carr, Edward Salisbury, Charles Darwin, Bernard Ashmole, William Holford, Maurice Dean, Hugh Casson, Halsbury and Trenchard Cox. I was only a listener, often an uncomprehending listener. Any member who does not attend one of the eight dinners in two years is reckoned to have resigned. And so, after more than twenty instructive years, and very sadly, I resigned when I left London. I had made one small but welcomed contribution: the printing of the list of members and rules.

Am I a snob? Honestly, no—not since my childhood, despite my obvious enjoyment in name-dropping. And I have one piece of evidence to offer. When I retired to the country and the distance as well as lessened income made my membership of two London clubs nonsensical, it was from the august and regnant Athenaeum, not from the familiar Savile, that I chose to resign.

XVI
London's Burning

Despite my profound absorption with my changes of loves and lives in the years between the wars, I never lost my feeling for the politics of the left, my concern for the betterment of the then Ill-fare State. My political gestures were made, I fear, as much to quieten my own conscience as in the hope of influencing anyone. They were in general feeble and futile. When Ramsay MacDonald was in process of forming the first Labour administration I sought him out and said, 'Do demonstrate at once the difference between Labour and the old political parties by announcing a reduction in the salaries of Cabinet Ministers'. He said, 'It will be my care to show how like we are to previous governments, not how unlike'.

During the General Strike in 1926 Vera and I drove hundreds of miles as couriers of the Trades Union Congress: I think some of our missions were invented simply to get rid of us from strike headquarters.

In 1927 we were holidaying in Yugoslavia. At our little café table on the sea-front at Spalato I opened a few-days-old English newspaper. It reported the execution in the United States of Sacco and Vanzetti, allegedly for murder but in reality for their Socialist activities. Near to us were seated groups of sailors from an American battleship in the harbour. I stormed over to their tables and shouted the foul news. They were unmoved. After a few minutes of my haranguing one of them asked me to say the names again. Then: 'Any of you fellows ever heard of those guys?' he asked. One way and another they made it clear that they had not. I turned unhappily away.

Ten years later Vera and I, estranged in every other way, made a tiny political gesture together—on a New Year card. The inscription was: 'In the hope of a more peaceful and Dictatorless year'. The Guernica and other bombings by Franco's Spanish fascists were in our minds. We reproduced a drawing by Leonard Beaumont of a torrent and torment of falling bombs and faced it with this text:

> Peace on earth and mercy mild:
> Two for a woman and one for a child.

I argued on relevant and irrelevant occasions that Hitler should be stopped by force from entering the Ruhr in 1935. I was a vociferous supporter of sanctions against Mussolini's invasion of Abyssinia. Like most leftists, I became disillusioned with Stalin's Russia.

In 1935 I let it be known at Labour Party headquarters that I would like to find a parliamentary seat if my political past did not in their view debar me. Herbert Morrison was precisely reassuring on this point. Soon I received a letter from the Labour Party agent of the Yardley Division of Birmingham, asking if I would like my name to go forward for consideration as their candidate. I felt bound to remind them of the fact that I had once been a member of the Communist Party, that I was a very busy man in the film industry, that I lived remotely so that I could not spend much time in the constituency. That was, not surprisingly, the end of that. Was I half-hearted in my approach? I think so, but I wanted to believe that I had not deserted politics, but that politics had deserted me.

Refugees from Hitler's Germany seeking asylum here in the 'thirties had to have English sponsors. People of all political colours and creeds helped, but above all the Quakers. In Germany and Austria even children had to wear badges to distinguish them from German super-men. Train-loads of these Jewish children arrived at Victoria Station to be met by their new foster-parents here; a boy of eight was sponsored by Bay's family.

I was asked by a young Jewish art student already in England if

I would stand sponsor for his mother, who was still in Hitler-land. Vera agreed. Through the Society of Friends the lady in question, Mrs Elsa Fabian, was told that she might come to us. She wrote a grateful letter of reply. To my surprise a little later I received another letter of gratitude from Mrs Fabian in a different hand and from a different address; and then another. I assumed that she had had to move about Germany to be sure of her escape and had repeated her intention to come to us in carefully disguised handwriting. This surmise was quickly confounded. The Society of Friends reported that they had made a little error. Three Mrs Fabians, no less, one with two children, had been told that we would welcome them. All three had parted with their homes. There was nothing for it but to agree to accommodate them all. They came to our house at Toppesfield. They were of different social classes; it was not an easy admixture. In the country, gossip abounds and now too there were spy scares. Soon I was visited by a police sergeant: 'You got a lot of German friends here, haven't you, sir?' I assented. Then came his trick question: 'This Hitler, he ain't really a bad chap, is he, sir?' He was startled by the vigour of my reply.

Bay was in the department of the Board of Trade which vetted entry applications from refugee industrialists. She tells me that everyone stretched the regulations to the limit. This was on practical as well as on humanitarian grounds. Often an applicant's particular skills were correctly judged to be able to foster employment in our depressed 'Special Areas'. The new industries they brought have enriched both the local and national economy—a repetition of what refugees from the Low Countries did at the end of the fourteenth century for our wool trade.

For my part, I was able to be of use to two German typographical designers. I have already told how Stanley Baldwin made possible Berthold Wolpe's entry into England. Thus I was one of the sponsors for his settling in this country. Elizabeth

Friedlander, notable calligrapher and designer of a type-face, had reached England by way of Italy, but without any suitable job. She came to see me at Mather's and became an important influence in our art department.

Two widely spaced invitations gave me my chance to snap at the English admirers of both Hitlerite Germany and Stalinist Russia. In December 1936 I wrote to 'The Anglo-German Fellowship':

"I have received your invitation to a dinner in honour of the Nazi Ambassador. I do not willingly consort with people who persecute democrats, exile intellectuals and bait Jews, or with their agents: and I would not willingly consort with Herr von Ribbentrop."

And when Stalin died the 'Society for Cultural Relations with the U.S.S.R.' invited me to join in a message of 'profound condolences to the Soviet Government and people in their great sorrow at the death of Stalin'. I replied:

"I tend to mourn a little for the death of anyone at all, but for Marshal Stalin's death less than for anybody's in the world. And I don't see what, dead or alive, he has to do with cultural relations between peoples."

Despite the illusions of Chamberlain's 'peace with honour' in September 1938, there was suddenly feverish trench-digging in the parks in London and the issue of gas masks for all. War was on its inevitable way. Bay's father tried to dissuade her and Evelyn Sharp from buying the lease of a house in London, since, he said, they would be paying for what might soon become a 'smoking ruin'. Nevertheless, with open eyes they took possession of 19 Cliveden Place, an amiable mid-Victorian house, halfway between Eaton Square and Sloane Square, with easy access to the government departments in which they worked.

On the day that Chamberlain announced that we were at war, I was very much *en familles* (note the plural) at the cottage at

Greatham with my first wife Hilda and my daughter Cynthia, and with my second wife Vera and our nine-years-old son Ben, whom I had met at Southampton at the end of their sharply cut-off holiday in France. We listened together to Chamberlain's even tones. Peace-lovers all, we nevertheless shared a solemn thankfulness that there was to be no last-minute retreat. I had never been a pacifist in the full Quaker sense: my stand in World War I was far more political than religious. Now I had no religion and the political issues were utterly different. So were my convictions. This was neither a conversion nor (as a few of my pacifist friends saw it) a perversion. Now there was no glory-sentiment, no plan of aggrandisement, nothing at all of 'my country right or wrong'; as I saw it, England had become a partisan of humanity.

That evening I kept a dinner date with Alan Barlow, then Under Secretary at the Treasury. Of all my friends he was nearest to the seat of power and knowledge. Our talk was, of course, wholly of the war. He told me that it would be a long one. In mitigation of our solemnity he offered me a cigar. I told him that I hadn't smoked for two years. 'Don't be a fool,' he said, 'you may never again be offered a Havana.' I fell, and fallen I have remained.

I did not meet Bay until late that night. After a day's work on the setting up of an emergency import control by the Board of Trade, she had spent the Saturday night with her parents in the country. On the fateful Sunday she was due to resume that work. She was driving a Board of Trade colleague back to town when the first siren sounded. They went into the air-raid shelter at a garage on the Great West Road. She told me that her main thought was that she didn't know her companion well enough to wish to die with him.

I realised that there would still be many men, including the Quakers, who in utter good faith would repudiate the war. Meetings were arranged for conscientious objectors to rehearse their intended statements to the tribunal they would have to face. I helped in those 'mock trials', using my First War experience.

Vera now took Benedict from London to Cambridge. A wise move, for later our house in Woburn Square was destroyed by a bomb. They could not comfortably go to our house at Toppesfield because it was fully occupied by the Fabian families, who now, as enemy aliens, were subject to an official standstill for six months. Cambridge provided schooling for Ben and friends for Vera. George Macy persuasively offered them shelter in the United States, but Vera went no further than the getting of visas. Moyna Macgill, Edgar Lansbury's widow, was able to take their children, I helping with a little money and much advice: the stage and television in the United States were to benefit years later through the talents of the children—Angela and her brothers.

Bay accepted me in her half of 19 Cliveden Place. There I stayed with her for the whole of the war. It was an indescribable comfort for both of us that we should be together.

I was forty-eight, too old and, I suspect, too cowardly to make a good soldier. (Later, because of my age, I failed to make even the Board of Trade Home Guard.) What, then, could I do? My one appropriate skill was in propaganda. The Ministry of Information was manned by brilliant writers who had no notion of the essential techniques of informing and persuading public opinion. To Nevil Rucker, an acquaintance who was Chamberlain's Private Secretary, I wrote about one of its bulletins which began 'The Ministry of Information is officially informed that', etc. This, I pointed out, was as convincing as if an advertisement said, 'The advertising agency is told by the manufacturers that . . .' Other valid points I made, partly to correct nonsenses, partly in the hope of being given a place in the Ministry. Rucker replied, 'We all recognise that the Ministry has not got properly going yet' . . . I heard no more. Duff Cooper, an old and easy acquaintance, became the third Minister of Information in 1940. I appealed to him. A pleasant interview was all that followed—Duff could never be anything but pleasant.

Harold Nicolson was now in the Ministry. I asked him whether it was my political history that kept me out. He assured both me and Dick Plummer, who intervened to help me, that the Ministry 'did not pay much attention to the Communist record of people who are now anxious to beat Hitler. In fact, we are now trying to get people like Joad and John Strachey to speak on the wireless'. Even so that didn't let me in.

My last try was through Eddie Marsh. In his reply I was, I saw with pleasure, still his 'Dearest Francis', though we had not seen each other for some years: 'Dearest Francis, I am writing to a broad-minded friend of mine at the M.O.I. I hope good may come of it'. Eddie's friend was Leigh Ashton, from whom came an honest statement: 'Nobody seems to want to have him here. . . It is pretty generally known that he goes about complaining of the shortcomings of the Ministry. That is never the best approach'. Indeed it is not, and I was a fool not to have realised it long before.

I turned to other Ministries. As an occasional pre-war broadcaster, I had met John Reith, the admirable first Director-General of the then compact BBC. In 1940 he was Minister of Works. I went to see him, arguing that he needed an Information Officer and that I was the man for the job. He showed no interest—either in me or indeed in his Ministry. Something else was on his mind. The mounting emphasis of his talk was about his qualifications to be our Ambassador in Washington. He strode up and down, showing me what was, in a purely literal sense, his two-facedness. When he passed me in one direction I saw that his expression was sensitive and mild; my hope was a little encouraged. When he went the other way, his profile was stern, set, unmoved; and I felt that I hadn't any chance at all. Slowly I realised that the set expression was due to the facial wound he had suffered in the

First War. Finally a gentle and abstracted handshake was my dismissal.

I had another string to pull. Ernest Bevin, old-time socialist warrior, was now Minister of Labour. I had known him first in happy agreement and then in sad controversy during my *Daily Herald* days. I was allowed a formal interview at the Ministry. Clearly Bevin had not realised who it was he was committed to see. His astonished greeting was ' *You*, my boy?' (I was nearly fifty and only ten years his junior.) 'What! *You*, my boy?' Then a burst of his wide laughter and another dismissive handshake.

Though for myself I could find no place in wartime propaganda I could for two of my friends. Zoë Farmer, introduced to me by Sidney Bernstein, had the task of recruiting suitable people for propaganda abroad. She accepted my recommendation of Elizabeth Friedlander and Stanhope Shelton, both working at Mather and Crowther. He was sent to Cairo and did brilliantly for Military Intelligence. And for himself; for there he met and later happily married Irène Lefèvre, who combines with all her charm a precise intellectual and independent mind.

Despite my failure to find a place in the Ministry of Information it was my luck to conduct the Government main 'Home Front' campaign. Food rationing was very severe, its processes had to be explained, and, most important, its pains had to be modified as much as possible by the best use of the little that was available. Howard Marshall, a Savile Club friend of mine, was Head of Information at the Ministry of Food. He asked me if Mather's would suggest a plan of campaign. What was needed was the publication week by week of recipes tied always to changing supplies. We looked for a confidence-commanding banner headline. Stanhope Shelton proposed just that: 'Food Facts'. I took the first draft advertisement to Lord Woolton, who was Minister of Food. I had prepared myself for a recondite sales talk. He looked at the draft and lay-out with the eye of the experienced salesman that he had lately been. Then he held up his hand to stop my sales-patter and said, 'You've hit it. That's just what we need'.

Woolton, whose frequent pomposity and affected speech disguised a most competent administrator, suggested that he and I should meet once a week at lunch. His engagements and mine in the event reduced these occasions to perhaps half-a-dozen a year. At the first of them he was my guest at the Ecu de France. Wisely, I had an exploratory lunch there the day before. Against strict regulation they offered me rolls of bread. I let the maître d'hotel have it good and proper. The sumptuary rules were obeyed next day and thereafter.

There was joy at Mather's. This account was a life-line to the agency, whose business had been whittled down by the war. We made 'Food Facts' into an expert economy cookery guide, with phrases that were usually colloquial and sometimes persuasively vulgar. This induced a vast and helpful correspondence from readers. One good lady submitted an economical recipe based on onions, at that moment in easy supply. We quoted it gratefully, and to give her credit I added 'Mrs Tucker knows her onions'. This phrase brought a still-cherished letter which reminded me that England was still Old-England.

"Mrs Tucker is always pleased to be of small use to everyone; but she is deeply distressed at the notice of herself in various newspapers today. She has the *Daily Telegraph*. She is a gentlewoman of very distinguished birth, and she has no idea of such a very vulgar expression as 'knows her onions' being in use, and it pains her deeply. The King's English is degraded and Mrs Tucker is degraded also. She will avoid writing in future."

But her desire 'to be of small use to everyone' broke down that resolve forthwith, for her letter ends with two more recipes . . . Dear Mrs Tucker, my smiles are truly respectful.

Occasionally we broke into doggerel. When there was precious little bacon:

> Aunt Mary threw her rinds away;
> To the lock-up she was taken.
> There she is and there she'll stay
> Till she learns to save her bacon.

Even potatoes had to be cherished:

> Those who have the will to win
> Eat potatoes in their skin—
> Knowing that the thought of peelings
> Gravely hurts Lord Woolton's feelings.

We did in fact do well on the food front over the war years. In the less public-spirited days after the war, with rationing still necessary, the Ministry commissioned one of those mysterious readership surveys. The number of housewives 'likely to have used the recipes' in a particular advertisement was reckoned even then to be more than 150,000.

'Food Facts' advertising, the biggest Government account, could not in justice stay for ever with Mather's alone. In due course it was shared with two other agencies. This enlarged our weekly meetings at the Ministry as well as our ideas. When the one-hundredth 'Food Facts' appeared I was given a proof of it flatteringly inscribed to me by Woolton and, amongst others, by Sir Henry French (the Ministry's Permanent Secretary), Howard Marshall, Evelyn Forbes (a constant copywriter) and the heads of the other two agencies. 'Editor-in-Chief' they named me; and this I remained not only through the war but as late as 1948.

By the early spring of 1940 the 'phoney' war was coming to an end. I was one of the little people of England who in our millions

wanted to get rid of Chamberlain. On May 7 I sent a telegram to
R. A. Butler (our local M.P. in the country):

"Urge you put country before political friendships and oust
old gang of bus-missers."

To the doubters at the Savile who said 'But who else is there?'
I replied, 'Anyone at all. The doorman at Claridges'.

On May 10, the day that Hitler invaded the Low Countries,
Winston Churchill became Prime Minister.

On May 28 Alan Barlow dined with us at Cliveden Place. The
news was bad: the Dutch had surrendered and Belgian, French and
British troops were being pressed back towards the coast. 'We
are keeping back the worst news,' said Alan, who must have fore-
seen Dunkirk. I told him that H. G. Wells had said to me, 'I do
not believe in invasion because I believe in arithmetic. They cannot get enough men over here to be worth their while.' Alan disagreed. He told me that the East Anglian bridges were already
mined and a great deal of defensive flooding had been done. We
had seen concrete 'tank traps' on our major roads. They were not
always what they seemed. Bay and I, driving to London from
Toppesfield in a fierce wind, saw one that had been blown over: it
was made of well-disguised canvas.

This was a time when everything was being tried, however
fantastic: Gordon Waterfield, a close friend of ours who had lived
in Egypt and could speak Arabic, found himself in his late thirties
removed from the BBC, trained in Scotland as a commando—he is
a man of strong but unsoldierly build—and despatched to Egypt
carrying a suitcase of poisoned arrows and sticks of gelignite with
instructions to blow up a certain railway bridge and to distribute
the arrows to tribesmen. When he got to Cairo he found that the
military command on the spot wanted to preserve the bridge and
that tribesmen expected guns, not arrows.

Bay and I, for our part, were full of ideas and inventions for the
defence of England, and Alan Barlow even undertook to send

some of them to 'those concerned'. Bay had an idea for a flying minefield; my favourite proposal was about petrol storage tanks. The current plan was to set them on fire if they were likely to fall into enemy hands. My scheme was instead to put sugar into them so as to gum up the carburettors of invading vehicles. This would mean not a mere denial of petrol but an actual counter-attack. How had I come by this notion? When I was driving for the T.U.C. during the General Strike in 1926, sugar was once dropped into my car's petrol tank; carburettor, feed-pipes, the tank itself had all to be dismantled and cleaned.

Munitions and other war supplies required the transfer of labour from the normal consumer-goods industries. The Board of Trade set up a new section to achieve this. Laurence Watkinson was put in charge of this and he had to find premises. A portion of the A.A. headquarters at Fanum House in Leicester Square was requisitioned. He had to find people: he appealed to university dons to serve as clerks during the long vacation. Bay, his junior colleague and admirer, introduced me to Watkinson. Was this my chance after my many frustrations? Would he accept me as a pseudo-don? He did, for he knew that the effects of the restrictions needed watching and that I had market-research experience. When his letter came I bought a new fountain-pen and wrote on a large virgin sheet of paper over and over and over again 'Francis Meynell, Civil Servant'. Quickly I possessed myself of that badge of office, the civil servant's briefcase, a little dingy but ample, designed (I am told) more than a hundred years ago to carry not only papers but two bottles of port.

My joyful pride was doubtless due in part to my love of Bay and my admiration of her devoted skill in her work; but over all was the sense that now I was at last held acceptable by Authority ('Establishment' was not then the vogue word), which I had so long resisted but in this war wished wholly to serve.

In fact my new appointment was soon in jeopardy. Murmuring

something about knowing my political past Sir William Brown, the Civil Service head of the Board of Trade, told Watkinson that I was to go as soon as the early problems of the section had been solved. An indignant Watkinson suggested that the Board of Trade owed me at least a letter of thanks. His first draft for Brown's signature was returned as over-warm. He made his second even more effulgent. The file happened to reach the President, Sir Andrew Duncan, who knew me well in business and at the bridge table. He minuted: 'I wish Mr Meynell to continue with his work'. That was decisive.

Mather's and the Board of Trade came to flexible terms. I was to give the Board of Trade as much time as was necessary for my job there; Mather's were to continue as my paymasters and I was to remain as Director of their Creative Department with a special responsibility for 'Food Facts'. Pamela Zander, now my secretary at Mather's, guarded my door and my desk from all but essential callers and business.

My years of service under Watkinson ('Wattie', as he was known to all) convinced me, as Bay and many of his colleagues were convinced, that he did more than any other man on the home front to make possible the winning of the war. Practically all the controls over civilian goods other than food were invented and set up by him. Besides being an exact administrator, he was a remarkable and courageous innovator who knew exactly when not to consult his superiors; he tells me that he still shudders to remember that he launched the import licensing department just before the outbreak of war without first consulting the Treasury, the Cabinet Office, or even his own Permanent Secretary. Short, bright-eyed, confidential-voiced, utterly unpompous, with no vestige of the expected Civil Service aura of public school, university and club, he had the capacity to make all his staff, including cleaners and messengers, feel that they were valued individuals, all necessary to the smooth working of the department.

On my first day as a civil servant at Fanum House I was a wishful-to-learn intruder at a deputation that Bay was receiving from angry hosiery manufacturers who were now subject to restrictions in their home market. Bay could not give the main reason for the policy—to release labour for munitions—because as usual Wattie had acted before getting approval, this time from the Ministry of Labour. The spokesman for the deputation came to the peroration of his long and laboured speech. Slamming the table he declaimed: 'Those, Madam Chairman, are the opinions on which I base my facts . . . I mean—' Before he could complete his correction Bay was off the mark. Smiling, she said, 'I am grateful for that adequate summary'. A stuffy meeting came to an almost jovial end. 'Madam Chairman' became one of my favourite ways of addressing my beloved Bay.

My section had to grow fast to meet the ever-growing shortages and Leonard Skevington, an industrialist, came as my full-time assistant and was my organiser-in-chief. Our job was to seek out and report on shortages of all kinds, from overalls to razor blades, from tea-cups to trousers, and then to suggest ways of mitigating the differing degrees of hardship in the regions.

This work could not be done solely from our headquarters, now separately established in Neville House, close to I.C.I. House, where the main Board of Trade had moved after the War Cabinet took over its Whitehall offices. We therefore appointed a number of Area Distribution Officers ('ADOS') to report on any local or special deprivations. (North Wales, I remember, figured as a land denuded of 'ladies' outsize combinations'.) Matches were one of the hundred scarcities. I have a letter I wrote to my father telling him in all seriousness that I was trying to get him a box of matches as his birthday present. Sanitary towels were an awkward shortage which was even discussed at a War Cabinet meeting, ministers having been lobbied by their wives. We had to ask for help from the United States and a special shipment relieved that situation.

All my staff were temporaries and I chaired the board that interviewed applicants. We welcomed Reg Hicklin from Unilever's advertising department, a man of letters whose versatility quickly allowed him to become the man of figures that we needed at head-quarters. Later there was Clarissa Bell, whose devotion to our work and workers amounted almost to a passion. Most of the staff were female and the section soon became famous for its pulchritude. A first inspection of our out-housed section by the current President of the Board of Trade was a formality, but when it was repeated beyond any official expectation I guessed that it was due to the call of beauty rather than of duty. It remains a little embarrassing, even today, to name our lovelies. I yield to the temptation. There was Varda Procter (ex-*Vogue* model and ballet-dancer), who wrote poetry and whose reports were always wise and sometimes witty; there was Anne Cloake, whose eyes were as bright as her mind, with her gypsy-like hair falling over her lovely small face in a manner which would still look fashionable today; there was Susan Wyatt (now Hicklin) with her mass of yellow hair and a meaning smile that was as indicative as a long minute of agreement.

War-time leave in the Civil Service was reduced to one week. For ours, in September 1940, Bay and I and Evelyn Sharp went to Toppesfield, now no longer occupied by the Fabian families. There we were joined by Stephen and Att Potter and their two boys. We tried to make that week as like as possible to our pre-war holidays together at Talloires. It was magnificent weather. We bathed in our pool before breakfast and spent most of the day playing tennis at the nearby house of Dick and Beattie Plummer. They joined us in bicycling picnics. Being air-raid wardens, they felt it their duty to ride carrying gas masks and tin-hats—inconvenient *impedimenta* on bicycles. Our week coincided with the beginning of the Battle of Britain, and we returned to a sterner London and the onset of bombing.

A letter in May from Bay's brother, Robin, had given us reassurance. He was in the Fleet Air Arm, which was then operating in support of British forces in France. Wisely, I think, he thought it proper to break an order of silence. He asked me to start a loud morale-whisper to the effect that 'the bombs the Germans are dropping in France are extraordinarily ineffective except for a direct hit. They do little damage horizontally, even at 10 yards. It seems to me worth while spreading good news. God knows we have enough bad'. A characteristically humble letter reported that he was leading his squadron 'with great caution and cowardice'. It arrived on the very day on which we read that his courage had won him the Distinguished Flying Cross.

The Savile Club had an old and unoccupied member who had sensibly removed himself to the country. On his occasional visits to London and the club he used to buttonhole member after member, telling each of us at length what we must have felt during a raid ... he became known as the 'bomb-bore'. At the risk of myself being a bomb-bore, I continue with this theme.

Except for our brief holidays and some weekends, Bay and I were in London throughout the war. We found to our surprise that the crescendo of approaching bombers, the roar of explosions, the sinister short intervals of quiet, were not in the event as insupportable as we had imagined when we had read of the bombings of cities in Spain. In an early raid the front of a house four doors away from us was demolished and the occupants, who were in the back of the house, were uninjured. So Robin's information was confirmed. Other bombs fell in the road and blew up the water and gas mains, making fountains of fire and of water. Our house was undamaged. By a strange chance, on this night and on no other, I had filled our bath with water against emergency. We invited our harried neighbours into the house for a drink. I had a precious bottle of whisky, kept unopened for such a crisis. To my surprise and delight every incomer opted for tea, which we alone in the neighbourhood were able to provide because of our store of bath-water.

I spent many evenings at the Savile. When I bicycled there, Bay made me wear a paper-back book in my hat as a protection against 'flack' from our guns. Usually I drove, until petrol rationing made this impossible. If an air-raid warning sounded I went home at once to Bay. On one such night I was getting into my car outside the Savile when I saw in the otherwise deserted street an elderly small man, bowler-hatted and carrying a briefcase. I told him where I was going and asked if he would like a lift. First he hesitated and then explained: 'That will be on my way, but I have never been in a private car before'. Then he thanked me and joined me. He was a retired accountant now recalled to work. As we approached Sloane Square, he said that he was specially glad that Peter Jones was still undamaged. 'I always call it the house with a thousand windows,' he said. And then the accountant in him pushed aside the artist: 'You must understand, sir, that I have never counted them,' he said.

Eric (Sir Frederic) Hooper* entertained us at the Savile with many Churchill anecdotes, which we enjoyed the more because he told them in Churchillian accents. One was about an interview with the Archbishop of Canterbury: 'Archbishop, what precautions are you taking for your shafety if the Nayzeys come to Canterbury? You will shelter in the crypt? No, that will not shuffishe. I will arrange for the roof to be strengthened with shteel girdersh and a double layer of shandbagsh above. And then, Archbishop, then I think you will be shafe—unlesh you shushtain a direct hit from a 500-pound bomb. And if, Archbishop, if that should befall, I fear you must take it as a shummonsh.'

A bomb anecdote that went the rounds was of the woman who

* 1892–1963. Managing Director of the Schweppes Group of Companies; Director of the Political Research Centre, 1942–44.

was being rescued during a midnight raid from a high storey of a burning house. To the fireman at the top of his ladder she said: 'Wait one moment, please. I must fetch my teeth'. His answer: 'Hitler ain't dropping sandwiches, Ma'.

I once asked a taxi-driver, since his trade gave him no cover, how he reacted to the flying bombs. His answer was so helpful to my own morale that I scribbled it down: 'Well, I figure it out like this. First they got to make it; then they got to put me name on it; then they got to launch it; then they got to get it over the Channel; then it's got to dodge the fighters and ack-ack; then it's got to find number 92 Paradise Lane; and then ten-to-one I'll be out at the local'.

My daughter Cynthia served with the Red Cross at an exposed post near Lots Road Power Station. She was involved, therefore, in all the horrors of bombing. At a Greatham weekend she told Hilda that she could not bring herself to go back to London. She stayed away for two days, and then courageously returned to duty. Her commandant, Bridget Patterson, foresighted and cleverly-kind, received her without a sign of surprise or reproach, and Cynthia worked devotedly with her until the war's end. It was a comfort to Hilda and to me that Cynthia sometimes stayed with me and Bay. When she was off duty and there was a raid she often could not sleep and read to herself by torchlight under the blankets so as not to wake Bay or me. The three of us slept in a basement room. Bay and I found as we lay together that here was an assembly of the things we most cared for: all-embracing close-ness that meant 'if one of us, then both'.

As the type of blitz 'progressed' from ordinary high-explosive to land-mine, to doodle-bug, to the silent V2, it became more difficult to maintain a show of calm confidence. Nevertheless Bay managed to achieve this, except in one night-time particular. Her general calm and this one exception I put into a till-now-private verse that I addressed to her:

It 'isn't on' that you would change your tricks
Of mind and movement when you 'meet your Saviour'.
A Channel crossing or the final Styx
Would bring the same cool competent behaviour.
You'll quell an interrupter with 'I'm reading'—
Whether he be your lodger or the Lord;
But beggar or cherubim, if they be needing,
Will have your hand and most considerate word.

Yes, when death threatens, silky-smooth or bleeding,
You will find nothing special to rehearse.
You'll make a personal call to your relations,
Cast a wide eye for spectacles and purse
And cancel all outstanding invitations . . .
Your Board of Trade voice, adequate but terse.

The bombs fell—not exactly pitter-patter.
I scarce could hear them, for your teeth's loud chatter.

Civilian life in war proved to have many of the same components as in peace, but more intense and spaced-out by the extra
duties of wartime. There were still some theatres to go to, some
clubs to dance at, with always a little surprise that they had survived the last night's raids. Bay and I continued with our poetry-
reading evenings, in which Pamela McKenna and Alan Barlow
were our most regular partners. Sometimes with Evelyn Sharp, we
read aloud many of Dickens's novels. After the fall of France there
was a general wish to entertain and distract the French soldiers in
London. We took three of them to the Gargoyle, still our favourite
dancing place. I was perplexed that one of them, young, quick-
moving, handsome, failed to dance with Bay or with the other
women who made up our party. One of his companions drew me
aside and explained. The non-dancer was in private life a priest.
The war as we saw it in London had its minor eyesores as well as

its major horrors. Streets were filthy, people dishevelled, laundry very scarce, windows unmended, houses unpainted. Nevertheless there were compensations. Willow-herb quickly established itself in the bomb ruins; the black-out allowed one to see the stars; stucco houses lit only by the moon had new faces; the barrage balloons, shaped like fishes, gleamed in the sun and glowed as the searchlights found them momentarily at night. I put my gratitude for these little mercies into a verse which the *Evening Standard* passed on to my fellow-Londoners:

> In all the random sluttishness of war
> Let us record
> The town's recovery of moon and star,
> And praise the Lord
> For silk-and-silver fish
> Ballooning in their bowl of sky;
> And wish
> That London's willow-herb will never die.

In the spring of 1941 the more knowledgeable people at the Board of Trade—as usual this meant chiefly Wattie—realised the imminence of a famine in clothing. Only rationing could safeguard essential, and equal, supplies for the rich and the rest. It was a complex and secret undertaking. Any leakage could produce a dangerous clearance of the shops by even a few irresponsible people—the 'private spirited' as Alan Barlow called them. This made impossible the 'market research' which would have been helpful. The little that we could do was to make a wardrobe count among the staff actually at work on the project. The wide variation, ranging from Oliver Lyttelton's forty suits to my two-and-a-half, gave us plenty of smiles but no guide-lines.

After much cogitation it was decided that the grown-up ration would be 66 coupons for a year and that a man's suit, which consumed more cloth than anything else, would need 26 coupons. Shops would be able to replace their stocks only against the coupons they received. 'What about giants?' somebody asked. 'They have to have their suits made for them and 26 coupons won't give the tailor replacement for the extra cloth he has had to use.' This was a dodgy question and I made a dodging answer: 'Refer the problem to Stats'. From the Statistics Division came this answer: 'It is true that a giant (6 ft. 7 in. and over by our definition) will need for a suit twice as much cloth as does the average man for his. It is true also that a dwarf (by our definition 3 ft. 10 in. and under) will need only half as much as does the average man. Fortunately there are twice as many dwarfs as there are giants: therefore the problem is self-solving'. In my plainer terms this meant that every time a giant went to order a suit he had to take with him two dwarfs to order theirs... When I circulated the minute I could not refrain from telling about the statistician who was drowned in a lake the average depth of which was not more than three inches. We did in fact decide to offer extra coupons to the few tailors who proved to be giant-ridden.

Mine was the job of arranging the advertisements which would give both shops and people the information they needed. (There was then no Census of Distribution and the shops, like the public, could be informed of the details of rationing only in the newspapers.) My draft of the first crucial announcement came before a committee presided over by the Parliamentary Secretary, Captain Charles Waterhouse. Its theme was 'Fair Shares'. The chairman questioned whether this had not a tinge of Socialism about it. Reg Hicklin, usually a man of eloquent silence, now spoke up for the text and it was agreed:

"There is enough for all if we share and share alike. Rationing is the way to get fair shares. *Fair shares*—when workers are producing bombs and aeroplanes and guns instead of frocks, suits and shoes. *Fair shares*—when ships must carry

[269]

munitions and food rather than wool and cotton. *Fair shares*—when movements of population outrun local supplies."

The plans for rationing were finally evolved and all the staff engaged (but not knowing why) and two hotels in Bournemouth requisitioned for offices. We had chosen Whit Sunday as our D-day so that retailers would have the Whit Monday holiday to label their goods with the ration values. Now, only ten days before Whitsun, Winston Churchill, who hated any form of rationing, refused the go-ahead for the scheme. The President, Oliver Lyttelton,* went to the War Cabinet to restate his case. After a long wait he was told that the Cabinet had been too busy with other problems to hear him. Next day I was bemoaning the situation with Lyttleton in his office when his private secretary hurried into the room: 'Downing Street—the Prime Minister himself on the phone'. I made to go, but Lyttelton motioned me to stay. As he held the telephone to his ear his face changed from gravity to pleasure. Then he told me what Churchill had said: 'We've shunk the *Bishmark*. So you can have your clothes rationing'. Typical Churchill this: illogical in terms of economics, for the sinking of this, the most successful of marauding ships, actually lessened our immediate need, but masterfully aware that this news would heighten morale and so make rationing more acceptable.

Clothes rationing added greatly to the duties of my section at the Board of Trade. Special anomalies and hardships had to be dealt with. At the beginning relaxations were as necessary as enforcement. For example, many shops were caught with large stocks of 'frivolity' goods—dress-suits, evening dresses, sports clothes, spats and sandals—on which no one could afford to spend coupons. This problem was solved by allowing them individually to hold 'white elephant' sales at trifling coupon values.

Sir Thomas Barlow was the most effective of all the business

* Now Lord Chandos.

men brought into the Board of Trade. Amongst his concerns was the introduction of 'utility clothing' and simplifications in labour and materials—such things as the abolition of double-breasted jackets, turn-ups to trousers, superfluous pockets. Naturally enough, I remember only economies in men's wear, but more importantly he employed London couturiers to design women's dresses with the maximum economy of materials and labour. All this was a supplement to the rationing of clothes, so our duties brought us together. I chanced to be in Tommy Barlow's room when he had to question a clothing manufacturer who was suspected of rigging the restrictions to his firm's advantage. The defence was unconvincing. Tommy began his address in his most direct manner, pushing back the mass of iron-grey hair which topped his large, handsome face: 'I wonder if you have any idea, Mr X, how I long to be relieved of this job? Yes, Mr X, I dare say you have. But I wonder, Mr X, if you have any idea of my reason? No, Mr X, I doubt if you are with me there'. Then, using the charm which he habitually reserved for an insult, he finger-tipped his hands, smiled and in a wooing tone said: 'It is, Mr X, because I shall never have to meet a man like you again'.

Retired army officers anxious to 'do their bit' were sometimes applicants for jobs in my section. Among these, Oliver Lyttelton sent me, without any recommendation, a young and hearty sixty-year-old. I asked him for his views on rationing: Does it work fairly? Is it justified? 'Of course I saw what was coming, so I laid in half-a-dozen suits', he said. 'You must be well off for coupons then?' 'Not one to me name—the ladies get 'em, God bless 'em.' This was fun, so I asked him what he thought of utility suits. 'I haven't seen them, but let me tell you that this notion of trousers without turn-ups is worse than a blunder—it's a crime.' No, we did not employ him.

When the Board of Trade had to undertake a difficult new project its habit was to mix a businessman's prestige and skills, and too often innocent new view, with a civil servant's disciplined experience. So it came to pass that Bay was appointed joint part-time head of my section. What reassurance, what fun even, for both of us! In October 1941, when my section had proved itself for a year and a half, I was formally appointed 'Adviser to the Board of Trade on Consumer Needs'. What tickled my fancy was the *Daily Mail* headline: 'Poet as Nation's Housekeeper'. The *Evening Standard* said that I was going 'from limited editions to limited clothing'.

In 1943, when the war had begun to turn in our favour, Hugh Dalton, now President of the Board of Trade set up a committee to devise plans for post-war improvement in the design of consumer goods. This committee, like its plans, was a mixture of idealism (design for its own sake) and practicality (improved exports). Its members included Kenneth Clark, E. A. Goodale, J. E. Sieff and Josiah Wedgwood; Bay was the official and I the unofficial representative of the Board of Trade—another happy collusion. The heart of our agreed recommendation was for a strong Design Council. I was deputed to put our detailed scheme before the recently appointed Minister of Reconstruction, Lord Woolton. I waited on him in his charming but fragile office in Richmond Terrace, Whitehall. He was at his most lordly and assured, I at my most diffident. My mission was of great future importance for British industry, but a difficult one to justify while the war still dominated the scene. I was in the middle of my first *ers* and *ums* when a 'doodle' (flying-bomb) alert sounded. We instantly obeyed the official instructions—and our own instinct—to take the nearest available cover. Down we went under Woolton's table, he still the lordly Minister, I his suppliant. Then came an 'imminent' followed by the crash of a nearby bomb. When the 'all-clear' sounded we arose from our head-to-head posture on an equality, two frightened men. All was easy after that. Woolton promised a recommendation of our plan to the Cabinet. It was

Alix (Bay) and F.M. at 19 Cliveden Place soon after their marriage. Photographed for *Harper's Bazaar*.

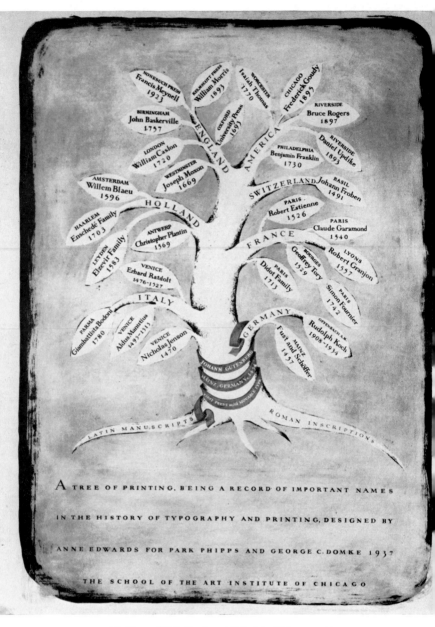

'A Tree of Printing', published in Chicago, 1937.

accepted. The Council of Industrial Design was appointed in December 1944. Tommy Barlow was its chairman and I was one of its seventeen members. Under its three successive directors—C. E. M. Leslie, Gordon Russell and Paul Reilly—it has done, and is doing, great things for industry and for the public.

In his private and social life Dalton was a charming man, but he was not always popular with his civil servants; like many a Labour Minister since, he started with a foolish distrust of them. He red-inked unflattering comments on their minutes and he liked to do his admonishing of a 'permanent' in front of a 'temporary' like me. The time came for his departure from the Board, and this meant a gathering in his office to bid him farewell. Sir Arnold Overton, the Permanent Secretary, made the formal address. He was a man who would in no circumstances say a word that he did not mean. What he now did was to recite a history of the Board from the days of its foundation as 'the Board of Trade and Plantations' down to the present day. Not a word to or about the President until his final sentence: 'And now, sir, I am able to tell you that your civil servants were grateful that you agreed with them that to implement the policy of providing more shoes it was necessary to have more shoe leather'. There was an awkward silence instead of the to-be-expected applause. Sir Charles Bruce-Gardiner, chief businessman adviser to the Board, was the second speaker. He peered at the speech that someone had written for him. His first words were 'After the moving and eloquent tribute to which we have just listened . . .' He was interrupted by a titter from all of us, including the President himself.

In his speech of reply Hugh Dalton made his last and undoubt-edly his best showing to his civil servants. He spoke for half an hour without a note and dealt amusingly and knowingly with the work of every one of the thirty or so people in the room—to my delight offering wise praise to Bay among the rest.

I did much broadcasting during the war. By far the most

popular of the BBC's programmes was the Brains Trust. It was the parent of today's quiz programmes. Donald McCulloch was its regular chairman. He was relieved every now and then by Geoffrey Crowther,* Lord Elton or me. I was, I think, a long way the most frequent substitute, appearing once a month in 1944, for instance. The groups over which I presided included at various times Professor Gilbert Murray, Margaret Rawlings, Cyril Joad, Lord Vansittart, Malcolm Sargent, Julian Huxley, Emanuel Shinwell, Kenneth Clark, Professor Andrade. This gives a notion of the serious discussions which I was expected to compère. The BBC persisted with me though there were sundry protests that I exceeded my duties as chairman by posing supplementary questions and joining volubly in the discussion thereof. (I have never learnt to hold my tongue.) The discussions were off-the-cuff and as we might by mischance say something that might help German Intelligence, the programme was not put on the air until two days after its recording, when the censor had had his say. Thus I could listen-in and hear my own voice as others heard it. This surprised and distressed me, and I did much private practice with vowels and pitch of voice and with the elimination of *ers* and *wells*. (The current disease of 'you know' and 'I mean' had not then struck broadcasters.)

The anxieties of war increased one's sensibility, and in my case made me write more poetry. The *Sunday Times* and the *Observer* were my occasional outlets, and in 1944 I published my *Fifteen Poems* with a return dedication to Walter Turner, Osbert Sitwell and Rodney Hobson, all of whom had dedicated poems to me. In my foreword I explained why I had written so little. 'I have never put work before life; I have satisfied my senses, enjoyed companionship, played games with more than Australian determination though less than village skill. A full life has meant an empty book.'

* For many years editor of the *Economist*. Now, as Lord Crowther, chairman of Trust Houses Ltd.

The first blitz bit as deep into the hearts of ex-Londoners as it did into our own. Jan Struther, who was safeguarding her children in America, showed this in a moving poem she sent to me. The BBC welcomed my proposal that I should broadcast it. Despite the formal trappings of the studio and the watchful eye and ear of the producer, I found it very hard to keep my voice wholly under control. I want to give this poem a renewal of life. It is called 'A Londoner in New England 1941'.

I was a citizen once of a great city.
　　Its buildings were of mellowed brick and of weathered stone.
I woke up every morning to its sparrows' chatter
　　And lay down every evening to its traffic's drone.

Its sky-signs were my earliest constellations.
　　My nursery rhymes were the legends of the town.
I sang, 'London's burning, London's burning'.
　　I sang, 'London Bridge is falling down'.

It is peaceful here. Yet here, where maple and sumach
　　Cut unfamiliar patterns on a moonlit sky,
I am a citizen still of the same city:
　　I feel its houses crumble and its people die.

Heavy at heart, I lie awake at midnight
　　And hear a voice, five hours nearer the sun,
Speaking across the ether from a grim daybreak,
　　Calmly reciting what the night has done.

I think, 'London's burning, London's burning'.
　　I think, 'London bridge is falling down'.
Then something wiser than thought says, 'Heart, take comfort:
　　Buildings and bridges do not make a town.

[275]

'A city is greater than its bricks and mortar;
   It is greater than tower or palace, church or hall:
A city's as great as the little people that live there.
   You know those people. How can London fall?'

These words of courage and comfort were of the kind we needed and welcomed. If you, my reader, or those you love lived in London through the blitz, please read this poem aloud. . . Tell me, was there not a break in your voice?

XVII

Annus Mirabilis

Peace. At last, on May 8 1945 the hideous Nazi threat was destroyed. This, not victory in the old boastful and cruel sense, was what we celebrated in our public cheers and private tears of thanksgiving. Our immediate celebration was to keep open door at 19 Cliveden Place and to summon in any passer-by who cared for a drink. Among the strangers were three beautiful girls with platinum-coloured hair from the Icelandic Legation; they helped us to entertain many American G.I.s, who generously returned later in the day with full bottles of drink to replace the half-bottles they had emptied.

During the many desperate days that were now passed, J. B. Priestley's broadcasts had expressed and thereby reinforced public resolution. In his homely Yorkshire voice he spoke man to man—the most difficult form of rhetoric. He held out no false expectations but expressed true and general desires—for an equal and poverty-free society at home and in the family of nations. We were out of earshot of his peace-day broadcast, but he sent us a printed copy. It is a masterly look-back and a hopeful look-forward. What makes it read sadly is the fashion in which the world has come to accept armament trades as vital to 'the economy'—and you need to keep enemies in order to justify arms. Compare his allusion to Russia with the general attitude today, and remember our failure to take the hand that Khrushchev was to offer us:

"And then came a hot Sunday in June when we heard that Hitler had gone roaring East and thus brought us a great new ally: the lean giant in overalls—Russia—which saw, with mounting fury, all the great works for which its people had sacrificed immediate comforts—all the dams and power stations and factories, blasted and overrun. And we said—and the Prime Minister said it, and the shop stewards said it—'These people are our friends, and their suffering shall be our suffering, and their triumph shall be our triumph.'"

Stafford Cripps, that remarkably selfless man, became President of the Board of Trade in the new Labour administration of 1945. He was a man of ideals, unfamiliar with the processes of administration but reliant on his civil servants, and capable of making dreams come true. He instituted a regular first-thing-in-the-morning meeting (we called it 'Morning Prayers') with the heads of his department. At the first of these his precise definition of problems and policies gave me the large hope that here was a Government with the will and the power to bring us something akin to social justice in our time. That hope has been largely though not wholly satisfied. In our Welfare State there is no longer a whole class of 'the Poor'. Yes, there are still poor and deprived people, particularly among the elderly, but there is not the desperate and unhelped poverty that horrified me when I was young. Today the major problems, as the young protesters recognise, are international. We are still under sentence of war: a suspended sentence—but suspended for how long? Over everything is the spectre of the bomb.

This year 1945 was Annus Terribilis as well as Annus Mirabilis. On August 6 the atom bomb was dropped on Hiroshima, and mankind for the first time in its history found that it possessed the techniques of self-extinction. Bay's brother was Flight Commander on one our aircraft-carriers in the Far East; he wrote that he thought it likely that his was one of the lives saved by the dropping of the bomb and the consequent Japanese surrender, but that he would rather have died than have been so saved. Like multitudes of people wiser than I am, I did not at once realise the horror and the implications. We were playing bridge with A. D. Peters and his wife when the news was broadcast; it did not affect our concentration on the cards. Gradually, helped by the *New Yorker*, which devoted two whole issues to John Hersey's report of the devastation at Hiroshima, realisation grew. Bay and I joined the C.N.D. movement, which the Priestleys did much to promote. It has been sad to see its enormous propaganda power diminish over the years by its mixture of other worthy but irrelevant causes.

But enough of politics. This year was Annus Mirabilis in a private as well as a public sense for Bay and me. Vera told me that she was now prepared to divorce me; she thought that our son was old enough to accommodate to the truth. Bay was anxious that there should not be the usual subterfuge and that she should be named as the co-respondent. She went to see Harry Lintott, the Establishment Officer of her department. How would the Board of Trade view her involvement in a divorce? Harry said that this was a matter private to her and no affair of her employers. And so 'a little man in a bowler hat' came to 19 Cliveden Place one day at breakfast time and reported us as living together.

In this summer Bay and I took another momentous step to-gether. We bought Cobbold's Mill at Monks Eleigh in Suffolk, destined to be our happy home for twenty-two years. It is a combination of a water-mill and a miller's dwelling, and parts of it date back for many centuries. It had been a working corn mill until 1938. A little had been done to renovate it, but we began at once to a slow shaping of it to our eyes and needs. Is there a happier occupation?

I had other semi-public reasons for my private pleasure in this year. I was appointed one of the forty Royal Designers for Industry (that is what the R.D.I. after a name means) and I was made 'Typographical Adviser (unpaid) to His Majesty's Stationery Office'. Both appointments were in part a recognition of my Nonesuch work; the second was an exciting challenge, because the standard of government printing was then very poor.

Like scores of others who had been 'dollar a year' civil servants during the war, I now had to make plans for my livelihood. Should I go back full-time to Mather's? Gordon Boggon, its vice-chairman, advised me not to; in the pinched post-war economy, he said, Mather's could not really afford to keep me; even Francis Ogilvy, the managing director, was hesitant about returning from his Cabinet Office post. So I decided to look for other work. Perhaps my Board of Trade success had made me vainglorious. If I could make my mark there, could I not make it, and profitably, in Big Business?

Halford Reddish opened that door for me. In practical terms the door was that of a room at the Savoy Hotel where Halford and George Earle, chairman of the Cement Makers' Federation, gave me lunch and scrutiny. Seemingly I passed, for quite fantastically I was soon asked to take charge of the Cement and Concrete Association, a body financed by the industry to promote the intelligent use of cement. Now it was proposed to enlarge the Association's responsibilities, particularly in its research function, where England lagged behind some other countries. I put to them a naive but critical question: what would be the cement makers' attitude if research showed the possibility of economy in the use of cement? Halford's reply was immediate: they would welcome it as making concrete even more competitive with other building materials. This made me feel that in the war-worn world, with so much to rebuild and to build, there might be a public as well as a private-enterprise interest in my task. Doubtless this was in part another of my self-justifications. My contract was to be for ten years, my salary £5,000 a year—a lot of money in those days—and all my conditions were agreed to. I was allowed to remain a director of Mather & Crowther, to continue for a time my weekly attendances at the Ministry of Food, and to carry out my duties at His Majesty's Stationery Office. Finally, and very importantly, I might bring with me from Mather's my invaluable help-friend-secretary, Pamela Zander.

I went to my new job with a pleasant secret. I had been offered a knighthood in the forthcoming New Year's honours. After doubts that were in the main pretended, I had accepted it. True, Trilby Ewer's verses that I had myself printed at the end of World War I were busy in my mind:

> Every wise democrat
> Who has the sense to rat
>   Honoured shall be.
> Knighted he's sure to get
> Or made a baronet,
> Shoved in the Cabinet
>   Or the P.C.

In its day this was all just. But now? All through this war, the monarchy had been a sustaining symbol, what Bay called 'a live flag'. Honours were part of the monarchy's trappings. I had worked hard, I had accepted discipline, and this offer was a re-assurance to me that I had played a useful part. Plain vanity was there, and a calculating and selfish motive: my honour would certainly help me in my new career. My fifteen-year-old son had a mixed but not too condemning view:

"Congratulations! I'm very pleased you've got the 'Knight Bachelor', because you, unlike probably many others, did something for it. I'm glad that it pleases you and I'm sure it will please most of your friends.

My feelings are very mingled. I would always rather think of you as a jailbird, whose principles were unshakeable. Still, there've got to be Knights, even under a Labour Government, so they might as well be good ones. Sorry to be so paternal or platitudinous to you! Don't get me wrong, and think that I feel as Vera does that it's unforgivable. I'm not awfully good at expressing myself. Even to say that emotionally

I'm very pleased and intellectually I'm just a bit sorry, doesn't really fill the bill."

To me Vera was in fact gentle and kind and understanding. She wrote:

"Congratulations, if you feel that way. You know, of course, that I agree with your Early Period of thinking that these pretties are a disadvantage to the body politic—and disagree with the Labour Party for doling them out. But maybe I'm a prig, or Peter Pan, or Has-Been.

I *think* that Ben is (secretly) delighted with your knighthood, but (publicly) rather embarrassed by having to reconcile it with your early history, of which he has already boasted to his young friends. The line to take is: that he may disapprove of you or me, but that you and I will not disapprove of his disapproval."

Ben and Cynthia came to the Palace to watch my accolade. They would have found a behind-the-scenes view more entertaining. The group of about-to-be-knighted were assembled 'offstage' and an obviously bored Admiral in full dress gave us our instructions: 'You will enter the Presence in alphabetical order', he chanted. Then, as he came to the significant instructions, he lowered his voice to what we heard as a diminishing yum-yum-yum ... The early-in-the-alphabet knights-to-be begged him to repeat his instructions; which he did, as inaudibly as before. Again the petition, again the diminuendo to nothingness. The door to the Great Chamber was thrown open and a quite uninstructed 'A' had to lead us in and fumble by trial and error for correct stances. Those of us who were as low in the alphabet as my 'M' placed me were unembarrassed; we learned from our predecessors' misadventures.

What really pleased me about my congratulatory letters was that so many of them added to the official citation, which referred only to my work at the Board of Trade. Thus Kenneth Clark wrote: 'I like to think that you have really been knighted for the Nonesuch Press, and because in the world of business and the Civil Service you have not forgotten poetry'. Halford Reddish added a footnote that now I should always be able to get domestic staff; and Stanley Morison pointed out that I should have to give larger tips. Ernest Pooley (himself a Knight Bachelor) sent me a gay postcard:

"I have just realised that this was what was lacking in the ranks of Knights Bachelor—the addition of one who really looks like a Knight, thinks like a Knight, and behaves as a Knight; who is agile in leaping forwards and sideways, the protector of many queens, and making full use of his pawns."

At the top of my letters of over-praise I have kept one salutary corrective. This is a postcard sent to me after a Brains Trust broadcast. It was addressed to Francis Menel and it said: 'We don't know how to spell your name. We don't want to know how to spell your name. We only want you to GET OFF THE AIR'. It was signed 'Several patient listeners'.

XVIII

Man of Business

When I arrived at the Cement and Concrete Association in 1946 I had a warm and expectant welcome from Philip Gooding, who was Head of Information, and a cautious and inquiring one from Harry Hastie, the Association's secretary and head of staff. Both became my close and kindly associates. My first task was to look for a skilled man to be Technical Director and so supply the scientific knowledge of cement and its uses that I wholly lacked. After many interviews I chose well, or luckily, and Dr Collins left the official Road Research Laboratory to recruit and lead our technical team.

The Association had its pleasant office in Grosvenor Gardens. My work there proved to be serene and happy. My function was far from heavy in detail yet astonishingly large in outcome; I was the decider, others were the proposers, the preparers and doers.

The more profound reason for my happiness was that Bay and I were at last married, in August 1946. I was fifty-five, she forty-three; we have 'lived happily ever after'. Every year we joyfully celebrate what we call our 'aggregation-of-income-tax day'. (We reckoned that if we had continued to 'live in sin' we should have saved £600 a year.) The Board of Trade gave us a wedding present and Bay an extra fortnight's 'honeymooning' leave; and Björn Prytz gave the wedding lunch at the Swedish Legation. Then we spent a gay afternoon and evening at our beloved Cobbold's Mill with Björn, Evelyn Sharp and the Potters as our guests.

The next day we started on our wedding trip to Sweden. For some days we were happily lodged by Björn's wife, Aino, in the guest-house of their lovely island home near Gothenburg, and thereafter toured the country. We had a lesson in the breadth of Swedish education. Björn had lent us his car. As we drove through

Jönkoping its horn began blasting of its own accord. Horn-sounding is forbidden in Swedish towns, and a policeman quickly stopped the car and addressed me severely in Swedish. 'Being English,' I said, 'I don't understand your words, but I can guess your meaning.' He went to the front of the car and gazed meaningly at the Swedish number plates. Then he spoke to me in Swedish again. Again I protested that I was English and ignorant of Swedish; whereupon he challenged me in English: 'If what you are saying is true then speak a piece of Shakespeare.' I gave him the whole twenty-two lines of the 'quality of mercy' speech. Now he was all smiles and took us to a garage, where the horn was silenced.

After six months at my new job I presented with some trepidation my first report to my bosses of the Cement Makers' Federation; they finance the c. & c.a. by a levy on every ton of cement sold. My thesis was that a large-scale research station was needed to develop such new techniques as pre-stressing (used abroad but not then in England), shell roofs, light-weight concrete and pleasant surface finishes. My report was discussed at a Federation meeting of the top men of the top companies, who brought with them their seconds-in-command. Thus George Earle, the gentlest of gentlemen, brought John Reiss, Max Jensen brought Jim Mackintosh. These, I was told, would in future represent their companies at our meetings. With my talent for gaucherie, I asked, 'Does that mean I shall in future be playing with the second eleven?' The top men looked embarrassed, but John Reiss and Jim Mackintosh, soon to head their companies, merely smiled. In fact these two forgiving 'substitutes' gave me warm support and continuing friendship.

It was John Reiss who organised assent to the greatest project of my 'reign'—the purchase of Wexham Springs near Slough as the basis of our research station. This was a fine 20-room house in 31 acres of garden. Planning permission for our necessary extensions was not easy to come by. One welcome stipulation was that we should resuscitate and even develop the beauties of the gardens; so when a cement-maker more money-minded than the rest questioned me about the extravagance of employing three full-time gardeners, I had a ready answer.

In 1947 Vera wrote this to me: 'If, as may be, I have Parkinson's Disease, that is not what I shall die of. Ask your cronies'. I took this as a declaration of her belief that her illness—her 'may be' illness—would not be a mortal one. Her and my medical cronies, Joan Malleson and Portia Holman, told me that in their belief she did not in fact suffer from that fell disease. I was reassured, and I was wrong. Some weeks later she killed herself; and then it was easy to see her letter as an announcement of that intention. If I had read her letter aright would I have tried to deter her? I doubt it. It was and is my view that one has an absolute right to end one's life when one wants to. (That is why I am a life-member—or should it be a death-member?—of the Euthanasia Society.)

I had letters from many people who in the old days had been close to us both. Why do I print phrases from three of them? In self-justification no doubt, but also because they add to my inadequate description of Vera. In all her doings and designs she had sought something that she was never able to find, neither in herself nor by means of the psychoanalysis which she suffered (my carefully chosen word) both in the United States before I knew her and in England during her last years, when she was herself training to be an analyst. Margaret Cole, speaking the compassionate truth in words that were almost my own, wrote: 'I remember Vera so beautiful. I think she had the loveliest bone shapes of any woman I ever knew. So intelligent, but demanding things of life that it wouldn't give. I do so wish it need not have happened; but I don't believe that anything or anybody could have prevented it sooner or later'. Joan Malleson, who had been her capable and generous doctor, made a characteristic self-accusation: 'I would have done more for Vera, but I am not tough enough for such a personality'.

David Garnett wrote: 'I am glad she found the courage; as Charmian said of Cleopatra, it was well done'.

At the cremation Portia Holman, Vera's friend more consistently than anyone else, spoke movingly and wisely. Raymond Postgate read 'Tissue of Time', a poem that I had addressed to Vera in our ecstatic early days together. Is there a foreboding in the last two verses ?

> There is no means to annul
> One gesture, one word.
> These are tissue of Time, these are all
> Immortal. I have heard
>
> Egypt and her Antony
> With their first love fulfilled
> Cry out, and again cry;
> Nor ever are they stilled.
>
> Though Helen's lips are dust
> The kisses of her lips
> Still burn the towers, and must
> Still launch the thousand ships.
>
> When your love's flight shall falter
> Shall fall, like a wounded bird,
> You too cannot alter
> The said or the unsaid word.
>
> So this is the sum of it, this—
> (Say not it is not much)
> You cannot unkiss that kiss;
> You cannot untouch that touch.

Now, at this acutely sensitive time of her death, I wrote verses which, when they were published in the *Sunday Times*, our closest old-time friends, Vera's and mine, welcomed as just. Most important of all, our son Benedict after early doubts approved their publication. The covering title was FOR ONE WHO CHOSE TO DIE.

> Add up our griefs, count all regrets and guilt—
> They do not match, in pain, a sensible part
> Of her close chaos, arduously built,
> Or the bright torture she held to her heart.
> So, in the audit, piteously one says
> 'The world without her is a happier place'.

> Of mind, tall as a tower,
> Of beauty, she had her hour—
> Brightness unshaded.
> She would not keep the flower
> When it was faded.

Cobbold's Mill was Bay's and my weekend home, and in the long days of summer we sometimes commuted during the week, but that was rare because we both had demanding jobs to do and petrol was still rationed. Weekends were short, for civil servants worked then on Saturday mornings and any Saturday off counted as a whole day's leave. Many members of our two families and a host of our friends spent holidays and weekends with us. Among them very often was my dear first wife Hilda. She and Bay had an equal and close friendship until Hilda's death in 1962. Evelyn Sharp and Stephen and Att Potter were our most frequent guests. One weekend in 1946 Stephen put into my hands the typescript of a book he had just finished writing. 'Please read it at once', he said, 'and tell me what you think of it.' Then he left the room. Bay and I read the first chapter together and laughed and laughed again. 'Find Stephen and tell him how funny it is', said Bay. He was not hard to find, for there he was kneeling on the other side of our door, with his ear to the keyhole. 'I wanted to hear if it made

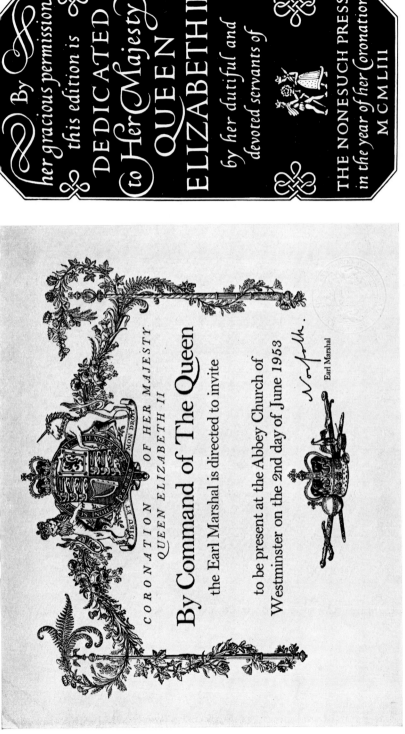

(*Left*) Invitation to the Coronation (*see page 301*). (*Right*) Engraving by Reynolds Stone for the second complete Nonesuch Shakespeare. (Original 6 × 3 inches.)

My dear Ernest: you have repri-
manded Miss Hayman for her
use of the capital R shape as a
"small" letter to such good effect
that she has reverted to the am-
biguous r shape. I am more incompetent and so more obstinate.
The fact with me is that I cannot
quickly (and writing must be quick
or it becomes drawing) make an r
which has an incontestable r-ness.
My capital R is not therefore an
embellishment: it is a confession
of weakness; a confession truly
without much contrition and with
little hope of amendment, but humbly
made nonetheless.

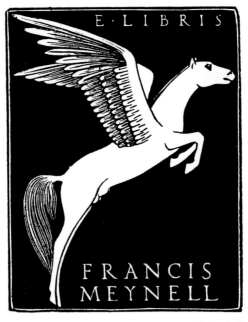

(*Above*) F.M.'s handwriting from *Written by Hand*, by Aubrey West.
Allen & Unwin, 1951. F.M. was a founder member of the Italic Handwriting Society. (*Below*) Bookplate wood-engraved by Eric Gill.

you laugh', he explained. The book was *Gamesmanship*, one of the shaping books of its time. When it was published he dedicated it to me, and nominated me 'Gamesman Number One', a tribute to our perennial and always slightly spoof competitions with each other. One word I contributed to this internationally famous book. Stephen's sub-title was 'How to Win at Games without Cheating'. He accepted my emendation: 'without *actually* cheating'.

Neither my work nor my age debarred me from playing games. When I was in my fifties I thought it appropriate to ask Joan Malleson whether I was still fit to play squash. I was put through my paces and told: 'Yes, you may go on playing, but only against opponents you can be sure of beating'. She told me that in the previous year she had had a like inquiry from a rich sixty-year-old patient who had his own squash court and a chauffeur of thirty, chosen more for his skill at squash than with a car. 'I told my patient', said Joan, 'that if he went on playing he would probably fall down dead in his squash court.' He had replied that this would be a happy death and that he would continue to play. 'Sure enough,' said Joan, 'three weeks later I had an emergency telephone call from his house to report a death on the squash-court. It was the chauffeur who had fallen down dead.' I found this an effective gamesmanship story to tell my younger opponents before we began our games.

Tennis—family tennis—I continued well into my sixties and I still took my cricket seriously enough to have lessons. I have a 1949 bill from 'Sandham, Strudwick and Gover' (all fine county players), who had a cricket school at Wandsworth: '18 lessons at 10s. each'. And my modest skill as a batsman increased with my years. Within two years of my sixtieth birthday I played for Sudbury against Braintree and hit 61 runs out of the side's total of 84. I have a cherished cutting from the local newspaper with a three-column heading:

'KNIGHT IN PADS TO THE RESCUE'

What follows is, I fear, a continuous boast. Any visitor to the Research Station at Wexham Springs will be astonished by its acres of natural and architectural beauty combined with its obvious 'fitness for purposes'. There is nothing comparable with it for any other industry in England, nor have I found its like in the many countries—including the United States—to which I have made visits of inspection.

For our new buildings we employed good architects. The Structures Laboratory, the most difficult of these, proved to be the handsomest. It was designed by my Savile friend Kit Nicholson, son of the great 'Billy Nick', the painter. Kit died in a glider accident and it was Hugh Casson who handsomely completed it. Later we had a first-rate architect on our staff, W. R. Oram, and he designed many of our buildings, including our first Training Centre.

We had formal openings of our new buildings by successive Ministers of Works, George Brown and Hugh Molson among them. They made their speeches, I made mine. Indeed for me speech-making now became the habit of my life—in England, Sweden, Italy and the United States. Since I could not talk technically I was forced to be anecdotal—a relief, I think, to listeners at learned conferences. On occasion I dared to speak in Italian, once at a welcome we gave in England to Dr Nervi, hero of remarkable advances in concrete technology, and once at an international conference in Rome—but only after my words had been carefully Italianised and phoneticised for me.

In my third year at the Cement and Concrete Association I found that the growth of my responsibilities there compelled me to abandon my remaining executive task for Mather & Crowther. This meant the end of my many years' attendance at the Ministry of Food weekly meetings, where the intent and text of the next issue of its food economy advertisements were discussed. My retirement was no hurt to the Ministry, for my place was taken by

Stanhope Shelton (the inventor, remember, of the compelling title, 'Food Facts') and Gordon Boggon, Mather's vice-chairman. I remained a non-executive Director of Mather's.

The last executive job for Mather's in which I had a hand proved to be, I suppose, one of the most significant. David Ogilvy had proposed the setting up under his command of an advertising agency in the United States. He had obtained the moral and financial support of Laurie Mather and of Bobby Bevan, head of Benson's, another prominent English advertising agency, but in Britain's dire financial state official permission for the necessary purchase of dollars to set it up was hard to come by. Ogilvy's plan would promote our exports by providing our exporters with local selling propaganda. I made this case, first by letter to the Board of Trade and then less formally to Stafford Cripps, its President, and to John Henry Woods, its Permanent Secretary, who came to lunch with Bay and me at Cliveden Place. My part, the exposition, was obvious and easy; Bay's part in designing the meal was more difficult, for Stafford Cripps was a vegetarian, a meagre eater and a teetotaller, whereas John Henry, a charming man-of-the-world, was a robust gourmet and wine-bibber. David Ogilvy in his book *Confessions of an Advertising Man** gives me credit for securing the needed permission, but his scheme was so clearly desirable that it spoke for itself. 'Ogilvy, Benson & Mather' proved to be a fantastic dollar winner. Now as 'Ogilvy & Mather International' (Benson withdrew) it has offices all over Europe and in the U.S.A.

At the Board of Trade Bay was now in charge of clothes-rationing. For a time shortages were worse instead of better, but inevitably less easy to bear. The fashion trade were eager to introduce the 'New Look' with longer and much fuller skirts, and Bay held a widely reported meeting with the fashion editors to appeal to them to keep women fashionable without using a lot of extra material. It was, to her surprise, a very angry meeting and two of

* Atheneum, New York, 1963.

the editors, whom we were due, as it happened, to meet at dinner that evening with Jake and Ernestine Carter, refused to meet Bay. Next day a parcel arrived on her desk. It was sent anonymously and it contained three fig leaves: one marked for Stafford Cripps, one for John Henry Woods and one for her.

At Cobbold's Mill our factotum was Mrs Stowe, a self-possessed, kindly, hard-working, large-familied woman of the village, who had a local reputation for defensive witchcraft: if someone on purpose or by mistake claimed one of her bags of peas on a picking expedition, that someone always fell off her bicycle on her way home. When we made a south-facing window (the only one in the house) she was disturbed about it. I asked her why. She said, 'Don't you know? The Black Death came through the south windows and after that they was all boarded up.' More than five hundred years of living legend was parcelled into that phrase. 'Work' for her meant manual work: she wouldn't accept that we too were workers in London offices. When the first partial relaxation of clothes rationing came, Bay explained to Mrs Stowe that this was an example of her work. This was Mrs Stowe's polite answer: 'When I read it in the paper, m'lady, what I said to Stowe, m'lady, was, m'lady, the old girl's done something for us at last'. Bay repeated this to Harold Wilson, then President of the Board of Trade, and thereafter in discussions with his senior civil servants he used to inquire, 'What does the Old Girl think'?

In the autumn of 1948 Bay became the first executive secretary of the Monopolies Commission; and she was made a Dame of the Order of the British Empire—an appointment that put her above me, a mere Knight Bachelor, in the honorific scale. I went to see her receive her honour from George VI. In the box containing her insignia we noted that she was to wear it on her left 'side'. Yes, a substitute had been found for the shocking word 'breast', used in similar instructions for men.

A few weeks later I dutifully attended a Trade Association dinner in the Café Royal. The speeches at these functions are not things to remember, but this time I really enjoyed the terms in which my health was proposed. The Chairman, Sir Herbert Williams, had known Bay when she was Parliamentary Secretary to the Board of Trade. Now he rose and said: 'I would like to drink a toast to the husband of the most beautiful, most attractive and most efficient member of the Civil Service'.

Later in the year Bay was invited by the American government to go to the United States, at their expense, to study American anti-trust legislation. As I wanted to meet my American opposite numbers in the cement industry, I travelled with her. I was a bystander when she was interviewed by a young reporter from the *Daily Express* as soon as the ship made port. Bay was asked a number of seemingly ignorant or (as it turned out) 'loaded' questions. One was: 'Do you think it right to use American money to break up British business?' Her decisive answer was that her visit had no such object; her mission was to compare the processes of American and English legislation on monopolies. This was not the answer the interviewer wanted nor was it the answer reproduced in the *Daily Express*. '"We'll bust some Trusts" says Lady Meynell' was its headline, followed by '"No, I do not think it wrong to use American money to break up British business".' Naturally this made a stink. There were questions in Parliament and no good was done to Bay's career.

When we got back to England I asked Arthur Christiansen, the Editor of the *Daily Express*, to let me see the interviewer's short-hand note. Sure enough it recorded Bay's answers as she gave them, not as reported in the paper. Even so, Christiansen refused to make any adequate correction. He excused himself by saying 'The story's dead by now'. Later, and under the counter, I was shown the text of a Beaverbrook command that Bay's visit was to be slammed as part of his campaign against the Monopolies Commission.

This visit took Bay to Washington, me to New York and Boston, and we met in Chicago, where we both had business. Bay was dined there by the Chaos Club, a meeting-place for economists and lawyers of the two local universities. They criticised her for what they regarded as the over-mild anti-monopoly policy of the British Government. It was not a restful evening. I met her after her verbal tussle; there was a flurry of snow and she relieved her feelings and tickled mine by taking a deep breath and saying: 'These snowflakes are neither sweetened nor vitaminised'.

William Benton, a tycoon friend of ours—he was shortly to become a senator—arranged interviews for Bay with the heads of a number of corporations. He invited us to his New England home at Fairfield. When we arrived he marched us away from his gathered guests to the far end of his estate, where a plaque on the public road recorded that in such-and-such a year King George's troops had landed there and burned Fairfield to the ground. Our host watched our reaction with the quizzical air which is typical of him. 'Bill,' I said, 'there is now a different King George on the throne of England.' He pretended surprise at my news then led us back and gave us an excellent lunch.

Now we took a week's holiday to stay with Celia Tobin Clark who, thirty or more years before, had been a close friend of my mother's. She lived in San Mateo at House-on-Hill, carried stone by stone from the Cotswolds. Here we basked in the Californian sun, played tennis and greatly enjoyed this revival of an old friendship. She took us to a grand dinner-party given by friends of hers who had a mansion in the private canyon next to her own. Along the mile-long entrance-drive every great tree was floodlit. There was caviare with the drinks. The dinner was eaten off gold plates.

The evening ended unhappily. Bay was put next to a New York corporation lawyer, who, it was thought, could be informative about the American anti-trust law. Hoping to gratify him, Bay told of her visit to the Supreme Court in Washington and of her admiration for one of its judgements. 'Our Supreme Court,' screamed the attorney, 'nothing but a gang of Communists!' There was dead silence through the company of perhaps thirty people. Then Celia's brother, banker and owner of one of San Francisco's newspapers, leaned forward and called across the room, 'You will withdraw those remarks about our Supreme Court!' Then a pause and again, 'You will withdraw those remarks about our Supreme Court!' A stuttering withdrawal followed, but it was the end of the occasion, for almost immediately afterwards Celia took her party demonstratively away. Back at House-on-Hill she soothed our shared embarrassment with a bottle of champagne.

When my ten years' contract with the Cement and Concrete Association was up in 1956, and I was sixty-five, my masters asked me to stay on for two more years, with an addition of £2,000 to my salary. All the time the Association had been growing in function, in staff, in buildings, and in the development of agreeable surface finishes—a subject dear to my eye. Our training courses in concrete techniques were an immediate success. For every one of them we had more applications than available places. The 'participants'— we adopted that rather dreadful word because they were too senior to be called 'students' or 'trainees'—were architects, engineers, builders, officers of many local authorities and Government departments. There were five thousand of these in the first five years.

My last task for the Association, and, as it has proved, my most successful, was to find my successor. Leo Russell was an admired neighbour of ours in the country—admired for his war record, his personality, his expert farming. (Bay and I had become weekend farmers on a small scale, so we had means of judgement.) There were also the very relevant facts that he had been Director of the Institute of Management and, equally important, had shown his strength of mind by resigning from it when the Institute exchanged some of its original functions for what he judged to be unsuitable ones. To my delight he told me that he would take on my job if he were asked to; I made my recommendation to my masters and he was appointed.

So it became true that nothing I had done in office so became me, etc., etc. . . . When now I make visits to Wexham I see the development and innovations that he has produced there. Most important of these is the fine building to house, feed, entertain and instruct the hundreds who attend lecture courses. Generously he has given my name to the building which first served this purpose.

Politics. Both Bay and I were profoundly opposed to Eden's Suez escapade in 1956. It was a shaming thing that ours of all countries and Eden of all men should embark on this aggressive war. On the day of Eden's ultimatum to Egypt the *Guardian*, to its lasting honour, listed the names and addresses of every member of Parliament and asked 'the people' to express their opposition to the war. We wrote letters to our M.P. and to the papers; we went to the mass meeting in Trafalgar Square and afterwards to the Albert Hall rally. The next night we were at the theatre; in the silence following 'God Save the Queen' I shouted, 'Eden must go'—and was followed into the street by voluble, even fist-raising, Edenites. My son and my daughter and Bay made themselves my bodyguard.

My swan-song for the Cement and Concrete Association was at a conference in Rome in 1957. The delegates of twenty-seven countries gathered there, and Bay and I were housed (as were the rest of the English delegation) at the Excelsior Hotel in great grandeur; but after one night we moved out to a humbler place, irked by the combination of rich extravagance and staff contempt. At the final banquet of 900 guests the highlight was the moment when seventy-two waiters processed through the darkened ban-queting-hall each bearing a great silver platter, cunningly self-lit, on which were huge lobsters. I had as vis-à-vis a rather dour Italian whom I failed to engage to talk. How could I get on terms with him? I said, 'Would not the procession have been better still if the platters had been carried by naked girls?' It worked. Thereafter we chatted easily.

At the end of my extended term of office in 1958 the staff of the Association gave me a farewell lunch. Bay and Pamela Zander found the tributes moving even to tears. My masters too gave me a feast, and George Brown (a former Minister of Works) and Frederick Snow (President of the Institute of Structural Engineers) were jointly my hosts at a dinner-party in the House of Commons. Herbert Morrison was in the chair, and there was a cluster of architects and engineers. Bay, the only woman present, in her Civil Service fashion took a minute of the proceedings. On occasions like this all phrases are praises, but I indulge myself by quoting two that she recorded:

> "George Brown spoke about the Nonesuch Press: his generation had always regarded Francis as the William Morris of their time. . ."
> "Philip Gooding emphasised how wisely Francis dealt with the staff: 'It was no use trying to blind him with science'."

Cement was not all my life in these twelve years. There was my work at the Stationery Office; I was for a while an active member of the Council of Industrial Design; I was still a Director at Mather's; I sat on a plenitude of committees; and from 1953 I planned and designed books for the revivified Nonesuch Press.

XIX

Somesuch

I don't like serving on committees. Who does, except for a boast in *Who's Who*? As the most ignorant member of the Advisory Council of the Victoria and Albert Museum I cannot remember a single matter to which my voice made any contribution; nor as a member of an Arts Council sub-committee; nor as chairman of the Society of Typographical Designers; nor as a member of the Governing Body of the Royal College of Art. Even in the Council of Industrial Design my only significant actions were in helping to found it and deciding to leave it.

That last decision was an oddity. Gordon Russell was a sympathetic Director, but I couldn't abide the decision to start a new magazine which was bound to kill *Design and Industry*, a worthy venture which was already hard put to it to survive. Here is a surprising reversal of attitudes: the Committee which evolved the new magazine, to be backed by public money, was entirely composed of Tories, while I, the Socialist, was now set on protecting private enterprise. Of course I lost, and left. Anyway, I was right about the death-blow to the old magazine. I acknowledge that the new one, *Design*, has flourished and been most useful.

I learnt something of decorum when I was chairman of the Postmaster General's committee on the design of postage stamps. It was made clear that our function was simply to *advise* the Postmaster-General, who was then to *advise* the monarch. This was especially touchy when the monarch was George VI, because he was a keen philatelist. It is told that an earlier advisory committee decided to send for his ultimate judgement the best and the worst designs submitted by invited artists. That would satisfy his demand that he should have a choice and at the same time ensure that the right one was made. It didn't work out; and a devious excuse had to be made that for technical reasons the bad design he chose could not be printed. In my time, we recommended Lynton Lamb's landscape designs, and very good they were. Buck De La Warr was the Postmaster General and he told me: 'The Queen really likes our stamps and so does the Prime Minister [Winston Churchill]. I know this because he gave me a very large cigar when I showed them to him'. Lynton Lamb reminded me of these stamps years later, on my seventieth birthday, by making a fake addition to his series which showed our Cobbold's Mill as the landscape and his own portrait (he explained that he had no photograph of me) in place of the royal head.

My chief post-war public job that was a constant interest and (I dare say it) a success was my appointment in 1945 as the first Honorary Typographic Adviser to His Majesty's Stationery Office. Alan Barlow proposed me from the Treasury and Norman Scorgie, the Controller, made me welcome. He had a real interest in design, which H.M.S.O. had then no means of satisfying.

Among my conditions for accepting appointment were that work must not always be placed at the lowest tender and that a design unit should be established through which I would work. Scorgie's first letter to me was charmingly signed, 'And so, Adviser-Designate, I am, your well-advised'. He told good stories. An example: during the war, when it was his duty to secure economy in the use of paper by government departments, he noticed that the sheets of toilet paper issued to the Navy were nearly twice the size of those doled out to the Army, and he invited the Admiralty to explain. The answer: 'My Lords of the Admiralty are at one with the Controller of His Majesty's Stationery Office on the importance of avoiding all possible waste of paper in time of war, but My Lords feel that the Controller has failed to take into account the hazards of a rolling ship.' Scorgie could tell such stories with rich amusement, but where royalty was concerned he was (perhaps properly) pompous. At my first visit I asked him to show me examples of the printing done for the obsequies of George V and for the ensuing Coronation. Scorgie clearly had to overcome a feeling that there was something regicidal about my request.

My first task was to find a man to work with me and to form and head a design section, for though the Stationery Office was then the largest publisher in the world it had no more than one layout man and one graphic artist. I turned to Harry Carter, who had worked with me at Nonesuch before the war. He answered encouragingly from Palestine, where he was learning Arabic and also cutting Hebrew type-punches. One aspect of Carter's talents is in a land—in many lands—unknown to me. I have only a reader's, not a speaker's, French and Italian; Carter, whenever he goes to foreign parts, learns the appropriate language, and sometimes returns with a knowledge even of its patois. No wonder that he had a distinguished career in censorship during the war.

I was fortunate indeed to have him as executive brain and hand at the Stationery Office. He remains one of the least-known best-known men in the world of books. He has chosen nearly always to be an accompanist, a Gerald Moore, rather than the soloist he could be. Thus that great book *John Fell* (Oxford, 1967) says on its title page 'Stanley Morison' in large type and then 'with the assistance of Harry Carter' in small type—whereas in his preface Morison says that Carter 'carried unflinchingly the massive burden of editorial drudgery'.

It was impossible for Carter, full-time, and me, with half-hours snatched from my job at the Cement and Concrete Association, to influence or even to examine more than a tiny fraction of the vast Stationery Office output. The prime notion was that I was to recruit and guide a staff; but the fact was that Harry Carter and I had ourselves to do such significant typographical work as was done. What took most of my little time was the design of im-

portant new H.M.S.O. publications such as the Working Party
Reports of the Board of Trade and (most onerous by far) the
printing for the death of George VI and the Coronation of Queen
Elizabeth. That last was a vast job, since it involved some 200
items. There was a hierarchy of responsibles. Over all was the
Monarch. The Earl Marshal was top functionary with Garter
King of Arms as his chief of staff. Over their shoulders peered, as
an ecclesiastical uncle, the Archbishop of Canterbury. The handy-
man was Her Majesty's Stationery Office plus the University
Presses and 'The Queen's Printers', Eyre & Spottiswoode, for the
ceremonial in the Abbey.

Not long before her accession to the throne I had the chance of
a talk with Princess Elizabeth. The occasion was a meeting of the
Royal Designers for Industry, and one by one we were presented
to the Princess, who was well-instructed as to the functions of
each of us. So my talk with her was about design in printing and
I dared to say that I thought the typography of her wedding
invitations was utterly inappropriate—it looked like an auctioneer's
catalogue. This she may have remembered when the new Royal
Arms and the Cypher were being planned, for she expressed a
wish that I be consulted. Sir George Bellew, Garter King of Arms,
did not like what he regarded as my intrusion. The Royal College
of Heralds, he said, had for hundreds of years designed the
Royal Arms and the Monarch's Cypher. I for my part did not
accept the designs produced by the Royal College of Heralds and
proposed Reynolds Stone, the outstanding letterist and engraver.
Garter was in the end content with Reynolds's; and so indeed
was H.M.S.O., which had to print the Royal Arms on an in-
finity of documents, including the stationery of all government
departments.

For the Coronation printing in general Garter set up a small
committee of which I was the only non-heraldic member. Our
first task was the card of invitation to Westminster Abbey. We

commissioned a decorative border from Joan Hassall, making a clean breakaway from old ceremonial printing; it was light and gay and, as it were, younger than its predecessors. But this was the wording:

> By command of The Queen
> the Earl Marshal is directed to invite ...

One of my troubles is that I cannot hold my tongue when I am concerned with the printing of redundant or ungrammatical phrases; so now I pointed out the tautology of 'by command' and 'directed'. I failed to move the hierarchy.

I had had better luck with the text of the Memorial Card issued to the next-of-kin of those who died in the war. I was consulted about the design only, but I took exception to a repetitive phrase about 'commemorating' and 'remembering'. It had been composed by a committee presided over by the Poet Laureate, John Masefield, and it had been approved by the King. Its correction needed the intervention of people far more dignified than I. Alan Barlow devised a brilliant method. He sent proofs to the heads of government departments, nominally seeking their opinion as to the shade of yellow to be used to represent the gold of the Royal Arms. The Permanent Secretaries duly made their irrelevant choice of colour—and added that a much more important matter was the repetitive wording... They, we, won.

Perhaps the most handsome job that Harry Carter and I designed together was the ceremonial book—few in pages but vast in size—prepared for the laying of the foundation stone of the new Chamber of the House of Commons in 1948. This involved me in sundry visits to the Speaker, Colonel Clifton Brown. At each visit I was handed with slow care from policeman to Sergeant-at-Arms, and then through two layers of secretaries to 'Mr Speaker' himself. When the contents had been approved and the first proofs were shown I thought there was a distinct unease on the Speaker's part. I was right. He pointed at his name in the processional order, which was printed in the same size type as that used for the Prime Minister (Clement Attlee) and the Leader of the Opposition (Winston Churchill). 'My name must be bigger than theirs', he said; and a last-minute call to the printers, the Curwen Press, had to be made. Then all was well, and the Speaker gave me one of the twenty-four copies printed on hand-made paper 'For His Majesty the King and those who took part in the ceremony'. Clement Attlee left his typical mark on the ceremony, I am glad to say: he arranged that all the workmen engaged on the site should be invited to the proceedings.

Harry Carter left H.M.S.O. after eight years of almost solitary service there—'escaped' was the sad word he used to me. He had achieved as much as any one man could in that time. We are both proud that Ruari McLean was able to testify in his succinct treatise *Modern Book Design*★ that we had 'succeeded in making official publications look as if they had been written by and for human beings'. Now H.M.S.O. has a properly staffed Design Unit headed by John Westwood—with Ruari McLean succeeding me in 1966 as Honorary Typographic Adviser. This is indeed a happy *dénouement*, for twenty years earlier I had tried and failed to per-suade McLean to take a paid post at H.M.S.O. under Harry Carter. In his regretful letter of refusal he had said of our project: 'It seems to be the first step towards the founding of an "Imprimerie Royale", an institution I have long coveted for England'. Yes, something like that has indeed happened.

One other public function I want to add to my boast—my membership for sixteen years of the Royal Mint Advisory Com-mittee. It has Prince Philip, Master of the Mint, as its acute chairman—which is stimulating; and it has St James's Palace as its meeting-place—which is romantic. We pass judgements on the design of coins, here and in the Commonwealth. Design only, please notice, not policy. I therefore felt it possible, even useful,

★ Faber, 1959.

to stay on the committee when our work was almost wholly concerned with the trappings of the needless and nasty—as I see it—decimalisation of our currency. With Milner Gray, a fellow member, my interest was in the shape and disposition of the lettering on coins. The Prince, sometimes surprised by our vehement technology, asked for a brief on this subject, which Milner Gray (mainly) and I composed for him: and we have been proud to observe that it has received his studious attention.

The Royal Mint has nothing to do with the design of notes, and it was merely as a member of the public that I wrote to Lord Cobbold, the Governor of the Bank of England, when there was about to be issued the last 10s. note. My point was that the word 'promise' (in the sentence 'I promise to pay') should, as a verb, begin with a small letter, not with a capital. Pamela Zander wisely suggested that my letter should be written on Cobbold's Mill notepaper. That address did in fact intrigue Lord Cobbold. Instead of no answer or the automatic one from a secretary, I received a warm topographical as well as typographical note asking me to discuss my point at the Bank of England. Yes, the new 10s. note was printed with a small 'p' for 'promise'. It was a short-lived victory: the 10s. note is withdrawn and the notes of other denominations have stuck to the capital letter.

FIFTY FAVOURITE
FAIRY TALES

Chosen from the Colour Fairy Books of

ANDREW LANG by KATHLEEN LINES

With illustrations by MARGERY GILL

A Nonesuch Cygnet

LONDON: THE NONESUCH PRESS

10 EARLHAM STREET WC2

Title-page of one of the Nonesuch Cygnets (unlimited editions, distributed by the Bodley
Head), 1963. The device is by Joan Hassall. Page size 9¼ × 6 inches.

Dinner to celebrate the 70th birthday of Sir Francis Meynell RDI, Wednesday May 10th 1961

Sir Francis Meynell (1st Course)

G A R A M O N D

Sir Ernest Pooley	Mrs Alan Sainsbury
Lady Richardson	Alan Sainsbury
Sir Ralph Richardson	Mrs B O Prowse
Mrs L A Hart	B O Prowse
L A Hart	Mrs Cyrill Tomlby
Mrs Herbert Farjeon	Ruari McLean
Edward Knapp	Sir Gerald Barry
Miles Malleson	Lady Spence
Miss Irene Clephane	Sir Basil Spence
John Langdon Davies	Mrs Robert Bevan
Miss Anna Hornby	Robert Bevan
James Laver	Mrs James MacKintosh
Mrs James Laver	James MacKintosh
	Rowland Owen

Sir Francis Meynell (Coffee)

F E L L

Mrs Max Reinhardt	Lord Pethwick Lawrence
Max Reinhardt	Lady Pethwick Lawrence
Dame Alix Meynell	Sir Edmund Ritson
Björn Prytz	Dame Evelyn Sharp
Mrs Mary Potter	Stanley Sheldon
A N Other	Mrs Stanley Sheldon
Mrs John Dreyfus	Herbert Simon
John Dreyfus	Mrs Herbert Simon
Jack Randle	Samuel Gurney
Mrs Jack Randle	Mrs Murray Somerly
Sir George Earle	Sir George Hamilton
Harold Hobson	Lady Hamilton
Mrs Harold Hobson	Sir Maynard Jonour
Joseph Compton	

Sir Francis Meynell (4th Course)

P E R F D / A U T R E A

Lady Keynes	Lady Russell
Sir Geoffrey Keynes	Sir Gordon Russell
Dorothy Garnett	Miss Nathalie Knipff
Miss Alice Meynell	Anthony Heal
The Hon Eric Harmsworth	Cecil Notley
Martin Zander	Mrs Ruth Simon
Mrs Martin Zander	Hans Schlöger
William Hummerstone	Rupert Hart-Davis
Miss Joan Russell	Reynolds Stone
Stuart Rose	Mrs Hans Schmoller
Mrs Stuart Rose	Hans Schmoller
Berthold Wolpe	Mrs Will Carter
John Ryder	Will Carter
Joseph Compton	Lynton Lamb

Mrs Benedict Meynell (1st Course)

J A N S O N

John Glasg	Reginald Hicklin
Miss Nora Dawson	Mrs Reginald Hicklin
Mark Dawson	L M Skevington
Lady Streat	Percy Muir
Sir Raymond Streat	Wilfrid Meynell
James Shand	Mrs Stephen Potter
Sir Donald Sargent	Stephen Potter
Sir Laurence Watkinson	Sidney Bernstein
Lady Watkinson	Mrs Sidney Bernstein
Benedict Meynell	Basil Davidson
Miss Nellie Lansbury	Sir Leslie Plummer
Raymond Postgate	Lord Archibald
Mrs Raymond Postgate	Lady Plummer
	Sir Francis Meynell

The Hon Leo Russell (2nd Course)

P L A N T I N

Sir Robert Kisree	Frederick Snow
Mrs George McNicoll	Mrs Frederick Snow
George McNicoll	Geoffrey Smith
Thomas Baldwin	Mrs Geoffrey Smith
Mrs Ashley Havinden	Major Forbes
Ashley Havinden	Mrs Evelyn Forbes
Mrs Brooke Crutchley	Sir Allen Lane
Brooke Crutchley	Douglas Cleverdon
Stanley Morison	Mrs Douglas Cleverdon
Mrs Beatrice Warde	Harry Yoxall
John Carter	Mrs Harry Yoxall
Mrs John Carter	Sir Frederic Hooper
	Lady Hooper
	Sir Francis Meynell

Tables arranged after two forms. Calligraphy by Leo Vernon

Nonesuch Again

Though after the war George Macy and I did no more Nonesuch books together, George did employ me to design a number of books for his Limited Editions Club, in which his wife Helen was an effective partner. So devoted were she and George to the art of the book that they had procured type and hand-press and learned the skills of the compositor and the press-man for the production of pretty pieces for their friends.

The most meaningful in my eyes of the books I designed for the Limited Editions Club was *John Brown's Body*,* Stephen Vincent Benét's superb epic poem about the American Civil War. As a greeting and thanksgiving to that then unsullied nation I had broadcast for the BBC passages from Benét's moving 'Invocation' in this book when the United States came into World War II. The then existing edition was undistinguished; could I persuade George Macy to let me design another? He replied with a characteristic call to order: 'Your letter', he wrote, 'expressed a burst of enthusiasm for Benét's poem. There are of course many other tellings of the John Brown story. I will arrange to send you *God's Angry Man*, which seems a superior telling to me'.

However, two years later he wrote again: 'You will remember that you wrote to me recently [recently, mark you!] out of a burst of enthusiasm for *John Brown's Body* to say that you would like to plan a new edition typographically. The time has come'.

His conversion was clearly not because of my persuasion but because a painter whose work he admired, John Stuart Curry, had made illustrations for it. This book satisfied my need to combine the functions of editor and typographer. Type must be arranged

* New York, 1948.

by the typographer to a purpose (the author's purpose) but also to a convenience (the reader's convenience): Benet's text involves so many themes, sometimes separate, often interplaying with others, that I felt it necessary to invent a means of identifying them. I therefore supplied a number of descriptive headings and innumerable shoulder-notes. It was a large task. When George came to London, I showed him my typographic plan. It is an anxious moment, this immature, tentative, pencilled realisation of one's intention, whether one is designing for oneself or for another. I have always taken humble warning from what happened to the great Gibbon. It was Gibbon's custom to present by his own hand a copy of each volume of *Decline and Fall* to the Duke of Gloucester. 'One day,' says a contemporary chronicler, 'elated with pride at the delightful office, and imagining as he went what handsome things the Duke would say to him—all he got from his Royal Highness was: "What? ah! another damned thick square book, eh!"' No, George was more kind and more recondite than that. He said he liked my plan.

About Curry's illustrations George and I were not at one. I disliked them and argued vainly for their omission. A second-best nearly came off—their relegation to a pocket in the binding. 'Yes' said George and then 'No' said George. Crisis. He decided to employ another typographer. The characteristic here is George's loyalty to the wishes of the artist, who had lately died. Cold-war telegrams and letters passed, in which George was more temperate than I. For I said that if the book was issued in a format not mine he must not use my mountainous editorial work. We were reduced even to sending messages to each other by a third party... Then George came to London again and greeted me with his annoyingly persuasive charm. He won hands down. So J. S. Curry and I were both reinstated.

In 1951, with a typical but still surprising generosity, George Macy handed the title and style of Nonesuch back to me, 'so that', he said, 'you can get some fun out of being Mr Nonesuch again'. His magnanimity would have meant nothing practical had I not made a close Savile Club friendship with Max Reinhardt, now managing director of The Bodley Head but then early in his career as a publisher under his own name. I had no money to finance any new Nonesuch venture and no means of distributing or accounting. These needs Max Reinhardt was ready to supply. I hope, even think, that our easy and trustful understanding brought him then an added 'recognition' in the trade and even some financial recompense.

We formed a new company, the Nonesuch Press Limited, with me as managing director and Max Reinhardt, Pamela Zander, and my son Benedict as directors. In 1953 I started Nonesuch again and since then we have published twenty-three books.

What was my thesis now? It was what you might call a socio-logical one. The new world after the shattering war meant that people's homes are much smaller. Not large houses now, with a library and ample bookshelves, but small flats and divided houses. A new Bible, a new Shakespeare, a new Blake: could these be made in fine editions that would fit the new and narrowed scene and shelf? The key to the problem must be paper. I searched the mills for so-called India paper that would be marvellously thin and opaque but would yet have just the minimal roughness of surface that would prevent pages sticking together—the vast dis-advantage of standard India papers. My search was a failure. Then I had a brainwave. One of the most competent paper mills in England belonged to the Imperial Tobacco Company and made exclusively cigarette papers. To them I put my problem. Would they be interested in devising a book paper to meet my require-ments? They were intrigued by the notion, invited me to attend their experimentations and finally produced precisely what I needed. The new Shakespeare occupied 234 cubic inches as against the 720 of the old. The new Bible, 199 cubic inches, the old edition 864; and the Blake—even more remarkable because its text was expanded—was only one-tenth of the bulk of its forerunner.

The Queen accepted the dedication of the Shakespeare, published in her Coronation year, and Reynolds Stone engraved a grand dedication page. Random House agreed to publish it in New York. I wrote to Donald Klopfer of my delight at this renewal of my ancient and happy association with him and Bennett Cerf. I even told him some of the selling-points and in the same sentence explained: 'These are commonplaces to you, dear Donald, but remember that I haven't been a publisher for fifteen years and must talk myself into it'. His welcoming reply: 'My, but it was nice to hear from you again. I hope the great load of cement you've been carrying will soon be removed and that you'll be back full-time in publishing'.

In 1953 too I began work upon *The Verse of Hilaire Belloc*, published in 1954. Of all the 150 Nonesuch books, pre-war plus post-war, this was the only one which involved me in a chaos of arguments and cares. It was a book of modest size; Belloc himself had blessed the plan for it; in W. N. Roughead (introduced to me by A. D. Peters) it had a devoted editor—I should properly call him 'editor-in-chief', because he amiably addressed me as 'co-editor' and, for my part, I named Rupert Hart-Davis 'extra editor'. What then piled up the difficulties?

Belloc died while the contents were still being collected. He had named as his literary executors Monsignor Ronald Knox, Duff Cooper (Lord Norwich) and Katharine Asquith. They realised the difficulty of their position. Could they interfere with the decisions made by an editor chosen with Belloc's approval? Belloc was a master of ribaldry, even of impropriety. Should they be censors? There were also some uncertainties as to authorship. Belloc's old-age delight was in continual recitations—mostly his own lines, but sometimes others which amused him. One couldn't persuade him to identify—no, he was on to the next recitation. In its foretaste of our book, the *Sunday Times* ascribed to Belloc (the fault was ours) one poem which was in fact by John Phillimore.

We and the literary executors came to a full-stop with our written arguments. I decided on a confrontation. We met three-a-side: 'Roughie', Pamela Zander and me, and the three executors. They were much easier in the flesh than on the reams of paper that had passed between us. Duff Cooper and Katharine Asquith spoke to me of our long-ago meetings. My opening remarks, learnt by heart and intended to be pistol-shots, could now be said only haltingly.

Two sonnets to Lady Diana Manners (Duff Cooper) were subjects of contention. We compromised, printing one, omitting the other. Unpublished verses to Lady Juliet Duff—what a lovely series it is!—were accepted on condition that we did not assemble them all together because (they said) 'that might give rise to misunderstandings'. Another contentious matter was the ballade in which the master line is 'And Mrs — will entertain the King'. It passed the executors' tests for decency and, with some doubt, authenticity; but was it not disloyal to the memory of Edward VII? I appealed to Harold Nicolson, an ardent Bellocian. He told me that when he and John Betjeman and Rupert Hart-Davis had lately competed in pseudo-or-real Belloc recitations, they could come to no accord about this text. He was all in favour of printing it, but, he warned, children of Mrs — might object. It was not included—but surely there is a simple way of avoiding offence? I print it here without naming the lady or her house:

> Near XYZ in Sussex you may see
> A house of large dimensions on a slope,
> Diversified by many an ancient tree
> And spreading garden lawns of ample scope:

And here it is that, when the Dryads ope
Their first adventurous arms to catch the Spring,
There comes a coronetted envelope;
And Mrs X must entertain the King.

The party will be large and very free
And people will be given lots of rope.
The Duke of Surrey, M.F.H., K.G.,
Will bring a divorcee in heliotrope.
And Mr Hunt, who manufactures soap,
Will answer for Victoria, Lady Tring,
And Algernon will partner Mrs Scrope—
And Mrs X will entertain the King.

There will be bridge and booze till after three
And, after that, a lot of them will grope
Along the passages in *robes de nuit*
And dressing-gowns, in search of other dope.
And a trained nurse will be sent down to cope
With poor De Vere, who isn't quite the thing,
And give his wife the signal to elope—
And Mrs X will entertain the King.

Envoi.

PRINCE! Father Vaughan will entertain the Pope
And you will entertain the Jews at Tring.
And I will entertain a pious hope,
And Mrs X will entertain the King.

Of two other verses it was a matter of stern decision by Ronald
Knox and Duff Cooper that they must not be included though
(which they preferred to doubt) they might be true Belloc. They
considered them too indecent to show to Katharine Asquith. True
or false, since they still go the clubman rounds I print them here:

> The world is full of double-beds
> And very charming maidenheads.
> This being so there's no excuse
> For sodomy or self-abuse.

And:

> Silent beside her sleeping Antony
> Great Cleopatra gazes out to sea
> And gazing, not without a pang, recalls
> Imperial Caesar's memorable balls.

The editing of an expanded—perhaps too much expanded—edition of the *Week-End Book* in 1955 made fun and games for me and for my helpers, Gerald Barry and my niece Sylvia Mulvey. Virginia Woolf would have rejoiced, for it did not have anything like the success (so annoying to her) of its predecessors.

My full-time work in the cement industry was then growing in significance and in its demands on my leisure. Even so, Nonesuch remained a happy hobby. In the next nine years I designed for it seven books, of which most were immediate sell-outs—a tribute to Max Reinhardt's skill as their financier and distributor. I have close at heart the variorum *Blake* (1957), which Geoffrey Keynes (of course) edited—a renewal, or rather a continuation, of our happy personal and technical closeness. When our large edition was exhausted it was reprinted by the Oxford University Press in an over-imitative manner. No matter, it made Geoffrey's perfect text much more widely available.

The making of the Bible involved a mountain of my work and Max's money, and it was slow in selling as well as in making; started in 1956 it was not finished till 1963. It would have taken even longer but for an agreement between Vivian Ridler and Brooke Crutchley, respectively the University Printer of Oxford and of Cambridge, to share the cares of printing. I make bold to claim that its 2,200 pages, with reproductions of 105 of the seventeenth-century woodcuts of Bernard Salomon, is the easiest to read and most engaging library edition in existence. This was just before the invasion of the new chitter-chatter translations: we used, of course, the lovely Authorised Version, the literary value of which is for me so much more important than its theology.

Unlike its much larger 1925 prototype, my post-war Bible included the delightful and seldom reprinted preface to the master edition of 1611—'Translators to the Readers'. Bay introduced me to it in a convincing way by reading a passage which defends the use of many synonyms in the translation of any often-repeated word in the original, lest the translators 'might be charged (by scoffers) with some unequal dealing towards a great number of good English words ... as if we should say to certain words Stand up higher, and to others of like qualitie Get ye hence, be banished for ever'.

In these years I had a number of pleasant but onerous public recognitions of my position in the world of printing and publishing. I was asked to write *English Printed Books* for that excellent and wide-ranging propaganda series 'Britain in Pictures'. I joined with other R.D.I.'s in furnishing the little 'Royal Pavilion' for the King and Queen's restroom at the 1951 Exhibition—my contribution was to design the Visitors Book and to lend and arrange the Nonesuch books which helped to 'furnish' the room. And I was asked by the National Book League to join with Desmond Flower in choosing the one hundred books to be included in its 1951 exhibition 'to illustrate the arts of book production'. In the United States George Macy had invented an 'award', a bronze statuette of Aldus,* to be made to the outstanding typographer of the day. Bruce Rogers had properly been the first to receive it in 1950. After a four-year gap the second Aldus was awarded to me.

This was the time of the McCarthy witch-hunts in the United States and when I applied for a visa at the American Embassy I

* Venetian printer, 1450–1515.

was asked if I had ever been a member of the Communist Party. 'Yes indeed,' I claimed, and then admitted 'but only for eight months, and that was thirty-four years ago.' I was given an absolute refusal. George Macy secured the intervention of our mutual friend Harold Riegelman: 'He is a big-wig of the Republican Party, and has the ear of the President'. Harold wrote to the Ambassador, Winthrop Aldrich, who referred the matter to the State Department. When at last the visa was granted, only a few days before the date fixed for the Aldus presentation ceremony, I was too deeply involved in an international conference of concrete technologists to be able to leave London. David Ogilvy handsomely—in every sense—agreed to represent me in New York. I had my say tape-recorded and there were speeches by Tom Cleland, Bruce Rogers and Robert Frost. George Macy reported to me that 'David Ogilvy accepted the Aldus statue with wonderful grace'.

Two years later George died a pathetically early death. The Limited Editions Club, of which he was begetter, fashioner, in some ways even tyrant, flourishes still, in the care of his wife Helen and of their son Jonathan. George was often formidable as a taskmaster, always lovable as a man. He allowed himself to be thought of as a salesman, but he was so much besides. His return to me of the Nonesuch Press in 1951 was an example of his wide generosity. He had his European triumphs. In 1952 the British Museum put on a show of the books, nearly fifty of them, that he had caused to be edited, illustrated, or printed in England; and the Bibliothèque Nationale gave him a like show for his French-made books. I wrote a short introduction to the British Museum catalogue, and after his death I was able to have my say at length about him and his work. A collection of all the books he had sponsored was presented to Columbia University and Helen asked me to make the dedicatory speech. We were her guests on the *Queen Mary* and thereafter luxuriously at the Delmonico in New York. (Yes, there had been a repetition of the visa nonsense—what a dangerous fellow I am!)

At Helen's flat we met her parents and renewed our admiration for her daughter Linda and her son Jonathan, whom we had known in their 'teens. The Columbia ceremony was well attended. The applause at the end of my speech was amplified by great bursts of thunder. 'That was George's laughter', someone said to me afterwards. The storm flooded the streets and Bay followed the example of a number of elegantly dressed women who took off their stockings and shoes and paddled to the waiting cars.

My latest (my last) Nonesuch venture has been the series of young people's classics, the Nonesuch Cygnets. I have always chosen to make books that I myself wanted, books not otherwise available in an editorial or in a physical form that appealed to me. In the 'thirties I had published the 'Tootleoo' books of Bernard and Elinor Darwin, chiefly because I wanted them for my young son; now, a generation later, it was pleasing to make editions for my grand-daughters.

How comes the title 'Nonesuch Cygnets'? I fancied it for no better reason than that, having a doting couple of swans and their six cygnets in the mill-stream at Cobbold's Mill, I saw the cygnets as a symbol of youth and as a printer's mark in combination with the old Nonesuch Palace device. So I put it to the test. A list of four possible series-titles was sent to seventy-five booksellers, librarians and teachers. All had the kindness to answer, and 'Nonesuch Cygnets' had a thumping majority.

The first of the Nonesuch Cygnets came out forty years after I founded the Nonesuch Press. My old passion for typography had not in any way diminished, though now I was no longer an innovator in the matter of book design. My lay-out sketches, from which the printer has to produce his specimen pages, have always been a bit sloppy in appearance though exact in instruction. For the Cygnets, very much a series though each with its own individuality, and for all the post-war Nonesuch books, my 'roughs' were made definite and smooth and elegant by the skilled hand of Pamela Zander. Kathleen Lines guided the editorial side of the Cygnet books, just as David Garnett did for many books in the first phase of Nonesuch.

Included in the Cygnet series is *By Heart*. I was its editor-cum-designer. I gave myself the pleasure of dedicating it to my grand-daughters, Janet and Kate. It is an anthology of memorable poems. To be easily remembered a poem should have rhyme and rhythm. This governed my choice of poems for this wide anthology, planned for people of all ages who have heart and ear for poetry—the ear is specially important in my context. I have always been a retainer and spouter of poetry: the editing of this book was my retirement-offering to an unfailing passion of my life.

Harvest

To turn the earliest page of time,
To seek the nurse, the difficult stair,
The corner where all comforts were,
The closet one could scarcely dare—
This is the commonplace of rhyme.

Return for me is different. I'm
A revenant past my middle-age
With more than middling friends. I go
With joy to not-so-long-ago—
Stiff-necked, stiff-kneed, perhaps more sage.
Shake heads. Shake hands. And turn the page.

Yes, there comes in a long and full life a time of backwards-looking, of a sense of culmination. So it was with me on my seventieth birthday. Max Reinhardt convened a group of my friends to plan a feast at the Savoy. Despite its size the occasion was intimate. There was no 'high table': I was given a seat at all five tables for some minutes and mouthfuls.

Formal-informal speeches were made by Jake Carter, Eric Hooper, Dick Plummer, Stephen Potter, Max Reinhardt, Evelyn Sharp and Laurence Watkinson. For me the happiest thing was not what they said to and of me (for praise and praise again are the inevitable condiments of such a meal) but what I glowingly thought of them. They were admired leaders or companions in all my successive public and private lives.

In the printed list of guests was a mysterious 'A. N. Other'. I searched for the unnamed; it proved to be Helen Macy, flying from New York for this one night and anonymous lest traffic delays

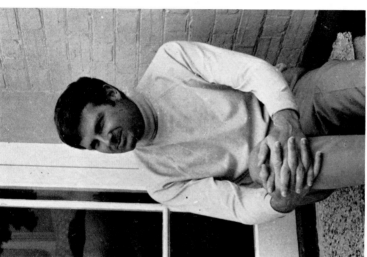

F.M.'s daughter Cynthia Lloyd, his son Benedict and Benedict's two children Janet (in front) and Kate.

Alix (Bay) and F.M. in France 1935, in Italy 1955, at home in Lavenham 1970.

might make her too late. She brought with her a handsome volume of amiable remarks from American bibliophiles.

A few days later Harry Carter put into my hands an album the equal of which I have never seen. He had collected salutations to me from typographers in Norway, Sweden, Denmark, France, Italy, Holland, the United States and from this country, and bound them in my favourite niger morocco. The pages were some of them printed, some calligraphed, some illuminated, some painted; making a gallery of designs, all typical of their makers. Its endpaper—but truly it is silk—was printed by the Oxford University Press with a surround of golden 'petits-fers' cut by Matthew Carter, Harry's son. Harry's introduction was this ingenious sonnet:

> F rancis, this album blackened by your friends
> R eceive from the U.P., who did it bind,
> A nd let the birthday greeting bring to mind
> N othing but pleasure in a spell that ends.
> C an any one of us by what he sends
> I nsure you well enough that he would choose
> S ucceeding pleasures for you great as those.
>
> M ay ninety winters never bring the bends!
> E diting this I gloried in the skill
> Y ou gathered round you, now intent to praise;
> N onesuch of art, of wit, how could there be
> E quals of theirs to draw or pen a phrase.
> L ook further to behold that galaxy
> L auding your gifts as being better still.

Other gifts give me continuing pleasure. From the Herbert Simons and the Zanders came a dozen china mugs decorated by transfers of engravings made by Reynolds Stone. One of these showed Cobbold's Mill and another proclaimed my fribbles and foibles in the lovely lettering of which Reynolds is the master. Lest professors of history should be bemused and beguiled in a matter of such universal importance I must correct an error! I am described on the mug as 'Originator of the Roof Game'. Not so, you pundits! Miles Malleson and Cyril Joad were my equal partners. (If the reader is ignorant of the rules of this mysterious game he can find them in *The Week-End Book*.)

I cannot resist telling of another gift from friends and one from me myself. Two of my poems were printed in an edition of fifty copies on hand-made paper by 's.m., b.c., v.r., d.c., r.s., j.d.' Typophiles need not be told that these initials signify Stanley Morison, Brooke Crutchley, Vivian Ridler, Douglas Cleverdon, Reynolds Stone (who engraved another lovely headpiece) and John Dreyfus. I am not ashamed of my poems, though they are outfaced by the beauty of the printing and paper and covers. To gratify myself in my retirement year I made, and published as a Nonesuch book, a final collection of my own verse. It is called *Poems & Pieces* and this is not an advertisement because the edition is exhausted. 'Anthologists, please note', wrote V. Sackville-West of an earlier collection. No, they have not noted; but the Library of Congress in Washington commissioned me to make a half-hour tape-recorded reading of my poems, and lately I have heard—yes, with proud pleasure—one of my poems read and re-read on the radio. But poetry is written essentially for its writer and for someone that he loves. Bay, my incomparable Bay, has reason to realise this.

Bay had resigned from the Civil Service at the end of 1955, some nine years before her due time, so that we could always be together at weekends (Saturdays were still workdays for civil servants) and when cement duties called me to conferences abroad. We called it our harvest and it has been a bumper one. My own retirement from the Cement and Concrete Association followed only two years after Bay's from the Board of Trade. True, neither of us was left taskless: I made a rather fruitless return to Mather's on a half-time basis; Bay sat on government committees and on the South-Eastern Gas Board. Nevertheless, in general our time was our own.

My four years half-time engagement being over, Mather's Creative Department gave me the kindest of farewells, expressed in drawings and verse. Facing yet another version of my Nonesuch Palace device, by Christopher Sharpe, was this verse by Paul Hoppé:

> Nonesuch the Palace, crumbled to clay;
> Nonesuch the Press, still alive as the day.
> If eternity you would own
> Build on paper, not in stone.

In 1966, when I was seventy-four, and still hale and hearty (I had to look often in the glass to remind myself—'Be your age') I made my latest visit to the United States, this time under the auspices of the Rockefeller University. My son-in-law, David Lloyd, was a professor there and he was part promoter of my visit. In England Nonesuch was now, I felt, something of a faded memory, so it was a surprise as well as a delight to find it alive in the esteem and on the collectors' shelves of New York bibliophiles.

My Rockefeller occasions were prepared with grace as well as enthusiasm. William Bayless and his right-hand man Rey Biemiller, of the Rockefeller University Press, arranged an exhibition of Nonesuch books; Joseph Blumenthal and the Spiral Press gave me a 'film-star' lunch at the Century Club, where the company of distinguished printers provided me with new neighbours at every course; the Grolier Club fed me good food and flattery. My own performances: a lecture on typography to 250 people at the university; a three-hour on-show stand-up at the opening of the Nonesuch Exhibition in the Rockefeller University library; a poetry lecture at Fordham University (not a success except for delightful chats afterwards with students); a speech at the None-such Cygnets promotion lunch given by Franklin Watts, their American publishers; a seminar (I am still in doubt as to what that word means) at the Rockefeller on the design of books; a lecture to Dr Leslie's bibliophilic group. Paul Bennett in the *Publishers' Weekly* gave eight pages of description to these events.

There were many delightful private occasions to which our journeys were made opulently easy by David Ogilvy, who lent us for a full fortnight his chauffeured Rolls-Royce. We wondered why people gathered at a red-light stop to peer into the car. They looked and then turned away in obvious disappointment. We found out why. The Duke of Edinburgh was in New York and he, of course, went about in a Rolls.

After our Rockefeller fortnight was over, Helen Macy put us up at her Park Avenue apartment and we had delightful renewals of old friendships with Laura Hobson (the novelist), Paul and Stella Standard (he the mentor of calligraphy at New York University, she the writer of cookery books), and Doris and Bill Robinson, Americans whom we had met on our voyage across the Atlantic in 1949 and who in 1957 had been our hosts in Cuba.

I don't know what the guide-books say about places to visit in New York, but *I* say to every English visitor, 'Don't miss the Cloisters'—those pieces of Europe in stone and tapestry that have been set up on the tip of Manhattan so lovingly that you can almost believe yourself back in Europe for an hour.

What a feast of kindness—knowing kindness—from Americans for my old-age farewell. Is it to be my last venture into the United States? As I write, this is the year in which I have regained my daughter (she and her husband are now settled in England) and mislaid my son. He is now Commercial Counsellor in the British Embassy in Washington. Even in my eighties there might, yes, there just might, be an irresistible desire to visit him there. . .

An autobiography is always something of a boast; otherwise it

would not be written. Have I given the impression that our mature
life was nothing but work and responsibilities? Indeed it was not.
Bay and I have always been devoted holidaymakers together. Before
the war, France was our holiday-ground—during the Mussolini
régime we would not go to Italy. Even during World War II we
managed a week each year, usually camping with our bicycles in
Scotland. Our post-war discovery of Italy was largely based on
Gordon Waterfield's castle at Aulla, which he lets to the luckier of
his acquaintances. There we have made no less than fourteen
annual holidays with family and friends. Bay has always kept a diary
of our holidays and these happy records led me to write the
following lines:

> We finger the pages, ruffle the seas apart,
> Follow the sun, his hours, on orchard and desert sand,
> On rivers gentle and sharp, their wild-flower tributaries,
> Siena, Rome, the Isles, the middle land,
> Padua, the Pyrenees—
> The places of your heart.
>
> Now put the book aside and draw your chair
> Close to the fire, and make new journeys there.
>
> There is all distance and all emptiness,
> There is all movement and all fireside ease.
> Read there the mathematics of access:
> Infinity as multiplier and
> Zero the multiplicand.
>
> Draw closer still. Put on
> The five times five times five-league boots of the mind.
> Travel, unravel, the unknown.
> Make early sunrise, and delay the moon.
> Learn many a heavenly patois as you fare
> Leisurely from Aldebaran to the Bear.

Visit Orion; bind
His belted sword against all possible war;
But most, but most of all,
While man premeditates his final fall,
Knead the Great Nebula into a star
To house a gentler fauna than mankind.

Return! Return
While still the embers burn.
Return a myriad miles to where you are.

In 1967 we left Cobbold's Mill, a home too large and too costly
to maintain for my old limbs and our deflated pensions. At
Lavenham, only four miles away from Cobbold's Mill, we live at
ease in an eighteenth-century timber-structured house that was
given a brick 'skin' a hundred years after it was built. It was called
'The Old Manse' when we bought it. We did not pursue my
suggestion that it should be called 'The Old Man's', and named it
descriptively 'The Grey House'. Much reshaping had to be done.
We added a sun-parlour and a games-room, where I can still beat
the young at ping-pong. Moving so short a distance, we have kept
all our circle of friends and we have made many new ones in this
paragon among the group of neighbouring and beautiful Suffolk
villages. Miss Leckie, our Scottish help for sixteen years, has come
with us. Cobbold's Mill is now in the possession of our friends
Stanhope and Irène Shelton, who keep its doors open to us.

We have felt happy and at home in Lavenham from the first day
of our move, and my son, my daughter and my two grand-
children, whose first place-loves will always be Cobbold's Mill
and Greatham, delight us by finding the Grey House a happy place
to visit. 'Lovely, we are going to G.G.', I once heard the grand-
children say. I took this to mean 'Gammer and Gaffer', as they
always call us, and showed my pleasure. They were confounded

and explained that it meant Gorgeous Grub. What of it? Bay was delighted, for she is the cook.

Most achievements of any man can be matters of doubt. Will the performances and attitudes of which I have told (even boasted) survive contemporary scrutiny? Clearly that isn't for me to say. But I can claim two things that cannot be denied me. Read and consider: (1) I persuaded my admired Robert Robinson's BBC programme to change from the American phrase 'Do you have any questions?' to 'Have you any questions?' by telling the story of the English woman in New York who had to see her gynaecologist. 'Do you have many children?' he asked her. Her astonished reply: 'No, never more than one a year.' (2) I designed a new comma, yes, a new comma, no less, for the italic letters of the O.U.P.'s seventeenth-century Fell type.

Now as I touch eighty, and inevitably come closer to death, I do not find it frightening. Non-existence extended as endlessly before one's birth as it will extend after one dies. True, the light dims now; but is not the twilight lovely?

INDEX

INDEX